FESTIVALS AND SONGS
OF ANCIENT CHINA

By

MARCEL GRANET

Professor at the School of Oriental Languages, Paris

TRANSLATED FROM THE FRENCH BY

E. D. EDWARDS, D.Litt.

Martino Publishing
Mansfield Centre, CT
2015

Martino Publishing
P.O. Box 373,
Mansfield Centre, CT 06250 USA

ISBN 978-1-61427-764-4

© *2015 Martino Publishing*

Cover design by T. Matarazzo

Printed in the United States of America On 100% Acid-Free Paper

FESTIVALS AND SONGS
OF ANCIENT CHINA

By

MARCEL GRANET

Professor at the School of Oriental Languages, Paris

TRANSLATED FROM THE FRENCH BY

E. D. EDWARDS, D.Litt.

E. P. Dutton
New York
1932

E. P. Dutton
New York
1932

TO THE MEMORY OF
ÉMILE DURKHEIM
AND
ÉDOUARD CHAVANNES

EDITOR'S NOTE

IN the French original of Professor Granet's work which appeared under the auspices of the Ministry of Public Instruction, the Chinese text of the odes which he discusses and interprets was given side by side with the translation. Chinese characters which greatly facilitated the use of the book by those acquainted with the language were given, wherever necessary, in the notes and elsewhere. They would, however, have been disconcerting to the general reader, and their reproduction in this English version would have rendered the price of it very much greater. Chinese scholars will doubtless regret their omission here, but it is almost inconceivable that any serious student of Chinese has not long ago possessed himself of the French edition. The Editor feels that the placing of this extremely important study at the disposition of a wider circle of readers more than justifies its appearance in its present form. Professor Granet is more than a sinologue. His work, which is much more than a study of the Book of Odes, throws new light upon the origins of one of the greatest civilisations the world has ever seen. It will be welcomed by many who are entirely unfamiliar with the Chinese language, and it is especially for them that this version has been prepared.

CONTENTS

INTRODUCTION

It is my desire to show that it is not impossible to learn something of the religious customs and beliefs of ancient China. Authentic documents relating to these early times are rare, and those which exist, date from a somewhat late period. We know that the Empire, when it abolished the Feudal System, determined to destroy the titles upon which that system rested, and burned the Books. No sooner, however, was the Empire itself established than it wished to produce titles for itself, and the Books were rewritten.[1] This was religiously done, and since, after all, it was from the institutions of the feudal period that those of the Empire emanated, when it became necessary to describe the former in order to formulate the latter, they were not so capriciously distorted that the historian cannot, with due care, draw satisfactory conclusions from them.[2] It is possible, then, to study the organization of the feudal period, and, by a comparative study of the texts, attempts have been made to describe this or that feudal cult.[3] But when this has been done, what do we know of the religious life of the ancient Chinese? All that has been arrived at is the official religion.

Description is all very well, but we must learn further from what sources in custom and belief the worship of the feudal states had sprung. If no attempt is made to discover in the texts anything beyond the shrunken forms of the state religion, as soon as one attempts to explain them one will find oneself at a loss. And, as a matter of fact, when one has discussed the primitive monotheism of the Chinese, or declared

---

[1] Cf. Chavannes, Introduction to the translation of Ssŭ-ma Ch'ien (referred to hereafter as SMC.), and Legge, *Prolegomena*.

[2] See, for example, the formulæ of investiture in Chavannes, *le T'ai Chan*, p. 453.

[3] See Chavannes' study, *Le Dieu du Sol* (*T'ai chan*, App. 437–525), a model of accurate scholarship and historical exactitude.

B

that they have always worshipped the forces of Nature and practised anceſtor worship, one has said all that can be said.[1]

A ſtudy which ſtops at such mediocre generalities misleads the ſtudent. Some, without attempting to grasp the fundamental elements of the religious notions prevalent in China, are content to take as their point of departure the facts that can be observed now.[2] They draw up liſts[3], elaborate documents, but what do they convey? Sometimes a positive value is attributed to the explanations of the Chinese themselves concerning their cuſtoms: if they ſtate that a certain ceremony serves to drive out evil spirits, it is accepted as a fact that it was actually devised for this purpose.[4] Or else, without authority and at random, the cuſtom which it is desired to explain is connected with one or another of the theories prevalent, and, according to whether Naturism or Animism is in favour at the moment, the cuſtom is explained by the universal belief in spirits, or by the not less general worship of the sun and the ſtars.[5] This is a loose method which hinders the accurate classifying of the facts, and even mars the cataloguing of them. It is enough to say that a feſtival takes place about the time of a solſtice or an equinox and it is at once labelled a solar feſtival. Having thus classified it, an attempt is made to deduce all its characteriſtics.[6] It is even better if it is a queſtion of the worship of the ſtars[7]; with a fine confidence in the antiquity of the civilization in queſtion and a skilful manipulation of the precession of the equinoxes, what cannot be explained! Occasionally hiſtory comes to the rescue and one has the curiosity to revert to the paſt to find the explanation of the present. The notion is excellent, but how many are the dangers to be avoided! The search

[1] Such is the attitude of the early missionaries, and of Réville, Courant, and Franke.
[2] E.g. de Groot, t. xii, of the *Annales du Musée Guimet*: *Les Fêtes annuellement célébrées à Emouy* (hereinafter referred to as: de Groot: *Emouy*). See the preface.
[3] E.g. the *Catalogue* of Grube, *le Folk-lore chinois* of Wieger.
[4] Cf. de Groot, *Emouy*, explanation of the fires of spring, p. 133.
[5] This is the attitude of M. de Groot, *Fêtes d'Emouy*.
[6] De Groot, *Emouy*, 5th month feaſts, p. 311 sqq.
[7] De Groot, *Emouy*, p. 436 sqq.

after the beginnings of things is generally misleading : particularly is this the case in China, where native scholars devote their attention to discovering, not the actual beginnings of things, but only the date when the characters employed to denote these things were first used.[1] Moreover, what is sought, even there, is confirmation of the conception formed of the Customs, rather by those who record them than by those who practised them, and, the more ancient the evidence, the greater the pleasure. In deference, as it were, to their rights, these notions are not considered with any idea of examining and judging them critically ; no attention is paid to the fact that they were apparently conceived at a later period ; it is not even thought necessary, in order to put them into positive language, to take into consideration all the system of notions, all the methods of interpretation, of their authors.

Neither the method of the historian who contents himself with arranging the texts simply with the expedients of outside criticism, nor that of the folklorist who is content to describe the facts in the language of his Chinese informant, or of a particular school, seems to me to be adequate, for neither is a really critical method. Results can only be hoped for, in my opinion, if a two-fold precaution is taken : in the first place, it is well to submit the documents from which it is hoped to draw the facts to a study which shall first of all determine the nature of these documents and thus allow the precise value of the facts to be decided ; second, the facts being obtained, and as soon as it is possible to translate them in positive language, it is wise to refrain from seeking anything outside themselves by which they may be interpreted. I have therefore divided the present study into two parts : in the first I have endeavoured to show what, precisely, is the nature of the principal document of which I propose to make use ; in the second, after having

---

[1] De Groot, *Emouy*, p. 231 sqq. *Recherches sur la fête de printemps* : investigations concerning the expression ' the first *ssŭ* day ', made with the help of the encyclopædias, and stopped when the term, as specially applied to a ceremonial gathering, no longer occurred in the texts.

given an account of such of the established facts as form a whole capable of being interpreted, I have endeavoured to make this interpretation.

The selection of documents is a very important matter : why do we select the love-songs of the *Shih ching* for our study ? The *Shih ching*[1] is an ancient text ; through which it should be easy to make the acquaintance of the ancient forms of Chinese religion. That is an important point ; but no one who has not a superstitious regard for the ancient texts should make his selection on the strength of this one advantage. For myself, I do not propose to seek in ancient facts the origin of modern facts. One thing of which I have become convinced in the course of this study is that it is useless to fix a sort of genealogical succession between similar facts in different periods. A verse of a Hakka song, collected in our own time, resembles in every detail a verse from the *Shih ching*, at least twenty-five centuries old[2] : the one is not a copy of the other ; both were improvised in analogous circumstances and every year, no doubt, during twenty-five centuries, similar lines have been composed.[3] Similarly, at every moment customs persist through perpetual renewal. A custom cannot be explained by showing that like customs existed previously : it is explained by establishing the link which makes it the

[1] For the purposes of this study of the *Shih ching* I have availed myself of the following editions : 1, the classic edition : *Sung pên* ; 2, the learned edition known as *Mao shih chu su* ; and, 3, the academic edition, *Shih ching ching i-chi ch'ao*. I have made use of the modern works included in the collections : *Huang ch'ing ching chieh* (HCCC.) and *Huang ch'ing ching chieh hsü pien* (HCCCHP.), particularly the *Mao shih ku hsün chuan* (HCCC. 600–29), the *Mao chêng shih k'ao chêng* (ibid., 557–60), the *Mao chih chuan chien t'ung shih* (HCCCHP., 416–47), the *Mao shih hou chien* (ibid., 448–77), the *Ch'i shih i shuo k'ao* (ibid., 778–807), the *Lu shih i shuo k'ao* (ibid., 1118–37), the *Ch'i shih i shuo k'ao* (ibid., 1138–49), the *Han shih i shuo k'ao* (ibid., 1150–8), and the *Shih ching ssŭ chia i wên k'ao* (ibid., 1171–5).

[2] Cf. xvii, and Hakka, vi (App. iii), xliv, and Hakka, xii, xxv, and xxviii, and Hakka, xxvii. It will be remarked that the Hakka poems have a more delicate atmosphere than the old Chinese songs. Cf. *Wei fêng* 8, stanzas 3 and 4, and Hakka, iii and iv.

[3] Cf. *Wang fêng*, 7, Couvreur, 81 : ' Unis entre eux sont les dolics ' : ' United are the dolichos plants ' and the lament of the Lolo bride (App. III) : ' L'herbe a l'herbe pour compagne ' : ' The grass has the grass for companion.'

inevitable outcome of certain series of circumstances. In some instances modern documents lend themselves better to the discovery of the basis of a belief than do the ancient ones ; if it had been so in this instance I should not have hesitated to make use of such documents, while taking care at the same time to demonstrate by an adequate mass of ancient facts that what is true of the present is true also of the past. I shall study the past directly because it is easier to understand ; that is all.

It happens that the documentary value of the *Shih ching*, or rather of such pieces in the collection as are love-songs, can be fairly accurately determined. This is the first reason for its selection. It also happens that this value is of the highest order : this is the principal reason.

Poems, even if collected over a period, are unlikely to be altered by the compilers of the collection. It is easier in poetry than in prose to differentiate between the original thought and the notions which may have arisen to obscure it ; here the commentaries have not found their way into the text.[1] The text can be examined apart from its various interpretations. On the one hand the text itself may be studied and, on the other, its history—and through its history the text becomes more intelligible.

The text, when it is ancient, must be a mirror of ancient things. If properly understood it is this certainly, but it is not easy to understand, and, without the assistance of the expositors, we should not see very much in it. I shall endeavour first of all to discover a method which, going deeper than the interpretation, reveals the original meaning. To find the key to the various interpretations it is only necessary to know the expositors : not that it is necessary to reconstruct their individual psychology ; they form a body whose composition decides the traditional principles of interpretation, which is of the symbolic order, and is based on a theory of public right : it

---

[1] This is not so in the case of ritual texts in prose : see for example the account of the festival of the Pa Cha in the *Li chi, Chiao t'ê chêng*, Couvreur, i, 594 sqq.

assumes a parallel between the carrying on of government and natural events.

I shall prove that this prejudice in favour of symbolism, to which the scholars feel themselves bound as by a professional bond of ethics, leads them into absurdities which they sometimes admit. Thus we shall know where to direct our attention. But we shall also see that these allegorical interpretations of the odes reveal an essential principle of their composition—a law of the species : this is the law of symmetry, the use of *correspondences*. He who knows that law is capable of understanding and translating the *Shih ching*.

Being able to read the text, and understanding the state of mind of the expositors, there is much to be gained by comparing the text with the commentaries. The poems of the *Shih ching*, read apart from the interpretations, are, one feels, popular songs, although tradition makes them learned works. It would be easy to say, " Let us set aside the traditional interpretation, for it has been proved that it leads to misconception of the text." It would be better to inquire how the mistake originated. How was it that the scholars—and excellent scholars at that—were unable to interpret their native language ? They were not merely scholars ; there is more of the official than the lover of literature about them ; they put the poems at the service of political ethics and thereafter were unable to admit their popular origin. For a government official the doctrine of moral duty emanated from above, and wherever a virtuous influence made itself felt, its scholarly origin was taken for granted.

Therefore the odes, which inculcate morals, cannot be the work of other than official poets. But whence do the odes derive their moral competency ? Let us put a case. If rules of life could be found in old love-songs, it was because, however imperfectly they were understood, their lines still re-echoed the ancient moral teaching. Their symbolic utilization would find no support at all, would not be intelligible, if these songs had not a ritual origin.

6

INTRODUCTION

It is very probable that the poems which at firſt sight seemed to be old popular songs, formerly possessed a ritual value. Moreover, the moral drawn from their symbolism had its inception in the notion that men, like Nature, muſt do things at the proper time. It may therefore be possible to find in the songs some traces of seasonal rules. Laſtly, since the poems themselves and the moral teaching which they express are given an interpretation which diſtorts their meaning, it is because that teaching is not in the leaſt that of the commentators themselves. It is possible then that the songs may introduce us to ancient cuſtoms which exiſted prior to the classic moral teachings. In short, they seem to be a document appropriate to the ſtudy of the beliefs which gave rise to the ancient seasonal ritual of the Chinese.

Their documentary value will be seen to increase if they are examined by their own light. They make it possible to ſtudy the operations of popular invention ; it will appear that they are the produ&t of a kind of traditional and colle&tive creation ; they were improvised, on certain set themes, in the course of ritual dances. It is evident from their content that the occasion of their composition was the important oral ceremony of the ancient agricultural feſtivals, and they are thus a dire&t teſtimony of the emotions which gave rise to these periodical gatherings. Their analysis may result in the discovery of the ancient fun&tion of seasonal ritual.

Thus the ſtudy of our chief document will enable us not merely to eſtablish the fa&ts but also to further their interpretation.

In the second part of the present work I shall examine the ancient feſtivals of whose general chara&teriſtics the odes will have already given some account.

Firſt of all I shall try to describe for their own sakes certain local feſtivals. In each case I shall present all the documents I have been able to gather, details of ritual, and explanations of pra&tices. Such grouping is not made with a view to a picturesque reconſtru&tion ; it will prove that the peculiarities

7

of local cuſtoms are only apparent, being in faɛt due to gaps in the texts or to their nature.

Four feſtivals can be reconſtruɛted : two in their ancient form and two in the form in which they appear in the worship of the feudal period. The relationship between the two groups is clear. Moreover, in the case of one of them, prototypes can be found which mark the ſtages of the transformation. It thus becomes possible to ſtudy the transition from popular ritual to the ceremonial of official worship.

The necessity for caution is evident from this ſtudy. It makes clear the accidental charaɛter of the representations which seem at firſt sight to explain the faɛts. It is necessary above all to diſtinguish between aɛtual beliefs and mere representation which is more or less personal and from which very little can be deduced. But, even in the case of the beliefs themselves, it may be misleading to conneɛt them too haſtily with the praɛtices. It is never certain that there is direɛt interdependence between the beliefs and the ceremonies. Such and such a ceremony or such and such a belief may originate, not the one from the other—the ceremony from the belief or the belief from the ceremony—but both from an earlier source ; and they may issue from it independently, in such a way that at the moment at which they are observed to coexiſt they may be at different ſtages of evolution.

Neither from the interpretation given to a modern ceremony, nor from the meaning attributed to each of the praɛtices of which it is composed, is it possible to deduce anything definite concerning either the funɛtion of the original assembly from which the ceremony sprang or the value of similar praɛtices which are found in that assembly. It will be proved that the cuſtoms have all been endowed with the moſt varied efficacies ; only their force remains unchanged. It is that which muſt firſt be explained before it is possible to see how it has become specialized.

I shall therefore begin with the ancient ritual assemblies and consider them in their moſt general aspeɛts. The ancient festivals are essentially seasonal : I shall show by means of a suitable example that they have, even in this guise, a human character out of which arises directly their power over natural events ; they are festivals of union by which good order is established in society and, at the same time, in Nature. They take place in a hallowed region of rivers and mountains. I shall show by the study of the representations included in the worship conducted by the ruler in honour of the Mountains and Rivers, that the power attributed to them is due to the reverence in which the holy places were held because they were formerly the traditional symbols of the social pact which the aboriginal communities celebrated at their seasonal gatherings. These festivals, in short, consist of a variety of contests with a verbal accompaniment of rival extempore poems. By the analysis of the emotions expressed in these poetic duels it will become evident why these ritual contests were chosen as a means of cementing friendship between individuals and groups. I shall also try to explain why it was especially in the Spring, by a contest in which the sexes were opposed, and by a kind of communal betrothal, that the alliance which bound different local groups into a traditional community was strengthened. Finally, by showing the cause of the atmosphere of impersonality found in both the sentiments and the songs of love in ancient China, it will be seen how it could happen that festivals, whose essential characteristic was the exercise of sexual rites, were never, unless at a later date, occasions of disorder.

I believe that this task will throw light on the origin of certain Chinese beliefs. It will give some information also about the creation of a literary form. It will bring into prominence the points of contact between symbolism and certain dominant conceptions of the Chinese mind. Finally, it will prepare the way for the study of the processes by which a learned ritual can issue from a popular ceremony. It seems to me to have furnished the means to set forth accurately the problems with which it has faced us ; problems with which it would be impossible to deal in full. I do not think that in the present condition of the study of the history of Chinese religion, an exhaustive research, as it is called, would be very useful. I shall be pleased if I have succeeded in fitly setting forth the questions and roughly outlining the work.[1]

---

[1] My best thanks are due to MM. Herr and Przyluski for their kindness in revising a large part of the proofs.

I

THE LOVE SONGS OF THE *SHIH CHING*

It is my intention to make a study of certain poems of the *Shih ching*, drawn chiefly from the first part which is distinguished by the title *Kuo fêng*. They are love-songs, plain-spoken and quite unambiguous.

How to Read a Classic

The *Shih ching*,[1] one of the classical books of China, is an ancient anthology of poetical compositions. It is known as the *Book of Odes* or the *Book of Poetry* and comprises four parts, the first being *a collection of local songs classified by States*,[2] while the remaining divisions contain, for the most part, songs of a ritual character.

Tradition maintains that the selection of the odes and songs was the work of Confucius : of all those preserved by the music-masters of the royal court only some three hundred pieces were adjudged by the Master to be worthy of inclusion in his collection.[3] It is said that the local songs (*Kuo fêng*) were collected periodically in the vassal states (*kuo*) because they exemplified the manners (*fêng*) brought about there by the feudal lords.[4] The odes of the first two sections of the *Kuo fêng* (*Chou nan* and *Shao nan*)[5] are generally allowed to

---

[1] Concerning the history of this text, see Couvreur, preface to his translation, and Legge, *Prolegomena*.

[2] I translate *fêng* by *airs*, *songs*, in accordance with Wang Ch'ung's usage of the word. Cf. p. 150, *Kuo fêng—Songs of the States*.

[3] Cf. Legge, *Prolegomena*.

[4] This is the theory expounded at great length in the preface to the *Shih ching*.

[5] The *Chou nan*, which describes the ideal of kingly virtue, is attributed to Chou Kung.—The *Shao nan*, in which the virtue of princes is set forth, is ascribed to Shao Kung.

have been composed in the royal palace, and, when sung afterwards in the villages of the various fiefs, they were the means of reforming morals.

If the evidence of the *Analects* [1] may be accepted, Confucius urged the study of his Anthology on the ground that from it the practice of virtue might be learned : the habit of moral reflection, respect for the social duties, and a strong antipathy to evil—these would be the benefits of such a study. Apart from moral lessons, much practical information would be found therein, and from the *Shih ching* a great deal might be learned about plants and animals.

Regarded as being of assistance in the development of the upright man and having the authority of a great saint, the *Book of Poetry* has become a book of instruction.

It was first used in schools, such as that which comprised the immediate followers of Confucius [2] : men of experience discussing [3] among themselves political theories, moral precepts and ritual laws—these were the men to whom was afterwards given the title " *literati* ".[4] These future government officials, these prospective masters of ceremonial, made the *Shih ching* the subject of their moral reflections and thus in course of time the traditional interpretation of the text became fixed.

In a company of prospective counsellors of state a knowledge of precedents is esteemed above all, and, according to the teaching of the Master, it is in this knowledge that the strength of counsellors lies.[5] This, no doubt, is why, at an early period, scholars desired to see in the poems of the *Shih ching* allusions to the events of history, and why, on the other hand, the poems were quoted in the speeches and dissertations recorded in the histories.

[1] *Lun yü*, xvii, 9.
[2] Cf. *SMC.*, v, Biogr. of Confucius.
[3] Regarding these discussions, see *Lun yü*, or *passim*, the *Li chi*.
[4] It is strange that the character used should have been regarded as the equivalent of another, which originally indicated the first rank of nobility.
[5] See the *Kuo yü*, a collection of speeches, advice, and reproofs.

LOVE SONGS OF THE SHIH CHING

Indeed almost all the poems of the *Shih ching* [1] are reproduced in the *Tso chuan*, and, conversely, almost all the poems are explained by events drawn from the *Tso chuan*. [2] Now, both the explanation of the *Shih ching* and the editing of the *Tso chuan* are attributed to the Confucian School. [3]

Thus the songs of the *Kuo fêng* were themselves associated with historical anecdotes and served to illustrate the precepts of moral philosophy and of politics.

Since there were in feudal China numbers of schools, itinerant and otherwise, all more or less independent of one another, it is easy to understand how different traditional interpretations of the *Shih ching* developed, and when, under the Han dynasty, the restoration of the Anthology burned by Ch'in Shih-huang Ti (246–209 B.C.) [4] was undertaken, four versions [5] made their appearance. Since, however, the differences lie only in details of orthography, there can be no doubt of the authenticity of the text, which has been handed down with only one of the systems of interpretation, that of Mao Ch'ang. It is referred to Tzŭ Hsia, a disciple of Confucius; to him is attributed a short gloss which forms the preface. The explanations given are always historical, moral, and symbolic.

From what remains of the other versions it is evident that this method of interpretation was general. Had they all been preserved in their entirety it would have been possible by a comparison of detail to understand the state of mind of the various schools and to know exactly the characteristics of each. In the present state of the text the work is still possible if all the quotations from the *Shih ching* found in the histories, especially in the *Tso chuan* and the *Lieh nü chuan*, are utilized.

---

[1] Cf. Legge, *Proleg.*

[2] See further on, the prefaces to the songs.

[3] See Legge, ibid.

[4] For the Burning of the Books see Legge, *Proleg.*, and Chavannes, preface to the translation of *Ssŭ-ma Ch'ien.*

[5] That of Mao (extant) and those of Lu, Ch'i and Han, of which only fragments remain. Cf. *HCCCHP.*, 1118–56.

Such a study would form a noteworthy contribution to the review of the origins of Chinese history, but would do nothing to further a knowledge of the original meaning of the songs and odes.

The essential thing is to note that, in the Han period, the symbolic interpretation was generally accepted. By this the educational value of the collection was still further increased. The *Shih ching* was studied not only in order to learn about natural history or national antiquities but also to understand the political history of the kingdom—to understand it better than it could be understood from the *Annals*, for side by side with the facts, were found, in symbolic form, opinions of weight.

Even a practical method of formulating moral judgments was discovered therein. In feudal times one of the most essential duties of the vassal was to offer advice. This was one of the ways in which his loyalty might be proved and his destiny be bound up with that of his liege lord. If his lord did evil the vassal was bound to rebuke him. *Admonitions*, indeed, form a large part of the subject matter of history.[1] An admonition, in order not to wound the dignity of the ruler, must not be direct. Thus it was a good plan to quote aptly and with proper emphasis, some lines from the *Shih ching*[2] which, for the occasion, assumed a symbolic value. Many songs are necessary for curbing absolute power. The habit persisted of quoting the *Shih ching* in the imperial councils. But the use of these poetical admonitions to correct the evil tendencies of a youthful prince whose future dignity already rendered him worthy of regard was also found to be a good method. Shortly before the beginning of the Christian era it became necessary to dethrone a bad emperor. His counsellors were punished and his tutor was also properly held responsible. He, however, avoided punishment by pleading in his own

---

[1] See principally the *Kuo yü*.
[2] E.g. *Tso chuan*, Hsi, twentieth yr. ; Legge, p. 177 ; ibid., Wên, second yr. ; Legge, p. 234 ; ibid., Chêng, twelfth yr. ; Legge, p. 378.

14

defence that he had made use of the three hundred and five poems of the *Shih ching* in his admonitions to the prince.[1]

Such a use of symbolism throws light upon its origin and its destiny alike. The *Shih ching* has become a book to be used in schools, a sort of manual of ethics for the use of the young. Even the love-songs themselves, provided they are not divorced from their allegorical interpretation, contribute to the growth of virtue in the young. By reason of the fact that they have served through the centuries to inculcate morality, the traditional interpretation of the *Shih ching*, which has been the cause of its inclusion among the classics, has become untouchable. It must be adhered to, at any rate when speaking officially and whenever it is necessary to show respect for orthodoxy. Possibly it is interpreted differently when read privately and for pleasure.[2]

A book so old and so closely bound up with the history of China might well arouse in various ways the interest of western scholars.

The earliest missionaries were chiefly sensible of the nobility of the ritual odes. In some of them they discerned traces of an ancient revelation[3]; they referred to the whole book with sympathy. Couvreur has definitely pointed out the inadequacy of the classical interpretation, and remarked that teachers never explain to children all the poems of an Anthology in which, officially, there is not one " licentious line ". He determined to make known what was the instruction given in the schools.[4] His translation is an exact reflection of the *Shih ching* as it is interpreted in our own times, and on this ground it is valuable.

Legge[5] appears to work upon the Classics rather with ancient China in view, but it must be admitted that his outlook on them is extraordinarily narrow. Often he seems to have no end in view beyond that of making an inventory of the literary

---

[1] *Ch'ien Han shu*, biography of Wang Shih, Shanghai edition, 88, p. 8, *recto* : 'I remonstrated, using the three hundred and five poems.'
[2] See farther on, p. 25 sqq.
[3] See Couvreur's note to his translation of the *Shih ching*, pp. 347–8.
[4] *Shu ching*, S. Couvreur, S.J., preface.
[5] See his translation in the *Chinese Classics*, and also the *Prolegomena*.

labours of Confucius and deciding whether or not he was really a great man. A rather brief review which does not appreciate the real problems; a too-industrious scholarship with, apparently, no rules to guide it; a desire to show at times the absurdity of the commentaries and at others to include in his translation injudiciously selected notes, all these factors combine to detract from the value of his work, notwithstanding the fact that it was done under the most favourable material conditions. The faults indicated are especially evident in his treatment of the Odes of the States.

Giles [1] and Grube,[2] in writing on Chinese literature, were most impressed by the simple natural beauty or the poetic charm of the Songs and have tried to communicate this impression by giving extracts. In the effort to be literary the translation has not always gained in accuracy. Giles, for example, in doing over again Legge's translation, does not, in my opinion, improve upon it by replacing useless explanations from the commentaries by poetic tags in the English manner. M. Laloy [3] has turned some of the songs into brief verse which, though sometimes pleasing, contains more of western literary bias than of the actual sentiment of the Chinese text.

Those who have given their attention to the *Shih ching* have sometimes been pursuing some practical point, whether historical or literary, and as it happens, they have been more or less successful, but either they have not imposed upon themselves the burden of systematic research, without which the original meaning of the odes cannot be discovered, or else they have been unaware of the necessity for effort in this direction. To tell the truth, it is no easy task.

The language of the *Shih ching* is both ancient and difficult. Neither the sinologue nor the educated Chinese himself has immediate access to it. This is most true of the odes of the

---

[1] H. A. Giles, *A History of Chinese Literature*, v, p. 12 sqq. Cf. the translation given by him on p. 15, and No. lxvi.

[2] W. Grube, *Geschichte der chinesischen Literatur*, p. 46 sqq.

[3] Laloy, *Les Chants des Royaumes*, preface and translation in *Nouvelle Revue Française*, 1909, ii, pp. 15, 130, 195.

16

first part of the book. How then can they be understood ?
One may apply to a literary Chinese or have recourse to the
learned editions. In making use of the commentaries there
is always the strong probability that one will be influenced by
their symbolic interpretation even while declaring from time
to time their absurdity. If, on the other hand, help is sought
from an educated Chinese, it is probable that he will, if he has
cast off the shackles of classical orthodoxy, be conscious of the
charm of the text, but he certainly will not seek in it anything
more than the satisfaction of his æsthetic taste. He will explain
an ode from the *Shih ching* just as one would explain a pleasing
poem, examining the *literary processes of the poet* and pointing
out the *art of the writer*. It will never occur to him that the
songs might be of popular origin.

I propose to show that it is possible to go beyond the simple
literary explanation, and, beyond the symbolic interpretation,
to discover the original meaning of the odes. I shall do so
by means of an example which is conclusive.

There is in the *Chou nan* a marriage song, the meaning of
which presents hardly any difficulty. In the state in which
it originated, the royal virtue had resulted in the regularizing
of marriage. Such is the historical explanation attached to
the song ; it is indefinite enough to absolve the commentators
from the duty of investing it with a very abstruse symbolism.
Let us rely on them to translate it.[1]

---

[1] In the translations of the odes which follow, the Roman numeral before the
title shows their order in this work. An Arabic numeral following the Roman
indicates (when necessary) the number of the line. The notes on the odes comprise :
1, information concerning the Chinese interpretations, and, in most instances, the
preface of Tzŭ Hsia ; 2, notes on the individual lines, taken for the most part,
from the commentaries of Mao Ch'ang (Mao) and Chêng K'ang-ch'êng (Chêng),
these notes being preceded by the number of the line ; 3, general information about
the meaning, or the ritual interpretations, or the beliefs connected with the ode ;
4, the principal themes. In order that a song or even a line may be read with profit
reference must be made to this assemblage of notes.
In the parentheses on the right of the title is given : 1, the section of the *Shih
ching* to which the ode belongs and its number in that section ; 2, the page on which
the poem is to be found in Couvreur's translation ; 3, the page on which it is to be
found in Legge's version. At the end of the book will be found a table of concordance
of the odes.

I. *The Beautiful Peach Tree* (*Chou nan* 6—Couvreur 10— Legge 12)

1. The peach tree, young and beautiful,
2. How profuse its flowers !
3. The girl is about to be married :
4. It is right that they should be wife and husband !

5. The peach tree, young and beautiful,
6. Abundant are its fruits !
7. The girl is about to be married :
8. It is right that they should be husband and wife !

9. The peach tree, young and beautiful,
10. Luxuriant its leaves !
11. The girl is about to be married :
12. It is right that they should wed !

I. *Preface* : " The song of the peach tree shows the effect of (the influence of) the queen. Because she was free from jealousy, men and women revered the rules ; marriages were made at the appointed times and there were no unmarried people in the state." (The queen is T'ai Ssŭ, wife of Wên Wang, the civilizing king.)

1 and 2. According to both Mao and Chêng these lines are a metaphor. The young vigour of the peach tree is depicted in the Chinese by a descriptive auxiliary which indicates in allegory that the person (the girl) symbolized by the tree has reached the age of marriage. Cf. *Li chi, Chiu li*, i, 1. Couvreur, i, p. 8 : ' A man of thirty is called vigorous, and he marries.' Applied to a woman the same term implies twenty years. A further descriptive auxiliary depicts the luxuriance of the flowers. For Mao it symbolizes the beauty of the girl. According to Chêng it indicates that marriages were made both at the proper season and at the proper age. (Chêng believes in the rule referring marriages to the spring-time.)

4. The text indicates that it is fitting to marry, since the age (Mao), or the age and the season (Chêng), are those prescribed in the rites.

19

6. According to Mao the fruits symbolize the feminine virtues of the girl. Chêng, in view of the meaning he has given to the flowers, makes no comment here.

10. According to Mao the descriptive auxiliary indicates the perfect physical condition of the girl.

12. Mao says these are the members of one household: Chêng gives them the same meaning as in 4 and 8.

Imperial Commentary of the Ch'ing Dynasty: The good government of the State is reflected in the proper ordering of the family . . . also (the government of K. Wên being good) it was inevitable that in all the states the women should be capable of ordering their households aright. Cf. *Ta Hsüeh, Li chi,* Couvreur, ii, p. 626.

The peach tree flowered: the time of flowering is referred by the calendar to the second month. Cf. *Yüeh ling.* Couvreur, *Li chi,* i, p. 340. Concerning the peach tree see de Groot: *Emouy,* pp. 88, 480.

A marriage-song. Theme: the growth of plants.

I have followed the interpretations of the commentators but have carefully avoided inserting their comments into my text. Attentive reading will show the many difficulties involved in the symbolic interpretation of even such a simple ode as this.

Thanks to King Wên, marriages were contracted according to rule; but what exactly were the rules of marriage to which these lines may, in figurative terms, refer?

At first sight it may seem to be a question of the age of the parties; they must not be too old. Further, the perfect age is symbolized by a flowering peach tree.[1] Still greater exactitude might identify the tree with a young girl of from fifteen to nineteen years of age. But, since it is allegorical, why stop there? The flowers represent the beauty of the girl, the fruits her wifely virtues, and the foliage the perfection of her physical state.

Marriages must take place not only at a certain age but also at a fixed season of the year, which in the opinion of certain writers is the spring-time, since it was in spring that the peach tree blossomed. There is yet another possible symbolism.[2] True, the fruit is mentioned after the flowers:

[1] I, 1, 2.   [2] Ibid.

were marriages also celebrated at the time when the peaches were ripe ? Much better not to inquire ! Let us be satisfied simply to know that the Civilizing King had successfully achieved the marrying of girls at the proper age and season.

So far, good ; and the old commentators were content, but the moderns [1] go further : the consciousness of over-emphasizing morals is invariably lacking in those who instruct.

The fourth line of each verse says that the marriage is fitting or proper : in each case the same word, meaning *it is right or fitting*, is employed, and in each verse a different term is used for husband and wife. In the first stanza *wife* is rendered by *apartments*, and *husband* by *house*, both these being regular usages of the words. In the second verse the same words are employed but the phrase is reversed, while in the third a new expression is used, meaning the members of one house, that is, a household. Shall the commentators assume that these lines are varied merely for the sake of the rhyme ? How much more instructive to prove that the effect of the royal virtue extends further than the mere regulation of marriages. The step is an easy one. All that is required is to give its literal meaning of *apartment* to the word indicating wife, that of *house* to husband, while to the verb, it is fitting, is given its transitive meaning *to set in proper order*. Hence, women, under the influence of King Wên, became capable of ordering aright their houses and the members of their households. So did the Ch'ing editors choose to render the ode, thus forcing Couvreur to translate : " These young girls are going to be married ; they will establish perfect order in their apartments and in their houses."

Into such errors does the symbolic interpretation lead, even in the case of one of the odes which it has least distorted. But setting aside the symbolic in favour of straightforward study, this ode is a marriage-song and the idea of marriage is associated with that of the development of plants and particularly with the fine growth of a young peach tree. The poem comprises

[1] *Imperial Commentary of the Ch'ing Dynasty.*

three almost identical stanzas, identical save for a slight variation in the second and fourth lines of each. In the first stanza, *flowers* rhymes with *husband*, in the second *fruits* with *wife*, and in the third a rather vague term is used to express husband and wife.

Let us pass to another ode. In reading Couvreur's translation of the *Shih ching* one cannot fail to experience a feeling of surprise when in the ode of the *Carambola Tree* one finds the lines :—

"(O tree !) I congratulate thee on being destitute of feeling."
"(O tree !) I congratulate thee on having no family ! "

The lord of Kuei, says Mao Ch'ang, was depraved, and his people suffered proportionately. They therefore wished that they might be deprived of feeling like the carambola, so that they might be the less acutely aware of their sufferings.

But the carambola had other advantages : it was young and already full of vigour, like the peach tree in the earlier ode ; moreover, it possessed branches, flowers, and fruit of vaunted charm. It is remarkable that the terms used to express that charm are equivalent, so we are told, to those employed to describe that graciousness which is the first essential of a wife.[1] There is, when one thinks of it, nothing surprising in that, for the poet, using the symbol of the carambola tree, is congratulating those who have no family. Not wish to have a family of one's own ! How extraordinary ! What a wicked ruler one must have lived under to conceive such a notion ! But, indeed, the trials of evil times were more easily borne had one no feeling and no family to care for . . . But what prince, after having thought over the ode to the carambola tree, would still be wicked enough to drive his people to such depths of despair ? These, briefly, are the ideas which the subtle poet-symbolist wished to imply in the *Carambola Tree*.

However, let us try to translate it word for word.

[1] II, 1 and 2.

Love Songs of the Shih Ching

II. *The Carambola Tree (Kuei fêng 3—C. 154—L. 217)*

1. In the valley is a carambola tree ;
2. Charming the grace of its branches !
3. How full of vigour its tender beauty !
4. What joy that thou haſt no *acquaintance* !

5. In the valley is a carambola tree.
6. Charming the grace of its flowers !
7. How full of vigour its tender beauty !
8. What joy that thou haſt no husband !

9. In the valley is a carambola tree.
10. Charming the grace of its fruits !
11. How full of vigour its tender beauty !
12. What joy that thou haſt no wife !

II. *Preface* : The carambola tree (is expressive of) the grief and trouble caused by depravity. The people of the ſtate suffered because their ruler was dissolute and they envied beings devoid of feelings and desires.

2. According to Mao the words descriptive of the branches mean compliance and docility, which two terms denote the virtues charaſteriſtic of woman ; they may denote the female sex. Cf. Couvreur's *Diſtionary*.

According to Chêng, the carambola tree, growing quite ſtraight and shooting out pliant branches as it grows, symbolizes a man who in youth is upright and simple-hearted, and who, as he grows older, will have no (evil) desires (but only desires which conform to the rules).

3. A descriptive auxiliary expresses the graceful vigour of the tree.

4. Chêng says that the Chinese word which I have translated by ' acquaintance ' = mate, companion. According to Chêng, the people are grieved by the wicked desires of the prince, and (by contraſt), using the carambola as a symbol, they praise a man who in the vigour of his youth is free from sexual desire.

8. Chêng says that the expression ' have no husband ' means to have no desire for conjugal (sexual) relations.

Chu Hsi explains *acquaintance* as feeling : men envy plants their lack of underſtanding and consequent immunity from pain.

In the Ch'ing Dynaſty editions the meaning of feeling is again

23

found. " It is generally considered a misfortune not to be married. The unmarried state is never referred to as a matter for congratulation. The people (of the country) of the carambola congratulate those who are not married. This indicates the extremity of distress."

The meaning given to ' acquaintance ' by Chu Hsi and the Ch'ing editors seems to approximate to that of the Preface. The latter being somewhat indefinite, Chêng, in order to give the word its real meaning without contradicting the Preface, has contrived a different application : in his view the carambola provides a model of behaviour which the prince is advised to follow.

A song of betrothal. Themes : the growth of plants, and accidental meetings in the valleys.

The composition of this ode is surprisingly like that of the *Beautiful Peach Tree*. Both describe a tree of fine growth, and apparently marriage is the subject of the latter as it is of the former. In one couplet *flowers* rhymes with *husband*, in another *fruits* with *wife*. May it be that in the other stanza the last word in the fourth line also refers more loosely to the betrothed pair, or, without specifying the sex, to either of them ? Read thus, the ode can be understood without recourse to symbolism ; it has nothing to do with the wicked Duke of Kuei : it is simply a song of betrothal. In one stanza the girl expresses in song her gladness that the youth of her choice is not engaged to another, and the young man in his turn, says the same ; but both may sing the first stanza, and without doubt they sing it in unison : " What joy that thou hast no *acquaintance* ! " [1]

I should not like to lay myself open to the accusation of translating Chinese by making bad puns in French. Even if translation be poor it should be serious, and with us it would be considered second-rate to employ the word " acquaintance " to express " friend " in this sense. Is it possible that in Chinese, always so dignified, in translations, the word might be so used without loss of dignity to the style ? As a matter of fact, the word *chih : knowledge, feeling, acquaintance* often has the meaning of *friend* even in books of a serious character. Nor is there anything surprising in that. But this is not enough.

[1] M. Granet uses the word " *connaissance* ".

24

Has the word the exact meaning of *friend* in this particular
ode ? Is it, in fact, I who make a pun and a mistranslation, or
is it the symbolic commentators ?

Mao Ch'ang gives no note at all on the word, but the preface
is precise : " The people think enviously of beings devoid of
feelings and desires." The preface is the work of Tzǔ Hsia,
a disciple of Confucius ; then I am wrong. Nevertheless, let
us examine the comment [1] of Chêng K'ang-ch'êng : " *Chih :
acquaintance*, means *mate, companion.*" Would Chêng accept
my version ? No, that would spoil the moral interpretation.
He adds then : " One rejoices that he has not . . ." What ?
A mate ? Feelings ? There is nothing else in the passage.
But no, that is *not* what Chêng says. He says : " One rejoices
that he has not the *desire* to take a mate, a wife." That is to
say, he (the carambola, presumably) is congratulated because
he (it) has been wise enough to avoid burdening himself with
the care of a wife under such a government. And that is how,
in conformity with the preface, he is without *desires.* So all
is consistent : the words have their correct meanings which
must not be ignored and morality has its rights which must
be respected. *Chih : acquaintance* really does mean *friend*
and not *feeling* and I am not wrong at all, but for all that the
Carambola is a satire directed against bad shepherds, and
Tzǔ Hsia, disciple of Confucius, was perfectly right. Chêng
K'ang-ch'êng [2] had sufficient ingenuity to avoid a bad misinter-
pretation without destroying the educative value of the poem.
By slightly forcing the passage he harmonizes his conscience
as philologist and his scruples as orthodox moralist.

At the same time he reveals to us a fact which is of the utmost
importance in a methodical study of the *Shih ching* : the
philology of the commentators is, in detail, *independent of their
moral theories.* It is one thing to point out, in the preface,
the services which the songs may render to good manners, and

---

[1] II, 4.

[2] Chêng K'ang-ch'êng (A.D. 127–200), the most eminent of the commentators
on the Classics, famous for his accurate scholarship as well as an acute perception
of the meaning of the ancient language.

quite another to read the text with accuracy. There is the *Shih ching* as explained and as quoted in the schools and in admonitions, and there is the *Shih ching* as enjoyed and analysed by the lover of art and antiquities. I do not see how Chêng could have stripped the old songs of the moral dress which is their official garb, but on the other hand I should have found it difficult to believe that such a fine scholar and man of the world could be misled by the unfortunate symbolism of the standard interpretation. With that rare wisdom which does not dispute the value of conformity to generally accepted social conventions, Chêng has expounded the *Shih ching* just as he found it, explanatory stories and prefaces included. He has benefited by its moral lessons to illumine as far as possible various points of history or law, and by its " lessons in things " to define with incomparable scholarship the meaning of ancient or technical words and, where the symbolic interpretation has been reduced to the necessity of straining somewhat the meaning of various expressions, he corrects it, mildly, in such a manner that the reasonably careful reader is not deceived while the moral may yet be preserved.

In reading the *Shih ching*, and particularly the *Kuo fêng*, the following rules will be observed :—

1. No attention will be paid to the classic interpretation, or to the variants of it which have survived. It should only be used in an attempt to discover the ritual usages *derived* from the *Shih ching* ; it must not be used in order to fathom the original meaning of the odes themselves.

2. The recognized distinction between odes which indicate a good state of morals and those which show a bad one, will be ignored. It may be that there are satirical odes [1] in the *Shih ching*, but to see a symbolic satire in an ode such as the *Carambola* is undoubtedly a misinterpretation.

3. Consequently, no distinction will be made between the first two and the remaining sections of the *Kuo fêng*. Odes

[1] No. LXII may be an instance.

26

classed in different sections [1] will be compared without hesitation. It has already been shown how useful such comparisons could be, and this method has resulted in the discovery that a supposed political satire was nothing more than a simple betrothal song.

4. All interpretations which are symbolic or which imply subtlety in the poet will be excluded.

5. All information concerning history or customs which may help to justify the symbolic interpretation will be carefully collected, but as independent data. For example, the fact will be noted that, according to Mao, all women must marry before twenty and all men before thirty years of age ; also that all marriages were, in the opinion of Chêng, bound to take place in spring, but these facts will not be made use of in translating the *Beautiful Peach Tree*.

6. Explanations of words or syntax will be welcomed, but a distinction will be made between those which are given out of desire for philological accuracy and those supplied merely to justify the academic interpretation. This is a rule difficult to adhere to ; to follow it closely requires : first, that the commentaries be read with great attention and in detail ; second, that some idea must have been grasped of the attitude of each commentator with reference to the particular passage he is interpreting ; third, that the special archæological theories of each school of commentators must be understood ; and, lastly, that from the beginning there must be an accurate conception of the general meaning of the ode under review. Good results can be obtained only by long practice and a careful application of the two rules which follow :—

7. The greatest attention will be paid to the rhythm of the odes. Experience shows that this rhythm reveals *certain correspondences of expression* allied to certain *correspondences between things*,[2] which illumine at the same time the special

---

[1] The classification which I have adopted has no reference to the official classification.

[2] The process of correspondences will be studied farther on.

meanings of words and the general meaning of the poem. Consequently, in the translation, every effort will be made to preserve the rhythm of the original ; the translation will follow line by line and in such a manner as to reveal repetitions or parallel expressions.[1]

8. The meaning of each ode will be decided by comparison with analogous poems. If in some instances it is impossible to discover the general meaning of an ode, this method will at least help to increase the collection of correspondences and in this way a series of poetic themes will be built up.

9. Experience shows that it is dangerous to interpret the songs of the *Shih ching* which have transmitted to us bare facts, by the aid of ritual regulations elaborated by an already developed religious principle, or reconstructed by devout archæologists. Every effort will be made to explain the *Shih ching* by the *Shih ching* : it is better to determine to know only the crude facts than to run the risk of directly relating these facts to notions or rules whose constitution is either derived from or independent of the *Shih ching*.

10. If it prove necessary to have recourse to outside sources, classical texts will yield to those which contain facts of folk-lore, ancient if possible, modern if necessary, borrowed at need from the arena of the civilization of the Far East—which will all have the advantage of having suffered the minimum of distortion as the result of judicial or religious thought.

11. The *Shih ching* is an artificial collection ; the origins of the poems contained in it differ widely, so it is said, as to origin, date, and author. Familiarity reveals the fact that in it no attention is, in effect, paid to provincial distinctions. Indeed, the study of the *Shih ching* gives a strong impression of *Chinese unity*.[2] On the other hand, it would be unwise not

---

[1] Observation of this rule has forced me to translate with absolute literalness. At times I have had to ignore the order of the Chinese characters, in which case I have endeavoured in my translation to make those words continue to correspond which correspond in the Chinese lines.

[2] At least within the *Confederacy of Chinese States* or ' Middle Kingdom '.

to be prepared to find in the collection, and even in the *Kuo fêng*, poems which are of later date or the work of scholars.[1]

12. It is not impossible, for example, that when the songs were committed to writing they underwent considerable alteration [2] : the fact must be kept in mind that the songs may be of secondary formation while the themes are of early construction.

13. The original themes, necessarily associated with sentimental situations, may appear in odes which give expression to analogous feelings without, on that account, any connection existing between these poems and the facts which are the source of the themes.[3]

14. Some themes, and even whole songs, may, at a given moment, have received in unmodified or only slightly modified form, a new ritual use or practice which, in return, has conferred on them a value or significance more or less new.[4]

15. In particular the love-songs and their themes may have received a new significance, whether by reason of the evolution of matrimonial institutions in the course of time, or because these institutions, in passing from one class of society to another, changed their value.[5]

16. From another point of view, certain themes or songs may have served, even without important modification, as counsels or as disguised satires, in accordance with the usage of counsels and admonitions mentioned above.[6] Such a use has been facilitated by the following facts : (1) The words which express friendship and comradeship-in-arms are also employed in the language of love [7] ; (2) a woman speaks

---

[1] E.g. v and lxvii (particularly the third stanza).

[2] E.g. xvii and liv B. Note, for example the evolution of the morning serenade. Cf. xlii ; *Ch'i fêng*, i, Couvreur, 103. *Hsiao ya*, iii, 8, Couvreur, 212.

[3] See p. 133.

[4] Comp. xxxiii, and *Wang fêng*, 4, Couvreur, p. 128.

[5] See the interpretations of lvi and lix. Cf. Granet : *Coutumes Matrimoniales de la Chine antique. T'oung pao*, xiii, p. 553.

[6] Compare the use of Malagasy songs. See Paulhan, *Les Hainteny Merinas*, 1913, preface. See Appendix I.

[7] See pp. 194–5.

of her husband, and a girl of her lover, as *lord*, or *my lord*, the same terms being generally used by a vassal ; (3) gender is not usually indicated—so that it is difficult to say whether a man or a woman speaks, and the reproaches of a forsaken mistress may—aside from their passionate character—pass for the remonstrances of a vassal or a friend. The possibility of such confusion is, in itself, an important fact, disclosing as it does the relationship of the various social affinities which may thus be mistaken one for the other.

All precautions being taken, the interpretation which can be given of the *Shih ching* must be regarded as practically certain so far as the themes are concerned, although it is not certain in every instance with regard to the songs. This limitation is not very important in the present study, which is concerned not with the examination of the literary value of the odes taken individually, but only with discovering the essential elements of a class. From this standpoint it is the themes rather than the poems themselves which are interesting.

The poems translated in the present work are the most important amongst those odes of the *Shih ching* which appear to be love-songs. I have arranged them in the order in which they seem best to explain one another ; they are classified according to their particular themes and are divided into three groups, each group being followed by the remarks which it suggests.

The songs which will be dealt with first are characterized by brief descriptions of subjects borrowed from nature. Similar descriptions are found in the ancient calendars. The study of these *rustic themes* will prove that the poetry of the odes is connected with seasonal customs, and one may wonder if it had not a ritual origin.

A second section will comprise those odes which depict *love in the village*. Is this rustic poetry of learned origin and moral in intention? I shall prove that if this suggestion has been put forward, it has been simply to justify the educational use of the *Shih ching*. But the reason why it has been possible to maintain it is because anxiety for moral orthodoxy prevented the understanding of the rural manners of ancient times. It is just these manners which will enable us to discover in what surroundings the songs originated. It will remain to study the content and the method of this rustic poetry and these will only become clear if we find that it originated amongst groups of dancers.

Finally, the last poems will indicate the *themes of the excursions on the hills and beside the rivers.* They will allow us to see how the songs of love, how both love and poetry originate in the rites of seasonal festivals. In conclusion, I shall show briefly what the love-poems, even when personal, have preserved of the primitive art of the song.

RUSTIC THEMES

III. *The Mulberry Trees in the Valley (Hsiao ya* VIII, 4— C. 310—L. 414)

1. The mulberries in the valley—how vigorous !
2. Their leaves, how beautiful !
3. As soon as I see my lord,
4. My joy, what is it not !

5. The mulberries in the valley—how vigorous !
6. Their leaves, how charming !
7. As soon as I see my lord
8. Ah ! what is not my joy !

9. The mulberries in the valley—how vigorous !
10. Their leaves how darkly green !
11. As soon as I see my lord
12. His fascination, how powerful it is !

13. Him, then, whom I love in my heart,
14. Is he too far off to dream of?
15. Him, whom I prize with all my heart
16. Him, when can I forget him?

III. *Preface*: *The mulberries in the valley*: a satire against King Yu. Mean men were in office, the sages in retirement. The poet longed for the sages that they might devote all their heart to the service of the king (that is to say, that the king might become sensible of their merits).

1 and 2. The fine appearance of the tree is depicted by a descriptive auxiliary.

Correspondence between lines 13 and 14 is proved by the use of the same terminal particle in each line, and between 15 and 16 similarly.

The use of the term *chün-tzŭ* lord, which also means sage, and the subjects of the poem, faithfulness and influence, explain how it has been possible to translate the search for the lover in the fields into a search for the sages who have gone into retirement because they were not invited to hold office.

Theme: the growth of plants. Auxiliary themes are accidental meetings in the valleys, influence (12), separation (14), and faithfulness (16).

IV. *The Poplars at the Gate* (*Ch'ên fêng* 5—C. 148—L. 209)

1. The poplars at the east gate!
2. How luxuriant their leaves!
3. At dusk we should be waiting for each other!
4. How bright the radiance of the stars!

IV. *Preface*: *The Poplars at the Gate*: A criticism of the times. Marriages were being made out of the proper season. Many youths and girls transgressed the rules. When the fiancé went in person to meet the girl she frequently did not come.

1 and 2. Youths and girls, taking no count of the seasons (not obeying the rules concerning the marriage season) did not wait for the arrival of autumn or winter. (Mao.)

The luxuriance of the foliage of the poplars indicates the middle of the third month. This is a picture showing that the season is too far advanced. (Chêng.) They have allowed the second month of spring to pass.

3 and 4. The ceremony in which the young man presents himself before his betrothed takes place in the dusk of evening. The girl, dallying with other lovers, was not at all willing to come at the usual time, and, when she did arrive, the stars were shining brightly. (Chêng.)

The third stanza differs from the others only in the descriptive auxiliary.

For Chêng (and no doubt the preface) the satire is twofold. Marriages took place neither at the season of the year, nor at the time of day prescribed. The marriage ceremony, *I li, Shih hun li,* ought to take place at dusk. Mao believes that the marriages took place too early (in spring or summer), for in his opinion the propitious seasons were autumn and winter. Chêng thinks they were concluded too late, the only proper month, in his view, being the second (spring equinox). For Chu Hsi: Meeting-place of lovers.

3. The word which is used in the terminology of marriage to indicate the day of the nuptial ceremony designates in the odes the time of the meetings or the trysting itself. Cf. XLIV, 5 ; XX, 7 ; LXVI, 7 and 10.

Themes: the growth of vegetation, trystings, and the shady places to the east of the towns.

V. *The Beautiful Flower (Shao nan* 13—C. 27—L. 35)

1. Is it not a beautiful flower,
2. The blossom of the wild cherry ?
3. Does one not feel her modesty
4. When gazing on the chariot of the Princess ?

V. The first four lines of a ceremonial poem describing the marriage of a princess to a noble. Such a marriage being beneath her, she must make a show of modesty. Cf. the story of the daughters of Yao. *SMC.,* Chavannes, i, 53.

Poem of courtship. Theme: blossom time.

VI. *Winged Locuſts (Chou nan 5—C. 10—L. 11)*

1. Ye winged locuſts,
2. How many you are !
3. May your descendants
4. Have great virtues !

VI. *Preface* : *Winged locuſts* : depiĉts the multitude of the descendants of the queen. The meaning is that, because, like the locuſts, she was never jealous, her descendants were very numerous.

2. The greatness of the multitude is depiĉted by a descriptive auxiliary. (Mao.) Of all beings endowed with sexual desire (lit. Yin and Yang desires) none is free from jealousy save the locuſts. Every female is able to receive the breath (of the male) and produce young. The virtue of the queen had equal powers.

Being free from jealousy she permitted all the women of the harem to approach their lord (cf. LVI, preface) and thus gave to her husband (and to herself) numerous descendants. (Chêng.)

4. A descriptive auxiliary indicates the social virtues of benevolence and kindness. Cf. *Chou nan*, XI, 2, and XIV, 5.

3 and 4. Chêng explains that the result of the virtue of the queen (freedom from jealousy) was that the children of the women of the harem were, without exception, good.

The second and third ſtanzas differ from the firſt only in the descriptive auxiliaries.

8. Respeĉt for the rules is indicated by a descriptive auxiliary. (Mao.)

10. The crowd is described by a descriptive auxiliary. (Mao.)

12. The harmony is depiĉted by a descriptive auxiliary. (Mao.)

Compare LIX, 1 and 2 ; the locuſt is conneĉted with the idea of sexual union.

Theme : the mating of animals.

It is difficult to avoid the impression that these lines carry a suggeſtion of a wish and incantation tending to promote the reproduĉtion of the species (human and animal).

VII *The Quails (Yung fêng 5—C. 56—L. 80)*

1. The quails go in couples
2. The magpies in pairs . . .
3. A man without goodness
4. Shall he be my brother ?

5. The magpies go in pairs
6. The quails in couples . . .
7. A man without goodness
8. Shall he be my lord ?

VII. *Preface* : *The Quails* : Criticism of Hsüan Chiang of Wei
(princess of the Chiang family, wife of Duke Hsüan of Wei
(718–699 B.C.). Cf. *SMC.*, iv, pp. 196 sqq.). The people of
Wei wished to declare that (the conduct of) Hsüan Chiang did not
accord with (that of) the quails and the magpies.

Hsüan Chiang (second wife of Duke Hsüan) abandoned herself
to dissipation and an irregular union with the heir-apparent, Huan
(son of Hsüan). Her conduct was not so exemplary as that of
animals. (Cf. Comments of K'ung Ying-ta on 3 and 4 : She did
not comply with the laws of mating which are observed even by
(animals such as) the magpies and the quails.) (Chêng.)

1 and 2. Descriptive auxiliaries used in lines 1 and 2 indicate that
the magpies and the quails produce their offspring in accordance
with the laws of mating. [Comment of K'ung Ying-ta : They do
not commit incest; lit. they have no irregular connections among
their own kind : i.e. relatives.] In flight the one follows the other :
i.e. the female follows the male with whom she should normally
pair. (It is this flight which the descriptive auxiliaries describe.)
Cf. LVI, 1 and 2. (Mao.)

4. Mao and Chêng say that the brother is the brother of the
prince, Huan, brother of Duke Hui (successor to Hsüan).—On
the word brother used to denote lover or husband, see XXXIII,
3 (n.), and *P'ei fêng*, x, 2nd stanza in f.

8. A princess, not a prince. Mao says the reference is to Hsüan
Chiang.

The political interpretation hangs upon the word *brother*, taken
in its literal sense, and *lord*, in its political sense. Themes : The
mating of wild creatures. Ironic refusal.

VIII. *The Mountains of the East (Pin fêng 3—C. 167
—L. 235)*

41. The oriole which takes its flight
42. How glistening are its wings !
43. This girl going to be married
44. Flecked with red are her horses !

VIII. Fragment of a military elegy.

41. *The song of the oriole*, theme taken from the calendar. *Calendar of Hsia*, 2nd month, *Yüeh ling*, id. (Couvreur, p. 340).

44. Theme : the horses of the marriage procession. Cf. XLVI.

IX. *The Magpie's Nest (Shao nan 1—C. 16—L. 20)*

1. The magpie has made a nest
2. The dove dwells in it !
3. This girl who is going to be married
4. Welcome her with a hundred chariots !

5. The magpie has made a nest :
6. The dove lodges in it !
7. This girl who is going to be married
8. Escort her with a hundred chariots !

9. The magpie has made a nest :
10. The doves fill it !
11. This girl who is going to be married
12. With a hundred chariots complete her glory !

IX. *Preface : The Magpie's Nest* (shows what constitutes) the virtue of a princess. A feudal prince endeavours by his actions, and strives by his labours, to attain to his honour and dignity (of lord). The princess in coming to marry him takes possession of (his dignity) and dwells in (his state). Her virtue is like that of the doves ; moreover she is capable of becoming the mate (of the prince).

1 and 2. The magpie typifies the prince ; the dove, the princess. (Mao.)

4. When the daughter of a noble marries a noble, a hundred carriages come to meet her and a like number accompany her.

4. Note that in the *I li*, in the chapter on marriage, the attendant of the bridegroom is called a charioteer. (Chêng.)

8. The attendants of the woman are called by a term which is interpreted by ' escort.' *I li* ; *Marriage*.

10. Chêng explains that the word *fill* is an allusion to the attendants of the woman who come to *fill* the house. A noble wedded at the

same time nine girls of the same surname, namely : a younger sister
(cousin) of the principal wife, one of her nieces (a girl of the next
generation to the chief wife), and two other similar groups of three
women (the principal of each group being called an "*escort*", the
others being a younger sister and a niece) chosen from two other
states, but bearing the same surname. Cf. chiefly *Tso chuan*, Duke
Yin, 1st year (Leg. 3) ; Glosses of Tu yu, K'ung Yang, Ho Hsiao.
Ku Liang—*Ch'un ch'iu*, Duke Ch'êng, 8th year (Leg. 366) ; Comment
of Tu yu, note from the *Tso chuan* ; comments of Tu yu and Kung
Yang.—Id., 9th year (Leg. 370) ; comments of Tu yu, Kung Yang,
Ho Hsiao—id., Duke Chuang, 19th year (Leg. 98). Comments of
Kung Yang and Ho Hsiao—*I li* : *Shih hun-li*—*Shih ching*, lxi,
and *Shao nan*, 11 ; Couvreur, p. 25.

12. According to Mao, the meaning of this line is 'fulfil all
the honours due to her on the occasion of the marriage procession '.

The number 100 indicates entirety. Cf. the hundred things =
all things.

The magpie is a bird of good omen which is deserving of the epithet
' happy ', and it is commonly associated with the idea of marriage.
See its rôle in the *Marriage of the Weaver and Ox-driver Constellations*
(cf. de Groot : *Emouy*, pp. 439–40, and this work *in fine*). The
magpie is an emblem of conjugal faithfulness. Cf. VII, and *Piao chi*,
Couvreur, *Li chi*, ii, 507. It makes its nest at the beginning of the
the 12th month ; *Yüeh ling*, Couvreur, i, p. 405.

The ring-dove or turtle-dove, whose song in the third month
(*Yüeh ling*, Couvreur, *Li chi*, i, 350) is associated with the gathering
of the mulberry-leaves, gave to the odes an air of spring. Cf. XLVI,
23 and 24. The hawk is changed into a dove in the second month of
spring (*Yüeh ling*, Couvreur, i, 340). Cf. *Hsia hsiao chêng*, first month.
The inverse change occurred in the eighth month (second month of
autumn), *Li chi*, *Wang shih*, ii, Couvreur, i, p. 283.

The rhythm is extremely simple, and is marked by the recurrence
of particles and balance of words.

The classic interpretation, although not far from the real meaning,
yet does violence to it.

The correspondence between the lines establishes a parallel between
the magpie and the bride, the doves and (the carriages in which
ride) her attendants. In the third stanza, Chêng and Mao admit,
however, that the doves are the symbols of the attendants. They do
not admit it for the first line, in order that they may be able, like
the preface, to emphasize the dependence of the wife upon the
husband.

A Marriage-song. Themes : birds ; the carriage of the bride.

37

X. *The Bind-weed* (*Chêng fêng* 20—C. 101—L. 147)

1. In the meadows is the bind-weed
2. All loaded with dew
3. He is a handsome fellow
4. With beautiful eyes.
5. Our meeting was by chance
6. And was all I could desire.

7. In the meadows is the bind-weed
8. All covered with dew.
9. He is a handsome fellow
10. With beautiful eyes.
11. Our meeting was by chance :
12. With thee all is well.

X. *Preface* : *The Bind-weed* : (The poet) is referring to the proper time for meetings. The influence of the prince no longer extends to the people. The people are exhausted by wars. Boys and girls miss the marriage-period. (The poet) thinks with regret of (the time when youths and girls) (all) went (to the gathering of young people appointed by the prince), but did not make special trysts with individuals. Cf. *Chou li, Ti kuan*, v, *Mei-shih*.

2. The dew is spread over the plants by the favour of heaven as the influence of the prince spreads over the people (Mao). For Chêng there is an indication of time, suggesting the second month of spring. The plants begin to shoot. The hoar-frost turns to dew. (Cf. LIV, where these events are reversed at corresponding periods of autumn.) Quotation from the *Chou li* to prove that at that period this was the time of matrimonial assemblies.

[For Mao : miss the time = pass the age. For Chêng : allow the favourable season (the second month) to pass.]

5. *Meeting* indicates that they met at the great assembly which was appointed by custom, without having made a previous appointment. (Mao.)

6. Agrees with my wish to marry at the proper age. (Mao.)

8. The abundance of dew is indicated by a descriptive auxiliary.

Chu Hsi : The meeting of youths and maidens in the fields among the plants all covered with dew.

Commentaries very important : they prove that, in the opinion of Chinese scholars, immorality does not lie in the rustic assemblies of girls and boys (authorized by the *Chou li*), but in the fact that in periods of disturbance these assemblies were made the occasion of pre-arranged meetings between individuals. Cf. The Contests, *in fine*.

Themes : dew ; meetings in the spring. Cf. LIV. (XI, pp. 12, 13, 14 ; see Appendix I.)

XI. *The Dew on the Roads (Shao nan 6—C. 20—L. 27)*

   1. The roads are dew-covered.
   2. Why then neither morning nor evening ?
   3. The roads are too wet with dew.

See the complete ode and commentaries in Appendix I.

XII. *The North Wind (Pei fêng 16—C. 48—L. 67)*

   1. The north wind, how chill.
   2. Rain and snow in squalls.
   3. Tenderly, oh, if you love me,
   4. With clasped hands let us go.
   5. Why stay ? Why delay ?
   6. The time is come, is urgent.

   7. The north wind, how boisterous.
   8. Rain and snow in drifts.
   9. Tenderly, oh, if you love me,
  10. With clasped hands let us go.
  11. Why stay ? Why delay ?
  12. The time is come, is urgent.

  13. Nothing so red as a fox.
  14. Nothing so black as a crow.
  15. Tenderly, oh, if you love me,
  16. With clasped hands let us go.
  17. Why stay ? Why delay ?
  18. The time is come, is urgent.

XII. *Preface* : *The North Wind,* a satire against cruelty. In the State of Wei everyone was hard and cruel. The members of different families (all the people) had no affection for one another. None gave a hand (to another) and (each) shunned the other.

2. Depicts the appearance of the wind and the rain.

The inclemency of the weather is symbolic of a cruel government (Chêng). Cf. X, Preface, 1 and 2.

7. The violence of the wind is depicted. (Mao.) Cf. XIII, 2.

13 and 14, according to Chêng, should be translated :—

> They are all red, the foxes,
> And all black the crows.

An allegory showing that lord and vassals (the latter owing to the evil influence of the prince) are all equally bad.

Invitation theme. Indication of the part played by forcible persuasion.

Themes : the weather ; invitation. Indication of the part played by forcible persuasion.

XIII. *Wind and Rain (Chêng fêng* 16—C. 98—L. 143)

1. Wind and rain. Oh ! how they rage.
2. Now crows the cock !

3. As soon as I have seen my lord
4. Ah, shall I not feel at rest ?

XIII. *Preface* : *Wind and Rain* : The poet thinks with longing of a sage. In a period of disturbance he longs for a sage who would not change his ordered conduct (to give himself to disorder like all the others).

1. Contains an auxiliary descriptive of the wind and rain.

2. Here a descriptive auxiliary represents the crowing of the cock. Cf. XII, 7.

1 and 2. Chêng and Mao : Just as inclement weather makes no change in the sound of the cock's crowing, so no disorders in the state can cause the sage to change his conduct.

The second and third stanzas are practically identical with the first, except for the rhymes.

Chu Hsi : A dissolute young girl announces that this is the time of the assignation she has made with a man, and she rejoices.

Themes : the weather ; meetings.

XIV. *The Thunder (Shao nan 8—C. 23—L. 29)*

 1. Now rolls the thunder
 2. On the south slopes of the southern hills.
 3. Why then does he remain away ?
 4. Dare he not take any leisure ?
 5. Oh, my good, oh, my good lord,
 6. Oh, return. Oh, return.

XIV. *Preface* : *The Thunder* : An exhortation to carry out public duty (due from the vassal to his lord). A high officer of the state of Shao nan being on a journey (beyond the borders of the state) in pursuit of the execution of the king's orders, and being unable to return home to rest, his wife is able, despite her distress over his hardship and toil, to exhort him to do his duty loyally.

 1. The noise of the thunder. (Mao.)
 2. The mountains produce (send forth) the clouds and the rain in order to give moisture to the earth. (Mao.)

According to Chêng the thunder is heard from all sides of the mountain, just as the high official travels in all directions.

The only changes in the second and third stanzas are the rhymes of the second and fourth lines.

Themes : absence ; the weather.

XV. *Withered Leaves (Chêng fêng* 11—C. 95—L. 138)

 1. Withered leaves. Withered leaves.
 2. The wind comes to blow upon you.
 3. Now Sirs. Now Sirs.
 4. Sing : we will accompany you.

5. Withered leaves. Withered leaves.
6. The wind comes to blow upon you.
7. Now Sirs. Now Sirs.
8. Sing, and we will follow you.

XV. *Preface*: *Withered Leaves*: Satire directed against Hu (Duke Chao of Chêng, 696–695). Lord feeble, vassal powerful; there is response even when there is no call. (Chêng: Lord and vassal, failing in their duty, do not call and respond in harmony.)

1 and 2. The leaves fly about only when the wind blows upon them; the vassal should respond only when his lord calls (Mao, Chêng.)

3. The vassals of different ages. (Mao.) Cf. XXXV, 9 and 13.

4. When the lord calls (in singing), (and only then), the vassals join him.

4. Suggests a response made in answer to a call, the response in an antiphonal song.

Cf. XXXV, Preface: The *Yang* (male) calls. The *Yin* (female) does not respond in harmony.

Symbolic interpretation founded on the notion that, in respect to his overlord, a vassal is in the same position of inferiority as the moon is to the sun, the *Yin* to the *Yang*, a wife to her husband. Hence the transposition of the theme.

Theme: withered leaves. Indication of antiphonal songs of autumn (10th month; cf. *Pin fêng*, I and LXVI, 31).

XVI. *The Rainbow* (*Yung fêng* 7—C. 58—L. 83)

1. The rainbow is in the east.
2. None dare point to it.
3. The girl when she marries,
4. Leaves behind brothers and relatives.

5. Morning mist in the west.
6. It will rain all the morning.
7. The girl when she marries,
8. Leaves behind brothers and relatives.

9. Now the girl whom you see
10. Dreams of being married
11. Without further keeping her purity
12. And before the marriage has been arranged.

XVI. *Preface*: *The Rainbow*: Putting a stop to marriage concluded without ceremonies. Duke Wên of Wei (650–634; cf. *SMC*., iv, p. 200) was able through his virtue (*tao*, his regulating power) to exercise a civilizing influence over his people. Dissipation and irregular unions became matters for shame. The people of the state no longer wished to forgather with the licentious (lit. take their places with them according to age).

1 and 2. Mao: When husband and wife transgress the rites the rainbow appears (lit. the vapours of which the rainbow is composed abound). The wise man, seeing this warning, is afraid (to break) the prohibitions : none dares point the finger at it.

Chêng : The rainbow, this heavenly warning ; one dares not point the finger at it. With how much greater reason should none dare to take notice of (associate with) a licentious girl ?

3 and 4. It is in the natural order of things (*tao*) that a woman, from birth should have to (go and) be married (outside her own family). But (since it is right that she should marry, gloss of K'ung Ying-ta) why should she grieve because she is not yet married (and, anticipating the marriage), why does she transgress the rules by licentious behaviour and a union without ceremonies ? That is very horrible.

6. From dawn to the time of food is the morning. (Mao.)

5 and 6. Chêng : When mists rise in the west in the morning it will rain before the morning is over : a natural result of the mists. (Metaphor) indicating : It is natural that from birth it should be a woman's duty to go and marry (out of her own family). From this fact also proceed natural feelings (namely those explained by Chêng in 3–4).

9 and 10. Thinking of the act of marriage. (Chêng.) Thus is expressed the magnitude of the infamous excesses of this licentious woman.

11 and 12. She does not wait for the command. (Mao.) This licentious girl is not in the least concerned to keep her virtue and does not know that she should await her parents' command to marry. (Chêng.) Cf. *I li*. Marriage : Marriage ceremonial.

Note the peculiar rhythm of the last stanza. The last word of each line is a final particle.

Themes : rain and the rainbow. The abandonment of one's relatives (a principle of exogamy).

43

Perhaps—and as a secondary application—a marriage-song ; ritual warning to the bride.

See the note on the rainbow. App. II.

XVII.   *The Escort (Ts'ao fêng* 2—C. 156—L. 222)

13.   Oh, the little, oh, the light
14.   Mists of morn on the southern hills.
15.   Oh, the pretty ; oh, the charming
16.   Young girls who are so hungry.

XVII.   The last stanza of a song which has certainly been distorted and is difficult to interpret.

13 and 15. Note the parallelism emphasized by the finals.

14. Theme : mist on the mountains. Cf. XVI, 5.

16. Theme : hunger. Cf. XLVII, 4. Comp. *Hill-songs of the Hakka*, vi, Appendix III.

XVIII.   *Harvesting (Wang fêng* 8—C. 82—L. 120)

1.   He is gathering the dolichos.
2.   One day without seeing him
3.   To me seems three months.

4.   He is gathering the artemisia.
5.   One day without seeing him
6.   To me seems three autumns.

7.   He is gathering the wormwood.
8.   One day without seeing him
9.   To me seems three years.

XVIII.   A very simple piece on the subjects of harvesting and absence. Cf. XXXVIII, 11.

Love Songs of the Shih Ching

XIX. *The Plantains (Chou nan 8—C. 12—L. 14)*

1. Let us gather, gather the plantains.
2. Come, let us gather them.
3. Let us gather, gather the plantains.
4. Come, let us collect them !

XIX. *Preface* : *The Plantains* (shows) the gentleness of the queen.
(She caused) harmony and peace (to prevail) and the women rejoiced
to bear children.

1 and 2. The plantain procures pregnancy (Mao), and allays the
pains of child-birth (K'ung Ying-ta).

Save for variations in the verbs the three stanzas are identical.

Note the monotony of the composition.

Harvesting song. Gathering herbs.

XX. *I gather the reeds (Hsiao ya 8²—C. 307—L. 411)*

1. All morning I gather the reeds
2. Without filling the cup of my hands.
3. See, my hair is all unbound.
4. Come, I will return and wash it.

5. All morning I gather the indigo
6. Without filling the hem of my skirt.
7. The fifth was the day he appointed :
8. By the sixth he has not appeared.

9. When thou goest a-hunting
10. I will put thy bow in its case.
11. When thou goest a-fishing,
12. I will twist the cord for thy line.

13. What fish hast thou caught in the fishing ?
14. There are bream and there are perch.
15. Bream there are and there are perch.
16. Come, come. How many they are.

XX.   *Preface* : *I Gather the reeds* : A satire upon (the fact that it is possible for) husbands and wives to remain alone.   In the time of King Yu there were many such.

1 and 2. A metaphor indicating inability to work resulting from prolonged separation of husband and wife.

3 and 4. A woman pays no attention to dress, etc., in the absence of her husband. (Mao.) In particular (Chêng) she does not dress her hair. Cf. *Li chi*, *Nei tsê*, Couvreur, i, 661, and *Wei fêng*, 8 ; Couvreur, p. 73, XXв.

XXв.   My lord, oh, how brave he is !
          In the state he has no peer.
          My lord, oh, he carries a lance
          In the van of the king's chariots.

          Since my lord went to the east,
          My head is like wind-driven seeds.
          Did I lack perfume or water ?
          But for whom should I deck myself?
                              (Cf. XXXVII, 4, 8, 12.)

          Oh for rain ! oh for rain !
          Brightly the sun shines forth.
          Longing I think of my lord
          With swelling heart and weary head.

          Oh where is the plant of oblivion ?
          I will plant it in front of my house.
          With longing I think of my lord
          Until my heart is overcome.

7 and 8. Mao: A wife should lie every five days with her husband. Cf. *Li chi*, *Nei tsê*, Couvreur, p. 661.   Chêng : 5th day = the days of the fifth month ; 6th day = the days of the sixth month, the meaning is that the normal time for his return had passed.

9–16.   Comp. XLII, 5–12.   Themes : conjugal intercourse ; harvesting ; fishing ; separation, and the communal feast.

XXI. *The Seventh Month (Pin fêng* 1—C. 160—L. 226)

14.   In spring when the days are mild
15.   It is then that the oriole sings.

46

16. The girls carrying their baskets,
17. Go along the little foot-paths
18. Picking the tender mulberry-leaves.
19. In spring when the days draw out
20. In crowds they gather the artemisia.
21. The hearts of the girls are anguished :
22. The time comes for them to go with the young lord.

XXI. The second ſtanza of a long ode in this manner entitled *The Works and the Days*, attributed to Chou Kung (about 1144 B.C.). He may have composed it as an address to King Ch'êng in the hope of inducing the prince to use his royal influence to make the occupations of men coincide with natural order.

15. Theme : the oriole. Cf. VIII, 41, and *Yüeh ling*, second month. See the remarks on this subjeċt in *Ruſtic Themes*.

21. Mao : In spring girls suffer the pangs of love, and boys in autumn. They feel its operation in their bodies. Chêng : In spring girls experience the *Yang* influence and think of boys. In autumn, youths experience the *Yin* influence and think of women. They undergo a physical change and they are in agony.

XXII. *The Plums (Shao nan 9—C. 24—L. 30)*

    1. Falling are the plums :
    2. Only seven remain.
    3. Ask for us, young men,
    4. It is the fortunate time.

    5. Falling are the plums :
    6. Only three remain.
    7. Ask for us, young men,
    8. This is the time—now !

    9. Falling are the plums :
10. Fill the baskets with them.
11. Ask for us, young men,
12. This is the time, speak of it !

XXII. *Preface*: *The Plums* (shows that) youths and girls await the fortunate time (to marry). The State of Shao nan having come under the civilizing influence of King Wên, boys and girls were able to await the proper time to marry.

The word here used may apply as well to the proper age as to the proper season for marriage. As a result of the divergences between archæological theories concerning the age and the season for marriage, the symbolic interpretations of the ode are both complicated and variable. To sum them up :—

(*a*) The proper age is supposed to be between 25 and 30 for men and between 15 and 20 for girls. The plums, more or less ripe— they fall more or less according to their State of maturity—symbolize the age of the affianced pair. In the first Stanza, seven remain— that is to say seven-tenths. Three-tenths have fallen. At this Stage of ripeness they represent the age of 26 or 27 for men and 16 or 17 for girls. In the second Stanza remain three = three-tenths. They symbolize 28 or 29 years of age in the men and 18 or 19 in the case of the girls. In the third Stanza none remain ; all are ripe ; the men are 30 and the girls 20. (Mao.)

(*b*) The compulsory age for marriage is supposed to be 20 for girls and 30 for men : there is no symbolic application in these ages.

(*c*) Spring is the season of marriages. Men and girls, ready for marriage since the plum season, will wait until the succeeding spring when they will mate of their own accord, without any of the ceremonies of marriage, in order to facilitate the repopulation of the State. (Chêng, with reference to the *Chou li, Ti kuan, Mei shih*.)

(*d*) The marriage season is in the fall of the year. When the plums have all fallen it is the last month of summer and it is time to ask the hand of a girl in marriage.

The phonetic part of *mei* (plum) is identical with the phonetic of *mei* (intermediary). Their pronunciation is the same. Colonel Bonifacy tells us that, in the *Man* poetry, the plum tree (or the flower of the plum tree) is an emblem of virginity. Cf. Appendix III.

Comp. LXIV, 4. The spring-time betrothals are concluded ; there remain the formalities of autumn, especially the sending of the intermediary.

A harvest song.

Theme : invitation.

It is evident that the odes of the *Shih ching* frequently contain lively and sparkling descriptions of subjects borrowed from Nature. These, with little change, are the topics which I have called *rustic themes*. Sometimes we are shown a tree

48

in the fullness of its vigorous growth, and, when its flowers, fruit, leaves and branches are praised, it seems that a parallel is being drawn between the growth of plants and the awakening of the human heart.[1]

Sometimes we see the beasts of the field calling to one another and flocking together, or we are given a description of the flight of birds which go, in groups or in pairs, singing together in harmony or answering each other's song, to gather in the densest parts of the woods, or to hide on the islets in the rivers.[2] Thus the loves of the beasts seem to be the counterpart of those of men. The state of the weather, the thunder, snow, wind, dew, rain and the rainbow, or the crops, the gathering of fruits or herbs also form a frame or an opportunity for the expression of the emotions.

We are accustomed to the poets borrowing images from Nature when they describe human feelings. When love is the theme a background of scenery seems essential, and tradition demands that the idyll should borrow its finest adornments from the countryside. Is it then by way of embellishment that the poets of the *Shih ching* have included these rustic subjects in their odes ?

The Chinese apparently think so[3] : these subjects, in their opinion, are metaphors, or allegories, that is to say, they are, apparently, literary devices employed to give poetic expression to the ideas. But what lack of imagination on the part of the poets ! What absence of variety in the imagery ! Even the selection of the pictures, if they are intended for embellishment, is difficult to understand. Flowers are less common than trees ; the blooming of flowers is scarcely mentioned ; usually it is of secondary importance, or else, if it stands for anything in itself, we discover by other means that the ode in which it occurs is different from the ordinary love-song.[4] The selection of images does not appear to have been a matter of

[1] Cf. I, II, III.
[2] Cf. VI, VII ; see also L, 9 ; LVI, LIX, 1–2 ; LX, 8.
[3] Cf. Preface to the *Shih ching*. Consult Couvreur, *Preface*, and Legge, *Prolegomena*.
[4] Cf. V. Ceremonial poem on the marriage of a royal princess to a prince of Ch'i.

taſte ; but, if it be necessary to know what images were pleasing to a poet of ancient times, we are not in a position to judge : it is juſt as well not to lay ſtress upon our observation. It is useful, however, for, having made it, it becomes necessary to ask whether the ruſtic themes have not something more than a decorative value.

When Chinese writers speak of metaphors or allegories we should take heed. These terms denote not so much a process used by men of letters as a syſtem used by moraliſts. Imagery is not employed merely to simplify the idea or make it more attraⅭtive : in itself it has a moral value. This is evident in the case of certain themes. For example, the piⅭture of birds flying in couples is, in itself, an exhortation to fidelity. If, then, metaphors borrowed from Nature are used to give expression to the emotions, it is due not so much to a consciousness of the beauty of Nature as to the faⅭt that it is moral to conform to Nature. Where, at firſt, one may be tempted to see an artiſtic intention, there may be a moral intention. From this new ſtandpoint it is already easier to underſtand why the ruſtic themes have so much importance and so little variety.

Often, beside the commentaries explaining a theme by the teachings which issue direⅭtly from it, others appear which find in it an indication of time. For example, a line referring to peach trees in bloom [1] shows, it is said, that the scene of the poem is laid in spring-time, while, at the same time, an allegorical meaning is given to the flowers. Between these two interpretations there is not as much difference as might be supposed. He who is able to conform to natural order ought further to imitate Nature by doing things at their appointed times. The birds which fly in couples and hide themselves in order to mate, exemplify the laws of wedded life ; and the time at which they mate is the proper time for marriages to be celebrated.

It will not be surprising to find men of letters regarding

[1] Cf. I, 1–2.

rustic themes as *maxims from the calendar*. This notion gives great support to the moral interpretation of the odes. Do two lovers meet when the dew covers the plants in the fields ?[1] This is a sure proof that spring is well advanced ; that, in consequence, the marriage-season is over, and, finally, since boys and girls still continue to meet, the lord of their state was not causing good customs to prevail in it. Does a young girl, on the other hand, refuse to go, either in the morning or the evening, along the roads too damp with dew ?[2] That proves that the Virtue (*tao tê*) of the prince,[3] and, consequently, the conduct of his people, were in accord with natural order (*tao*).

Certainly it is not necessary to follow in detail the explanations of the commentators ; but, on the other hand, it would be rash to assume that, in its own field, the symbolism which they make use of is without support. It is evident that it has no foundation if the rustic themes have their origin in some vague poetic sentiment of Nature. It is only supported if the themes spring from a seasonal ritual.

As a matter of fact, in the agricultural calendars, the rustic themes are found under their dates among similar maxims. There are several ancient calendars extant. Four in particular are worth comparing : the *Little Calendar of the Hsia*,[4] which is the oldest and which has been preserved in the *Rites of T'ai the Elder* ; the *Yüeh ling* or *Monthly Ordinances*,[5] which form a chapter of the *Li chi* and appear in more or less the same form in other works ; another which forms part of the third chapter of *Kuan Tzŭ*,[6] and lastly, one which is found in the sixth chapter of the *Chi chung Chou shu*.[7] From the study of these calendars the following facts may be established : (1) All are rural calendars which, by means of country sayings, show the divisions of the year. (2) All

[1] Cf. X. [2] Cf. XI.

[3] On *tao-tê*, virtue, the regulating power of the ruler over the world of men and Nature, see pp. 182 sqq. and p. 75, note 1. The translation given of *tao-tê* is required by the use of these characters, especially in the prefaces to the odes.

[4] *Hsia hsiao chêng*, see the edition given in HCCHP., 573–8.

[5] Couvreur, i, p. 331–410. [6] The chapter *Yu kuan*.

[7] In *Han Wei tsung shu*.

endeavour to allocate each of these sayings to a particular date in the astronomical year. (3) Several methods of classification are used with reference to the dividing of the year : Kuan Tzŭ divides the year into thirty periods of twelve days each (eight in spring and in autumn and seven in summer and in winter). The *Chi chung Chou shu* makes twenty-four periods of fifteen days, subdivided into three periods of five days, each period designated by a rural saying. The *Yüeh ling* and the *Lesser Calendar of the Hsia* merely divide the year into months, but in the *Yüeh ling*, grouped in one or two paragraphs for each month, are to be found the expressions which in the *Chi chung Chou shu* are used as titles for the periods of fifteen or five days. Most of them also occur in the *Lesser Calendar of the Hsia*, introduced into the topics for the month. (4) The sayings are not always referred to the same dates by different calendars. For example, the *Lesser Calendar of the Hsia* assigns the transformation of the hawk into a dove to the first month of spring, whereas the *Yüeh ling*, as also the *Chi chung Chou shu*, refers it to the second month.

The construction of these various calendars is easily explained : they are the result of a work of classification inspired by a variety of theoretical notions and a growing care for symmetry and accuracy. They are the work of archæologists working on a subject analogous to the rustic themes of the odes. The question then arises : Did the poets quote the sayings of the calendar in their poems or were the calendars composed of fragments of songs ?

The reader of the *Little Calendar of the Hsia* cannot fail to be struck by its peculiar construction. It is composed of very short, disconnected phrases, the longest seldom containing more than three or four characters, the order of which is so unusual [1] that the commentators append a note to the effect that the position of the words can be explained only by the

---

[1] First month, *Yen pei hsiang*. Second month, *Lai chiang yen nai ti*. *Shih yu chien ti shih shou*. Ninth month, *Tai hung yen chiang hsüan niao chê*. Eleventh month, *Yün mi chio*.

assumption that they are arranged in the order in which the things which they indicate strike the senses. Thus it is said, "It whistles, the kite [1]" because the cry is heard first and the kite is recognized afterwards.[2] Similarly, the phrase occurs[3] : "Now sings the oriole." This form of expression in a calendar seems strange, and, as a matter of fact, the *Yüeh ling* says, simply, "The oriole sings." [4] This is indeed the correct style and syntax of prose, while, on the other hand, the expression used in the *Calendar of the Hsia* is very poetic. Indeed, it occurs as a line in the *Shih ching* in exactly this form.[5]

Since examples of poetic language are found in the most ancient of the calendars, it would seem reasonable to suppose that the rustic themes of the odes are not sayings borrowed by the poets from the rural calendars, but are rather themselves composed with the assistance of rustic poetry. But it would be well not to be too hasty. The themes of the odes and the sayings from the calendars may proceed from a common source ; poets may have done the work of antiquaries and drawn, exactly as did the scholars, upon a store of proverbs. In this case the rustic themes would not at all prove that the poems in which they occur are not of learned origin ; they may possibly be the work of polished men of letters with a love for archaic language.

In the Collection edited by Confucius there is a very singular poem called *The Seventh Month*,[6] than which none is more honoured. The Duke of Chou, who was a great Sage,

---

[1] *Ming ko* : It whistles, the kite. Twelfth month.
[2] *Ming êrh hou chih ch'i ko yeh* : It whistles and afterwards the kite is recognized.
[3] *Yu ming ts'ang kêng* : now sings the oriole.
[4] *Li chi*, Couvreur, i, p. 340. *Ts'ang kêng ming* : The oriole sings.
[5] XXI, 14, Couvreur, p. 161 : This very line occurs in a festival ode, the *Seventh Month*, which is simply a calendar in verse. See below.
[6] *Ibid.*, Couvreur, p. 165, *8th strophe*. Compare *Chou Sung*, iii, 6, Couvreur, p. 441 (and the preceding poem). Concerning this tenth month festival, see further on page 168 sqq. The *Chou li* proves the ritual use of Ode 1 of *Pin fêng* in the article *Yüeh chang*. Cf. Biot, ii, pp. 65–6. The same passage refers to the ritual use of Ode 3 of Pin, which is full of sayings from the calendar, and which the commentators describe as a military ode. See also *T'ang fêng*, 1, Couvreur, p. 120.

composed it in olden times for the purpose of proving *that the Virtue of the Ruler sufficed to bring into harmony the occupations of men and the natural course of things.* This long poem is a calendar in verse, each line being a rustic saying which serves to indicate a period of the year. It is a kind of Chinese *Fasti*.

Now these Fasti are not a poetic diversion of the scholars, nor are they a learned collection of popular proverbs. The poem is an entity ; it has uniformity and significance ; it is an ode of whose ritual importance there can be no doubt. It was sung at the harvest festival which brought the agricultural year to a close, and a description of the festival itself is included at the end of the poem.[1] A threshing floor was cleared, wine was brought, a lamb was sacrificed, the cup of rhinoceros horn was used for drinking, toasts were proposed, and while the entertainment progressed the *works and the days* of the past year were sung. Doubtless such poems are the source of the more or less systematic calendars which have been preserved, and in this fact lies the explanation of the traces of poetic language found therein. Inversely, if sayings from the calendars occur in the poems, it may be possible to deduce the reason. Are we not indeed led to think that, like the song of the *Seventh Month,* the odes proceed more or less directly from seasonal festivals ?

One fact at least has been established : the importance of the rustic themes in the poetry of the *Shih ching* and for its expositors—even if, after all, the poetry is scholarly and the expositors are mistaken to some extent—is a certain sign of the importance of seasonal customs in the life and thought of the ancient Chinese.

VILLAGE LOVES

XXIII. *Outside the Gate (Chêng fêng* 19—C. 100—L. 146)

    1. Outside the east gate
    2. The girls are like a cloud.

[1] *Pin fêng,* 1, Couvreur, p. 161 ; see an extract in XXI.

3. Although they seem a cloud
4. None holds my thought.
5. White robe and grey cap,
6. She it is who can delight me.

7. Beyond the bastion of the gate
8. The girls are like white flowers.
9. Although they are like white flowers
10. None fills my thoughts.
11. White robe and madder cap,
12. She it is who can charm me.

XXIII. *Preface*: *Outside the Gate* (shows) the distress caused by disorder. Five times the Kung-tzŭ contested [the authority of Duke Chao of Chêng (696–695) = *viz*. Tu—Duke Li—twice; Hu, once; Tzŭ Wei, once; Tzŭ I, once. Cf. *SMC.*, iv, 458 sqq.] Wars were continuous. Boys and girls were unfaithful to one another. The common people wished to protect their union (against the instability consequent upon war). Cf. the preface to LII.

2. Are like a cloud: numerous. (Mao.) According to Chêng: loose women, or women who have left their husbands (families broken up by the troubles).

5. White clothes were worn by men. (Mao.) Grey head-dresses were part of the dress of women. (Mao.) The line is the symbolical expression of the wish that grey head-dresses and white clothes might remain united, that husbands and wives might not be separated. According to Chêng, the woman is referred to by her head-dress and her clothes.

8. Something light which flies about, a symbol of inconstancy. (Chêng.)

Theme: assemblies outside the village.

Compare *Chêng fêng*, 15. *On the level space* (XXIIIB). *Preface*: *On the level space*: a satire against disorder. There were men and women who did not observe the rites and formed irregular unions.

XXIIIB. 1. On the level space at the east gate,
2. On the embankments grows the madder.
3. Thy house is there, quite near,
4. Thyself art far away.

5. By the chestnuts at the east gate,
6. There are the low houses.
7. Do I not think of thee?
8. But thou comest not to me.

1 and 2. Chêng: The words of a woman anxious to form an irregular union with a man.
Despite Chêng, I think one should translate :—

3. Thy wife is there quite near.
6. There husbands and wives are gathered.

7. Cf. XLIII, 7.
Themes: meetings outside the gates. Also (separation and regrets or) invitation.

N.B.—If the translation suggested for 3 and 6 be accepted, compare the custom here described with the Japanese practice described in Appendix III.

XXIV. *The Hêng Gate (Ch'ên fêng, 3—C. 146—L. 207)*

1. Below the Hêng gate
2. One may rest at ease.
3. The spring flows and flows.
4. One may enjoy and eat.

5. When one would eat fish
6. Must one have bream from the River?
7. When one would take a wife
8. Must she be a princess of Ch'i?

9. When one would eat fish
10. Must one have carp from the River?
11. When one would take a wife
12. Must she be a princess of Sung?

XXIV. *Preface*: In praise of political moderation.
Theme: the communal feasts and the meetings outside the gates and on the river-banks.

XXV.   *The Ephemera (Tsʻao fêng* 1—C. 155—L. 220)

1. Oh, the wings of the ephemera.
2. Oh, the beautiful, beautiful garment.
3. How sad am I at heart. . . .
4. Come thou and dwell with me.

5. Oh, the wings of the ephemera.
6. Oh, the fine many-coloured robe.
7. How sad am I at heart. . . .
8. Come thou and rest with me.

9. It comes from the earth, the ephemera.
10. Hempen robe, white as snow.
11. How sad am I at heart. . . .
12. Come thou and be happy with me.

XXV.   Historical interpretation without interest.
Theme: invitation.

XXVI.   *The Solitary Service Tree (Tʻang fêng* 10—C. 129
—L. 185)

1. There is a solitary service tree
2. Which grows on the left of the road.
3. Oh, my Lord, oh, thou
4. Deign thou to come with me.
5. Thou whom I love from the depth of my heart,
6. Wilt thou not drink and eat ?

7. There is a solitary service tree
8. Which grows at the turning of the road.
9. Oh, my Lord, oh, thou
10. Deign thou to walk with me.
11. Thou whom I love from the depth of my heart,
12. Wilt thou not drink and eat ?

XXVI. *Preface* : A satire againſt a prince who was incapable of really uniting his relatives.

Themes : meetings, ſtrolls, and the communal feaſt. Cf. *T'ang fêng*, 6. Couvreur, 125.

XXVII. *The Hemp on the Knoll (Wang fêng* 10—C. 84— L. 122)

1. On the knoll there is hemp,
2. And there reſts Tzŭ Ch'ieh.
3. And there reſts Tzŭ Ch'ieh.
4. Oh that he would come and be happy.

5. On the knoll there is wheat,
6. And there reſts Tzŭ Kuo.
7. And there reſts Tzŭ Kuo.
8. Oh that he would come and eat.

9. On the knoll are plum trees,
10. And there reſts that Lord.
11. There reſts that Lord.
12. He presents me with girdle-charms.

XXVII. *Preface* : A satire againſt princes who do not search for men of worth.

Themes : a walk on the high ground ; presents.

XXVIII. *Quinces (Wei fêng* 10—C. 75—L. 107)

1. To him who gives me quinces
2. I will give my amulets in return.
3. This will not repay him ;
4. I will love him for ever and ever.

5. To him who gives me peaches
6. I will give fine stones in return.
7. This will not repay him;
8. I will love him for ever and ever.

9. To him who gives me plums
10. I will give diamonds in return.
11. This will not repay him;
12. I will love him for ever and ever.

XXVIII. *Preface* : In praise of the feudal custom of mutual aid.
Themes : presents, prestations.

XXIX. *The Ditches at the Gate (Ch'en fêng 4—C. 147—
L. 208)*

1. At the East gate, in the ditches
2. The hemp may be steeped.
3. With my fair chaste lady
4. One may sing in harmony.

5. At the East gate, in the ditches
6. The nettles may be steeped.
7. With my fair chaste lady
8. One may converse in harmony.

9. At the East gate, in the ditches
10. The rushes may be steeped.
11. With my fair chaste lady
12. One may talk in harmony.

XXIX. *Preface* : Satire upon the times. The light marriage of
the prince is reprobated and the poet thinks longingly of a good
woman who would have made a fit mate for the ruler.

3. The name of a princely family (that of the Chou) used to indicate a woman of good birth and noble character.

8. Antiphonal lines are implied.

Themes : the meeting outside the walls ; a song of work ; verbal accord.

XXX. *The Artful Fellow (Chêng fêng* 12—C. 95—L. 138)

1. Oh, such an artful fellow,
2. Who will not talk with me.
3. Shall I because of thee
4. Be unable to eat ?

5. Oh, such an artful fellow,
6. Who will not eat with me.
7. Shall I because of thee
8. Be unable to rest ?

XXX. *Preface : The Artful Fellow* : Satire against Hu (Duke Chao of Chêng, 696–695 ; cf. *SMC.,* iv, 458 sqq.). He was incapable of employing men of worth to manage the government. A powerful vassal usurps authority (viz. Chêng of Chai, cf. LI).

2. Who does not accept my opinions. (Chêng.)

6. Who does not give me employment ; lit. who gives me no salary for my support. (Mao.)

Chu Hsi : A dissolute woman, seeing that the man is breaking off relations with her, mocks him.

Themes : ironical invitation ; the communal banquet.

Symbolic interpretation, without any justification whatever, by transposition of institution. For example, the communal feasts of lovers and those of lords and vassals.

XXXI. *The Fu-su (Chêng fêng* 10—C. 94—L. 137)

1. The *fu-su* is on the hills,
2. The water-lily in the dells.
3. I do not see Tzŭ Tu
4. And I see none but fools.

60

5. The tall pines are on the hills,
6. The polygonum in the dells.
7. I do not see Tzŭ Ch'ung,
8. But I see artful fellows !

XXXI. The *Fu-su* : Satire against Hu (Duke Chao of Chêng, 696–695). Those whom he loved were unworthy of esteem.

1 and 2. As the hills and the valleys have appropriate vegetation, so Hu ought to appoint the most virtuous to the highest offices and the least virtuous to the lowest. (Mao.)

Chêng : The *fu-su* is symbolical of those who, despite their lack of talent, are appointed by Hu to high offices of State ; the water-lilies symbolize men of worth whom he neglects.

3. Tzŭ Tu : a man of the period who loved virtue. (Mao.)
4. These are the unworthy people employed by Hu. (Chêng.)
5 and 6. A metaphor : The tall pines on the hills ; a reference to the great vassals to whom Hu does not extend his favour. The polygonum : minor vassals whose counsels are listened to by Hu. (Chêng.)

7. Tzŭ Ch'ung : a man of worth. (Mao.)
8. The artful fellow is Hu, Duke Chao. (Mao.) An artful fellow has the appearance but not the reality, says Chêng.

Chu Hsi : A dissolute woman jests with her lover.
Themes : sarcastic invitation : hills and valleys ; vegetation.
Compare XXX and LI.
Symbolic interpretation : without any support whatever. No attempt even has been made to identify proper names.

XXXII. *Along the Highway (Chêng fêng 7—C. 92—L. 133)*

1. Along the highway
2. I take thee by the sleeve.
3. Do not be harsh with me.
4. Do not sever our past at a blow.

5. Along the highway
6. I take thee by the hand.
7. Do not be harsh with me.
8. Do not shatter our love at a blow.

XXXII. *Preface*: *Along the highway*: Thinking wistfully of men of worth. Duke Chuang (of Chêng, 743–701) failed in his princely duties. Men of worth forsook him. The people of the state longed to see a sage.

This ode is supposed to be the earnest entreaty of the people of Chêng to a sage whom they wished to retain in their state.

6. Forcible persuasion. Cf. LXVIII, 15. Cf. Maupetit, *Mœurs laotiennes. Bull. et Mém. de la Soc. d'Anthropol. de Paris*, 1913, p. 504.

Chu Hsi: A dissolute woman tries to detain her lover who is about to desert her.

Themes: quarrels; excursions; forcible persuasion.

XXXIII. *The Sluggish Flow (Chêng fêng* 18—C. 99— L.145)

1. The sluggish flow of the stream
2. Does not carry away a bundle of thorns.
3. To the end to live as brothers
4. Only we can do this, you and I.
5. Trust not the sayings of others.
6. They will certainly lie to you.

7. The sluggish flow of the stream
8. Does not carry away a bundle of branches
9. To the end to live as brothers
10. Only we can do that, we two.
11. Trust not the sayings of others:
12. They are sure to be insincere.

XXXIII. *Preface*: *The Sluggish Flow*: Mourning over the absence of vassals. Worthy men are grieved because Hu (Duke Chao of Chêng, 696–695) had neither faithful vassals nor good officers. In the end he died away from his own state

Both Mao and Chêng say that: Hu is no more capable of exerting his influence over his vassals than the feeble current of carrying away the bundle of thorns.

3. An allusion to the brothers of Hu who disputed the power with him. (Chêng.)

10. These two who are of one mind. (Mao.) Cf. *Pei fêng*, 10. Chu Hsi: Libertines talking together.

Observe the expression: to love as brothers, used with reference to lovers. Cf. VII, 4, and particularly *Pei fêng*, X, 2nd strophe: Thou art entertaining thy new wife. (Cf. LXVI, 55, 56, and LX, 29).

As an elder brother, as a younger brother. (The reference is to sworn-brothers.)

Themes: vows and faithfulness. Note the bundles of sticks and the banks of the river (perhaps omens drawn from the water-line. Cf. Sébillot, *Paganisme Contemporain*, p. 89). Cf. *Wang fêng*, 4. Couvreur, 78.

XXXIV. *The Nests on the Dam (Ch'ên fêng* 7—C. 149— L. 211)

1. The magpie nests are on the dam,
2. On the hill are beautiful peas.
3. Who then beguiles my beloved?
4. Oh my heart! Alas, what anguish!

XXXIV. *Preface*: Historical interpretations without interest. Chu Hsi: Secret amorous relations between young men and women.

Themes: the walk on the heights; slander. Cf. *T'ang fêng*, 12, Couvreur, 131.

XXXV. *The Fine Gentleman (Chêng Fêng* 14—C. 96— L. 141)

1. O Lord of the splendid mien,
2. Who waited for me in the way . . .
3. Alas, that I followed thee not! . . .

4. O Lord of the elegant figure,
5. Who waited for me in the hall . . .
6. Alas, that I followed thee not! . . .

7. In flowered robe, in plain robe,
8. In flowered skirt, in plain skirt,
9. Come sirs : Come sirs,
10. In your carriage take me with you.

11. In flowered skirt, in plain skirt,
12. In flowered robe, in plain robe,
13. Come sirs : Come sirs,
14. In your carriage take me home with you.

XXXV. *Preface* : *The Fine Gentleman* : A satire upon anarchy. The marriage rules were broken. The *Yang* (the male, the affianced man) called, but the *Yin* (the female, the affianced woman) failed to reply in harmony. The man came to seek the woman and she would not follow him. (Cf. *I li* : Marriage. 6th rite : the marriage ceremony : *Ch'in ying*.)

1, 2, 3. The bridegroom having come in person and having gone out (of the house of the woman after the ritual presentation of the wild goose) waits for the bride in the lane.

5. The reception-hall in which the presentation of the wild goose should take place (*I li* : Marriage). Cf. *Ch'i fêng*, 3. Couvreur, p. 105.

7 and 8. Mao : The marriage costume. As this is not the costume described in the *I li*, Chêng adds : the marriage costume of a *woman of the people*. Cf. *Wei fêng*, 3 ; Couvreur, p. 65 ; the same costume is described in the case of a *bride of noble birth*.

9. Would be addressed to the bridegroom (consequently in the singular). Cf. XV, 3, and the different interpretation.

Chu Hsi : The woman had made an assignation with the man who was actually waiting for her in the lane, but she, having changed her mind, did not keep the appointment, and afterwards, regretting that she had not gone, she made this song.

Themes : village assignations ; carriages.

XXXVI. *In the same Carriage* (*Chêng fêng* 9—C. 93—
L. 136)

1. The lady mounts the same carriage.
2. Fair is she as the candle-berry flower. . . .

3. Waving in the wind, waving in the wind,
4. Her amulets are of fine jades.
5. She is here, the fair Mêng Chiang,
6. Fair indeed and truly exalted.

7. The lady follows the same road.
8. Fair is she as the candle-berry flower . . .
9. Waving in the wind, waving in the wind,
10. Her amulets are tinkling.
11. She is here, the fair Mêng Chiang,
12. Her charm cannot be forgotten.

XXXVI. *Preface*: *In the same carriage*: A satire upon Hu (Duke Chao of Chêng, 696–695). The people of Chêng blame Hu for not allying himself in marriage to Ch'i. While he was heir-apparent Hu had earned the gratitude of Ch'i. The Marquis of Ch'i offered to him in marriage (a daughter of his house). The lady of Ch'i was good and he did not marry her. He perished for lack of the assistance of a great state. In the end he was exiled. The people of the country reproached him. Cf. *SMC.*, iv, 458 sqq.

2. The lady of Ch'i was beautiful, says Chêng; the people blamed the Duke for not presenting himself before her (6th marriage rite). Both would then (for a moment) be in the same carriage (when the procession set out from the house of the lady. Cf. *I li*: Marriage).

5. Mêng Chiang, eldest daughter of the lord of Ch'i (her name was Chiang) (Mao).

3 and 4. Suggest the speed of the journey—garments and pendants swinging in the wind. Cf. XLII, 5.

6. She was versed in the rites applying to women. (Chêng.)

10. The sound made by her pendant charms is indicated by a descriptive auxiliary.

12. (The memory of) her virtue will be handed down from generation to generation. (Chêng.)

Theme: chariot.

Observe the flower metaphors.

Mêng Chiang (a proper name which has been used as a peg on which to hang the symbolic interpretation): the beautiful princess. Mêng: the eldest, a term of respect; Chiang: name of a princely family; combined, they form a kind of collective name. Cf. XXIV, 8, and XLIV, 4 (n.).

XXXVII. *The Dolichos* (*T'ang fêng* 11—C. 130—L.186)

1. The dolichos grows on the bushes,
2. The bindweed spreads o'er the plains . . .
3. My beloved is far from here . . .
4. With whom ? . . . no, alone, I dwell . . .

5. The dolichos grows on the jujubes,
6. The bindweed spreads on the tombs . . .
7. My beloved is far from here . . .
8. With whom ? . . . no, alone, I rest . . .

9. Alas, the fine pillow of horn . . .
10. Alas, the gay brocade covers . . .
11. My beloved is far from here . . .
12. With whom ? . . . no, alone, I await the dawn . . .

13. Summer days . . .
14. Winter nights . . .
15. After a hundred years
16. I shall enter his abode.

17. Winter nights . . .
18. Summer days . . .
19. After a hundred years
20. I shall enter into his house.

XXXVII. *Preface* : A satire upon continual warfare.
15–16 and 19–20. Cf. XLIII, 9.
Theme : conjugal union and separations.

XXXVIII. *The Blue Collar* (*Chêng fêng* 17—C. 98—
L. 144)

1. Very blue is your collar
2. Very troubled my heart . . .

3. If I go not to you
4. Must you cease to sing ?

5. Very blue are your pendants
6. Very troubled my thoughts.
7. If I go not to you
8. Must you refuse to come ?

9. Go then !   And take a walk
10. On the wall and on the tower.
11. One day when I see you not
12. As three months is to me.

XXXVIII. *Preface* : *The Blue Collar* : Satire against relinquishing study. During times of disturbance learning falls into disuse.
1. The blue collar indicates the garb of a student. (Mao.)
4. In ancient times students studied the Odes (the *Shih ching*) and music. (Chêng.)
The nobles wore pendants attached to blue cords. (Mao.)
9. Idle students took delight in climbing hills. (Chêng.)
10 and 12. The study of the rites and of music must not be neglected even for a day. (Mao.)
Chu Hsi describes this poem as the song of a licentious person.
Theme : separation in the village. References to songs and to assignations. Compare the serenades of lovers in Formosa, see Appendix III.

XXXIX. *The Modest Girl (Pei fêng* 17—C. 49—L. 68)

1. The modest girl, how lovely.
2. She awaits me at the corner of the wall,
3. I love her, and, if I see her not,
4. I scratch my head, bewildered. . . .

5. The modest girl, how charming.
6. She gives me a red tube.
7. The red tube is brilliant ;
8. The girl's beauty is enchanting.

    9.   Plant which comes from the meadows,

10.   Truly as lovely as rare,

11.   Nay, 'tis not thou that art lovely :

12.   Thou art the gift of loveliness.

XXXIX. *Preface* : *The Modest Girl* : The customs of the period censured. The ruler of Wei was without Virtue (*tao*, the regulating power of the prince). The princess, his wife, was without Virtue (*tê*, delegation of the *tao*, the manifestation of *tao*, the active influence of *tao* the regulating power).

Chêng : Both ruler and princess lacking Virtue (*tao-tê*), a modest girl is offered—' given to me in accordance with the law of the red tube' (paraphrase of line 6). Her virtue being such (as the observance of this law suggests), she might take the place of (the princess) and be a fit mate for a Ruler.

1 and 2. The virtues of the girl being chastity and purity as well as respect for the rules, she was worthy to be loved. The ramparts of the town denote that which is lofty and may not be violated (viz. the rules). (Mao.)

The girl, being obedient to the rules, waits until the rites are all performed before she will make a move. She curbs her own inclinations (guards them) as if (with the help of) a rampart. Therefore she may be loved. (Chêng.)

This means that she does not offer herself as a dissolute woman would, and that she waits for the ceremony of the dispatch by the prince of an intermediary to ask for her in marriage.

3 and 4. She would like to go to the prince, but her behaviour remains correct. (Mao.) Her hesitations show her desire. (Chêng.) (These lines are supposed to be spoken by her.)

5 and 6. Because the girl is chaste, because she is beautiful, and because she may be given in accordance with the rule of the red tube which was practised in remote times, she is worthy to be mated with a prince. In ancient times the queen and the princesses were obliged to follow the custom of the red tube which was enforced by the Matron of the Women's Apartments (cf. *Chou li, T'ien Kuan*). The Matron who neglected to record breaches (of the rule of the red tube) incurred the risk of death. The queen and all the women of secondary rank visited the couch of the ruler in accordance with the rites. The Matron made a note of the day and the month. She gave them a ring to send them to the prince or to keep them (in their own apartments). When they were pregnant, in the last month before the child was born, (the Matron) gave them a gold

ring and sent them to their own apartments. (Cf. *Li chi, Nei tsê*, Couvreur, i, p. 662.) When they were to visit the apartment of the prince (the Matron) sent them, giving them a ring of silver which was worn on the right hand. After their visit the ring was changed to the left hand. In the service of the prince, everything, whatever its degree of importance, was recorded in a manner identical with that (of the red tube). (Mao.)

The red tube is the red tube containing the writing-brushes of the Matron. (Chêng.)

7. The tube is red because the Matron with her red heart (i.e. by the sincerity with which she performs her duty) corrects (the conduct of) the individuals (in the women's quarters). (Mao.)

8. The Matron, by making conspicuous (through the use of her red tube) the virtues of the queen and the concubines, causes their beauty to be seen. (Chêng.)

9. Shepherds, not meadows. (Mao.)

9. Young shoots of couch-grass. (Mao.) Just as these shoots will grow, so under the influence of the control which is exercised in the women's quarters, the girl will be worthy to be the mate of the prince. Cf. K'ung Ying-ta.

9 and 10. Chêng: Just as the shoots of couch-grass brought in by the shepherd may, thanks to their whiteness and their purity (cf. LXIV, 2), be used in the sacrifices, so the pure maiden who has lived in a place of retirement (cf. LVI, 3), after the intermediary has notified (her of the commands of the prince). (Cf. *I li*, Marriage, beginning: Chêng's comment on the intermediary), will be able to fill the position of wife to the prince.

11 and 12. It is not only that her beauty pleases me, but I admire her because it was possible for her to be offered to me in accordance with the rule of the red tube. (Mao.)

K'ung Ying-ta explains that lines 9–12 are metaphorical: Just as a shoot of couch-grass was brought by a shepherd, and, because it was beautiful and rare, might be used in the sacrifices, so it was necessary that the prince should be presented with a girl who was pure, faithful, and beautiful, who would therefore be a worthy mate for the prince and could take the place of the reigning wife.

Chêng (according to K'ung Ying-ta) says: If there were anyone who could offer me (as the beautiful flower is offered) a girl modest and pure, it would not be the girl whom I should find beautiful. I should admire the person who offered the girl to me.

Chu Hsi: Assignation-song of depraved persons.

A Village Assignation-song. Theme: love-tokens (flowers). Reference to pastoral life.

Observe the comparison (suggested by Chêng, 9 and 10, note) between the modest maiden who lived in retirement and the pure girl of LVI who went into retirement before she too became a fit mate and worthy consort for the ruler. Observe also the religious character of the shoots of couch-grass.

Although no interpretation is found for this poem analogous to those offered for LVI, LIX, LXVIIB, and *Shao nan*, 4, it is important for the study of the transposition of notions and rules applying to affianced girls of the peasant class to those of noble rank living in the women's quarters.

XL. *I Pray Thee (Chêng fêng 2—C. 86—L. 125)*

1. I pray thee, Master Chung,
2. Leap not into my village.
3. Break not my willow-trees . . .
4. How should I dare to love thee ? . . .
5. I am afraid of my parents . . .
6. Chung, I might love thee, indeed,
7. But my parents' words
8. Are also to be feared.

9. I pray thee, Master Chung,
10. Jump not over my wall.
11. Break not my mulberry-trees . . .
12. How should I dare to love thee ? . . .
13. I am afraid of my cousin . . .
14. Chung, I might love thee, indeed,
15. But my cousin's words
16. Are also to be feared.

17. I pray thee, Master Chung,
18. Leap not into my orchard.
19. Break not my plants of *t'an* . . .
20. How should I dare to love thee ?
21. I am afraid of the scandals . . .

70

22. Chung, I might love thee, indeed,
23. But the scandals which people talk.
24. Are also to be feared.

XL. *Preface*: *I Pray Thee*: Satire against Duke Chuang of Chêng (743–701). He did not (know how to) overcome (his affection for) his mother so as to curb (the ambition of) his younger brother. This younger brother (Tuan, surnamed T'ai-Shu) being lost to a sense of duty (in trying to dethrone his elder brother he was disobeying natural order), the duke failed to punish him. Chung (lord) of Chai reproved him and (the duke) paid no attention to him, being too lax to force himself to punish (those who incite to) disorder.

See *SMC.*, iv, p. 453.

Chu Hsi: The words of a depraved (woman).

1. Master Chung = Chung of Chai.

1, 2, 3. Chuang is supposed to be addressing Chung of Chai and refusing to listen to his advice, begging him figuratively not to rush violently into his village, over the hedge. To break the trees = to injure the younger brother Tuan. (Mao, Chêng.) Cf. *Ch'i fêng*, 5, st. 2, Couvreur, 107.

4. To love him: Tuan (the wicked brother). (Mao, Chêng.)

5. My parents, my father and mother, means only my mother, protectress of Tuan. (Chêng.)

6 and 7. Understand: I appreciate the advice of Chung but I dare not run counter to my mother's counsels. (Chêng.)

13. My cousins: the duke's family (who favoured Tuan). (Mao.)

Theme: an assignation (in the village of the girl, who was afraid of her parents; time of the engagement).

2. 25 families make up a *li* or village. The song shows that the village is occupied by the girl's family; the family unit is also a territorial unit, a local group. Observe the hedges and walls. The lover comes from outside, from another village: exogamy. Cf. *Ch'i fêng*, 5, Couvreur, p. 106.

An excellent example of the employment of a popular song as an admonition. A proper name (a very common one) serves as an excuse for thus employing it.

XLI. *Sun in the East* (*Ch'i fêng* 4—C. 106—L. 153)

1. Sun in the east.
2. She is a beautiful girl

3. Who is in my house . . .
4. She is in my house :
5. Following me she came.

6. Moon nearing the East.
7. She is a beautiful girl
8. Who is at my door . . .
9. She is at my door :
10. Following me she goes out.

XLI. *Preface* : Satire upon a prince of Ch'i. Lords and vassals had lost the sense of right reason. Illicit relations between the sexes were common and the influence of the rites was no longer felt.
Chu Hsi : Song of libertines.
Theme : village assignations. Cf. *Ch'ên fêng*, 8, Couvreur, 150.

XLII. *Cock-Crow* (*Chêng fêng* 8—C. 92—L. 134)

1. The cock has crowed, says the girl ;
2. The day has broken, says the man.
3. Arise, observe the night !
4. Is it the stars that shine ?
5. Quickly begone ! Quickly begone !
6. To hunt the duck and the wild goose.

7. When thou hast killed I will prepare them
8. And we will feast on them.
9. And, as we feast, we will drink.
10. Oh, that with thee I might grow old.
11. Beside us are lutes and guitars :
12. Everything makes tranquil our love.

13. If I were sure of thy coming,
14. I would give thee my trinkets.
15. If I were sure of thy favour,

16. I would send thee my trinkets.
17. If I were sure of thy love,
18. My trinkets should repay thee.

XLII. *Preface* : *Cock-crow* : A satire upon those who do not love virtue. The good manners of the paſt are exhibited as a reproach to the people of the present day who love not virtue but indulgence.

Chêng's comment (in order to explain ſtrophes 2 and 3) : Virtue= officers, great officers, virtuous gueſts.

1 and 2. Dialogue between husband and wife waking in the early morning shows that they do not forget themselves in indulgence. (Chêng.)

3 and 4. Only the greater ſtars are ſtill shining, the lesser ones having disappeared. (Mao.) The ſtars ſtill shine ; it is ſtill early for lovers to part. (Chêng.)

5. Line suggeſting a rapid step with garments flying. Cf. XXXVI, 3. (Which is identical in the Chinese.)

6. The spoils of the chase will serve to entertain the (virtuous) gueſts. (Chêng.)

8. Refers to the gueſts. (Chêng.)

10. Words of affeƈtion addressed to the gueſts. (Chêng.) See LXVIII, 16 ; LXVI, 51 ; *Yung fêng*, 3, line 1.

11. Music for the gueſts. (Chêng.) Cf. LX, 28, and *Hsiao ya*, i, 4, ſt. 7 ; Couvreur, 180.

13–18. Presents for the gueſts. (Chêng.)

Chu Hsi : Dialogue between virtuous husband and wife.

Themes : dawn ; separation at dawn (the affianced lovers have passed the night together) ; the chase, the communal feaſt, harmony (11, 12) ; presents and love-tokens ; conjugal vows (10).

Compare Hakka, xi. Cf. Maupetit, *Bull. et Mém. Soc. d'Anthropologie de Paris*, p. 510.

Compare *Ch'i fêng*, 1 and 5 ; *Hsiao ya*, iii, 8. (Transformations of the dawn theme.) The explanation of the original theme (in XLII) is based on the ideas which inspired its transformation.

XLIII. *The Chariot of the Ruler (Wang fêng* 9—C. 83— L. 121)

1. The chariot of the ruler, how it rumbles.
2. His robe is the colour of rushes.

3. How could I fail to think of thee? . . .
4. I fear him and I dare not . . .

5. The chariot of the ruler, how it rumbles.
6. His robe is the colour of rubies.
7. How could I fail to think of thee? . . .
8. I fear him and am afraid to go into the fields . . .

9. Alive, our rooms are apart,
10. Dead, we shall share the tomb.
11. If thou dost not think me faithful,
12. Be witness, oh radiant sun.

XLIII. *Preface*: Satire upon the great officers of Chou. The Rites and Duty were neglected. Men and women united in licence. The manners of the past are praised in order to satirize those of the present. The great officers no longer possessed the power to give audience (judicially) to disputes between men and women.
    1. Great chariot = chariot of a great officer. (Mao.)
    2. The dress of a great officer. (Mao.)
    4. Spoken by those who of old would have liked to give rein to licence but were restrained by fear of the laws. (Chêng.)
    9 and 10. All their lives women remained in the inner appartments; there is therefore a distinction between those who must remain at home (women) and those who alone have business abroad (men). After death, the spirits of husband and wife are reunited and merged in each other to form a single entity. (Mao.)
    It was the duty of the great officers not only to give audience to disputes between the sexes which arose among unmarried people, but also to enforce the regulations concerning conjugal morality, namely the rule of separation between husband and wife. (Chêng.)
    12. Formula of a vow.
    The themes are meetings in the fields, separation in the village; also faithfulness and vows. Auxiliary themes are the chariot and the splendour of festal garments.

If it is unwise to conclude from the study of the rustic themes alone that the poetry of the *Shih ching* is a rustic poetry, the preceding songs may, it would seem, henceforth justify the assumption. What indeed do they describe if not village love?

LOVE SONGS OF THE SHIH CHING

It is true that the same nice discrimination which has been capable of selecting rustic embellishments and of being inspired by the ancient sayings may also have been led to choose for scenes of love a rural dress and a rustic background. Is it not a fact that natural beauty and simple graces are acceptable even to the most delicate art? What is known of the history of these songs? Those who enjoyed and studied them, who classified and handed them down, were courtiers; those who had preserved them and attended to the performance of them at the palace ceremonies were the masters of music at the princely or royal courts. Why then should they not be the work of official poets? Why should the poetry of the *Shih ching* not be a *court poetry*? Tradition would have it that it is so, and gives good reasons for the belief.

The feudal lords ruled over an agricultural people; their government ensured alike the regularity of manners and of the seasons. The prosperity of Nature and the well-being of men both manifested the Good Fortune of princes. The contentment of men and things was evidence of the legality of their authority. The measure of their sway was the measure of the fertility of the soil, and their virtue was judged by the morality of their vassals.[1] As the lord, so the state; as the people, so the princes. "The rushes are strong": that is, the prince is good.[2] A peasant is too savage: that is because the government is conducted with violence.[3] Are families united? order reigns in the inner apartments of the palace.[4]

---

[1] This is the official theory concerning the regulating power of the prince; it is constantly referred to in the prefaces to the odes. One of the *Praise-songs of Lu* (*Lu sung*, 1, Couvreur, p. 445) describes dramatically the immediate and direct effect on things of the Royal Influence :—

> The thoughts of the prince have no limits.
> He thinks of the horses and they are strong . . .
> The thoughts of the prince are unfailing
> He thinks of the horses and they spring forward . . .
> The thoughts of the prince are undeviating
> He thinks of the horses and they go straight ahead.

Cf. *T'ang fêng*, 4. Couvreur, p. 124.
[2] *Shao nan*, 14. Couvreur, p. 28.
[3] Preface to XI and XLIV; see also that to XLVI.
[4] LVI and the *Chou nan* in general.

75

Has the wife of the prince, by reason of his influence, the Virtue which is worthy of a numerous posterity ? Then the women of the state wish to have children.[1] To praise a queen it is only necessary to describe peasant-women plucking the plantain which facilitated pregnancy, and the song which forms a rhythmical accompaniment to the picking is in itself a eulogy. Is there a style at once more delicate and more forceful, more subtle and yet more direct ? It is never necessary, for the court poet, when he would sing of a princess, to deck her in the guise of a shepherdess ; there is never any need of allegory—the links lie in the facts themselves : a true picture of things rural will suffice.

Thus, no matter how true to life the odes may seem to the reader, no matter how accurately they may portray rustic manners, there is nothing to prove that they are not the work of scholars.

If a poet proclaim in rustic strain his fidelity to his sovereign, then, since a moral lesson is to be drawn from rustic themes, he is helping his superiors stedfastly to pursue the right way. Now, not all rulers are good ; and often the princesses are monsters of iniquity[2] : were not the poets, then, as faithful servants, forced to represent the common people as sunk in vice, and to compose, by way of correction, rustic songs intentionally licentious ? But why, then, should Confucius be praised for having expurgated the *Shih ching* ? Why should the commentators insist that only a very limited number of love-songs is included in the collection ?

Frankly, apart from the poems of the *Chou nan* and the *Shao nan*, to all of which are attributed an official origin and a high moral tone, it is evident that the commentators find themselves in a dilemma.

Ssŭ-ma Ch'ien[3] relates that in 554 B.C. a certain sage named

---

[1] XIX, preface. Cf. the explanation of *Chou nan*, 7 ; Couvreur, p. 11 (which is supposed to prove that the Virtue of the queen ensures a large number of faithful subjects).

[2] See *SMC.* : the story of Pao-Ssŭ, which is typical, vol. i, p. 292.

[3] Vol. iv, p. 8 sqq. Cf. *Tso chuan*, Hsiang, 29th year.

Chi-ch'a, paid a visit to the court of Lu, and, in his honour, the music of the Chou was performed, that is the *Shih ching*, of which the poems were then arranged as they are at the present time. Chi-ch'a expressed his admiration, but the songs of Chêng and Ch'ên he found objectionable and, from their character, he predicted the downfall of these states.

In the *Analects*,[1] Confucius expressed the opinion that the melodies of Chêng were licentious. His disciple, Tzǔ Hsia, condemned not only the odes of Chêng and of Sung, but also those of Ch'i and Wei which Chi-ch'a had admired.[2] Such disagreement among the scholars at this early date is remarkable. But this is not all : Chi-ch'a, Confucius and Tzǔ Hsia agree in thinking the odes of Chêng baleful ; now, it is evident from the prefaces of Tzǔ Hsia which accompany them that they are intended to encourage virtue, and the fact that Confucius included them in his selection is further proof of this intention.

The *Chêng fêng* contains twenty-one poems, of which sixteen are without doubt love-songs[3] ; such is the opinion of Chu Hsi, that great scholar of the Sung dynasty, whose adherence to tradition is tempered by sound good sense. In his view they are all, with one exception,[4] songs of licentious persons presenting the illicit loves of young men and women. Now, if the prefaces are to be believed—and, since they are attributed to Tzǔ Hsia their authority carries great weight—of these sixteen songs, nine, or almost one-third of the total number, are praiseworthy political satires in which only men appear. Out of twenty-one poems there are fourteen in which there is no reference to love, and yet, on the other hand, Tzǔ Hsia declares the *Chêng fêng* immoral. It is true that the remaining seven are concerned with love, but two of them [5] depict good manners and were

---

[1] *Lun yü*, xv, 10.
[2] *SMC.*, iii, 275, and *Li chi*, *Yo chi*, Couvreur, ii, pp. 40 and 90.
[3] 2 (XL) ; 7 (XXXII) ; 8 (XLII) ; 9 (XXXVI) ; 10 (XXXI) ; 11 (XV) ; 12 (XXX) ; 13 (LI) ; 14 (XXV) ; 15 (XXIIIв) ; 16 (XIII) ; 17 (XXXVIII) ; 18 (XXXIII) ; 19 (XXIII) ; 20 (X) ; 21 (LII).
[4] 8 (XLII).
[5] 8 (XLII) ; 9 (XXXVI) ; and possibly 20 (X).

written in order that their presentation of virtue might recall bad rulers to the way of goodness ; thus they are noble and profitable admonitions. Five songs [1] portray deplorable manners ; the prefaces profess that three of them [2]—concerning the other two they are less positive—are also poetic reprimands. Disorder in government had brought with it military disturbances and the corruption of morals ; the portrayal of these dissolute manners would cause the rulers to ponder the consequences of disorder. Thus, after all, the whole of the *Chêng fêng* is prompted by good intentions.

Chu Hsi is less positive of the moral purpose of the writers ; often—and particularly in the case of the poems which he alone allows to be love-songs—he expresses himself as if they had been composed by the peasants of Chêng themselves in the midst of their excesses. For example, he says of the *Fine Gentleman* : " The man with whom the woman had made the assignation was actually waiting in the lane, but she, having changed her mind, did not go to meet him, and later, regretting the opportunity she had missed, she composed this song." [3]

The embarrassment of the Chinese tradition is evident. It may be expounded thus : After the *Shih ching* was used as a theme for exercises in rhetoric, and especially after it had become a classic and a subject of instruction, it was considered desirable to attribute to this educational work a moral value, independent both of the use to which it might be put and of the value which it would have had from the beginning. [4] The odes were used for purposes of instruction and it was imagined that they were composed for that purpose. They were employed to stimulate men to goodness and it was assumed that each one was specifically an exhortation to virtue. The purpose of the writers was examined, and, whenever it required artifice

---

[1] 14 (XXV) ; 15 (XXIIIв) ; 19 (XXIII) ; 20 (X) ; 21 (LII).
[2] 14 (XXV) ; 15 (XXIIIв) ; 21 (LII).
[3] Cf. XXXV. Chu Hsi refers to these songs as the sayings of libertines.
[4] See the Preface to the *Shih ching* : ' Former kings employed this book and men and women became filial and reverent, human relationships were adjusted, instruction and manners changed.'

to make their works seem as moral as they ought to be, the poets were credited with skill in craftsmanship. In the end it was believed that the *Shih ching*, which was employed by the scholars for purposes of instruction, had been composed by the learned tutors of the feudal courts.

This theory of the origin of the *Shih ching* scarcely conformed to the obvious meaning of the odes or to the tradition which saw in them the reflection of local customs. It was therefore assumed that the court poets, by the application of the theory of public right which declared the ruler to be the regulator of men and things, had given to their works not only the genuine atmosphere but even the actual substance of rustic songs.

Thus the circle would be complete—without a single difficulty. But for the moral which was to be inculcated some of the songs seemed too licentious; it was felt that they were not adequately excused by saying that the presentation of vice recalls to virtue—for tradition declared them to be licentious. Fortunately, opinion declared the expurgation of the *Shih ching* by a Sage, and that made it possible, since, officially, no licentious poems were to be found in the collection, to put forward for most of the poems an interpretation which rid them of all baleful influence by completely setting aside their character of love-songs. But in some instances, this method was defective, and it had to be admitted that a certain number of sensual poems were included in the *Shih ching*.

In certain cases it was still possible to avoid the difficulty, archæology helping to render the love-songs moral.[1] When a poem represented girls eagerly urging youths to " ask for "[2] them, the immodesty of the challenge was slurred over and the emphasis was laid upon their desire to be married at the plum-season, for it was possible to maintain that that was the proper time. When, in another ode,[3] a young girl regrets an unkept assignation, it is said that she is ashamed because she failed to accompany her betrothed when he came for the marriage ceremony. In addition to the fact that her penitence would

---

[1] Ibid., ' Cherishing the old customs.'   [2] XXII.   [3] XXXV.

suffice to render the poem moral, an opportunity is afforded to discourse upon an ancient custom. Is a girl represented as sharing the chariot [1] of her lover ? It is conveniently remembered that, on the departure of the bride from the home of her parents, it was customary for the bridegroom to remain for a moment in the chariot of the bride. This is the scene portrayed, no doubt, with the intention of advising a prince on no account to fail to contract a prudent marriage which had been suggested to him.

Do lovers part at dawn ? [2] They are supposed to be husband and wife, whose readiness to part shows contempt for sensual pleasures and, since it is the girl who urges the lover to go, she is extolled as the virtuous wife who does not seduce her husband from the labours of the day. For these poems which are acknowledged by scholarly interpretation to conform to morality, a moral and scholarly authorship is claimed.

At other times it is impossible to trace in the songs anything of the classic morality. They depict with simple directness the mingling of the sexes in the fields. Extraordinary custom ! Harangues on the subject of bad government could do little to soften the impression of licentiousness given by such poems. In order to bring them into line with the theory, they were held to be poems of censure composed by faithful vassals for the correction of their lord, but less effort was made to ascribe to them a learned origin. The commentators deemed it wise to pass rapidly over too glaring particulars. To a poem for which no subtle explanation was offered, what need was there to attribute a subtle author ?

Thus the interpretation of the *Shih ching* in accordance with the exigencies of morality resulted in the conclusion that there were two types of song to be found in what were admittedly love-songs. In one of these types the classic morality was recognized and the poems included in it were attributed to authors conceived by the expositor in his own likeness. The other type disclosed quite impossible manners,

[1] XXXVI. [2] XLII.

and there was consequently less disposition on the part of the
expositor to ascribe them to poets worthy of the name. Then
respect for authority amounted to a religion, and the two-fold
division of the *Shih ching* made possible its display. The moral
songs and the good poets were due to virtuous princes, especially
the king. The *Chou nan*, the *Shao nan* and even the *Wang
fêng* could not possibly include any save moral poems composed
in masterly manner : they were collected in the royal demesne.
It was assumed therefore that they were made in the palace
and afterwards sung in the villages for the improvement of
morals. On the other hand, there was not the same confidence
that the songs collected in the vassal states might in every
instance be directly attributed to scholarly authors. Thus was
salved, at least on political grounds, the morality of the *Shih
ching* ; and it was maintained despite the contradictions of the
work itself and the difficulties of the detailed interpretation of it.

In short, if the Chinese believe in the scholarly origin of the
Shih ching, it is because of the scholarly interpretation given
to it ; if they are forced to make that interpretation subtle,
it is because they desire to extract from it precepts which
accord with orthodox morality. The theory of the scholarly
origin of the Odes is closely connected with their educational
function. If, on occasion, the scholars feel somewhat uncertain
both of their moral value and of their scholarly origin, it is
because of the long interval of time which separates the manners
revealed in the Odes and those which they consider virtuous.
The dilemma in which the expositors find themselves is the
result of their belief in the immutability of moral principles.

But those who do not feel bound to revere the *Shih ching*
as a classic, or to accept the Confucian pronouncements as of
paramount importance, are not under the necessity of believing
that one song depicts vice and another virtue, or of proving
that customs were good only in the places to which the royal
influence extended. It is both simpler and safer to assume that
all the songs depict the manners which were prevalent in ancient
times.

They portray quite artlessly the loves of the country. It was in the fields[1] that girls and boys became acquainted with one another. Outside the gates[2] were recognized walks where they met—sometimes among the mulberry trees,[3] sometimes in the valleys, or it might be on a hillock or beside a spring which gushed out from the hillside.[4] The way thither led along the high road[5] and they often went hand in hand[6] and sharing the same chariot.[7]

The gatherings were attended by large numbers[8]; there seemed to be a cloud of girls; they were adorned with care: their parti-coloured garments,[9] their robes of flowered silk,[10] their head-dresses of grey or reddish colour,[11] their beauty, all were admired. The charmer was compared to white flowers, to flowers of the candleberry tree[12]; the choice was made and duly approached. Often the girls took the lead and made overtures to the boys.[13] Sometimes they were haughty, scorned the foolish youths[14] and afterwards repented.[15] The young folk wooed in rustic fashion, inviting one another to eat and drink in company.[16] They enjoyed themselves. Then followed presents and tokens of love,[17] declarations of faithfulness, vows[18]; for, after these betrothal ceremonies they must return home and live apart, each in his or her own village, until the next reunion. Sometimes faithless swains who refused to resume the old relations[19] were taken by the hand and implored, while, at other times, the girl tried to rouse them through jealousy.[20] Over all these manœuvres of the loving couples scandal held its way.[21] More than one complains of slander; another bewails her lost love; but rustic good-nature prevailed:

---

[1] XLIII, 8, and X.
[2] XXIII, XXIIIв, XXIV, XXIX; see also LXIII, LXVI, IV.
[3] XLIV.   [4] XXVII, XXXI, XXXIV; cf. I, II.
[5] XXXII.   [6] XXXII and XII.   [7] XXXVI and XII.
[8] XXIII.   [9] XXV.   [10] XXXV, XLIII.
[11] XXIII.   [12] XXXVI.   [13] XXXV, XXV, XXVI.
[14] XXX, XXXI.   [15] XXXV.   [16] XXIV, XXV, XXVI, XXVII.
[17] XXXIX, XXVII, XXVIII.   [18] XXVIII, XXXII, XLIII.
[19] XXXII, XII.   [20] XXX.   [21] XXXIII, XXXIV.

LOVE SONGS OF THE SHIH CHING

> When one would take a wife
> Muſt she be a princess of Sung ? [1]

Apparently, less freedom exiſted in the village. The period of separation was painfully tedious. While going about their work they mused upon their absent lovers, and these musings recur in the working-songs.[2] They tried to meet and made assignations ; the favourable time was in the twilight.[3] They waited for one another in the lanes [4] or at the corner of the walls.[5] When meetings were impossible they found delight in hearing the voice of the beloved, or watching him pass, all dressed up, along the top of the walls.[6] Sometimes they met again at night, the daring of too-bold lovers causing great agitation in the hearts of girls concerned about the possibility of scandal and of the reproaches of parents and brothers.[7] Nevertheless, they called them with all their heart. But if the young men succeeded in joining them, clambering over walls and fences in the village where the girl lived, at cock-crow she would urge them to go, and they would desiſt from their love-making.[8]

These ruſtic manners are too artless for any but a pedagogue to see in them an exhibition of depravity. But the pedagogues, in order to glorify their ſtandard of morality, would have liked to find that the country folk of ancient China had been ruled by the laws which prevailed in the feudal period, even before they had been formulated, for according to the scholars these laws were universal principles.[9] This shows a lack of the critical faculty. Is it not said that the rites did not apply to the common people ? [10] They were not allowed to have anceſtral temples [11] : how then should their daughters retire

[1] XXIV.
[2] XXIIIʙ, XVIII, XX, XXI.
[3] IV, XLI.
[4] XXXV.
[5] XXXIX.
[6] XXXVIII.
[7] XL.
[8] XLII.
[9] On the syſtem of moral duties imposed upon persons of rank, see *La Famille chinoise des temps feodaux*, chap. vii, which I hope to publish shortly. A large number of rules of life for persons of good family will be found in the chapter *Nei Tſè* of the *Li chi*.
[10] *Li chi, chiu li*, Couvreur, i, 53.
[11] *Li Chi, Wang ch'ê*, 3 ; Couvreur, i, 289.

thither at the age of fifteen to perform their ritual novitiate before marriage ? [1] It is very likely that from the time of the Chou an attempt was made to standardize customs. The ode called *The Chariot of the Ruler*,[2] if not simply a song of thwarted love, may possibly describe the arrival of an officer whose duty it will be to enforce the rules of the separation of the sexes as understood by the nobles. But, in that case, it is clear from the song how grievous such an innovation was. When they went to look for friends in the country or made assignations in the village, the country-girls were only breaking rules which were never meant to apply to them, and they were behaving in accordance with old customs. Betrothals took place in the fields [3] and were followed by a period of separation during which the girls only saw their lovers without the knowledge of their parents. This was the period of the engagement. The excitement of the meetings, longing for the absent, these are the feelings on which the poetry of the songs is based. Certainly they are unsuitable material from which to extract Confucian doctrines, but to find them immoral is to lack the historic sense. These ancient songs are moral after their fashion : they portray an ancient system of morality. But they do not portray it deliberately. They are not the work of moralists nor do they give the impression of having been produced by mental exertion, or of coming from a society as cultivated as that which took pleasure in them at a later date. Let who will believe the songs to be the work of *scholars*.

The rustic themes which they contain and the simple manners which they represent suggest that the songs of the *Shih ching* are of rustic origin. How were they composed ? The study of those which have been translated in the present work already allows the establishment of certain facts which render it possible to understand their origin.

A striking fact about these ancient songs is that they

---

[1] *I li*, Marriage.   [2] XLIII.
[3] See Granet : *Coutumes matrimoniales de la Chine antique. T'oung pao*, xiii, 543. See further, p. 129.

contain no element of personal feeling. It is not that poetry
of a personal character is lacking in the *Shih ching*—an example
will appear later—but it is not the personal element which
inspires the rustic poems grouped in this study. All these
lovers are alike and all express their feelings in the same way.
Not a single picture suggests a particular individual. A pronoun,
the word "lord", ready-made phrases such as a handsome
fellow,[1] the pure maiden,[2] the modest girl,[3] the one of whom
I am thinking, the fair lady,[4] serve in almost every instance
to indicate the loved one. If the second person is used it
seems to be so general in its denotation that it can always be
understood in the plural. The words most frequently used are
the most vague, boy, girl, which are also undoubtedly collective
words. None states the qualities which make the beloved
dear. At most there is a reference to her charm,[5] to her
beautiful garments,[6] and once to her beautiful eyes.[7] Similes
are rare. In one place girls are compared to white flowers [8] ;
the metaphor applies equally to all and is not intended to describe
anyone in particular. The beautiful Mêng Chiang,[9] who
shares the chariot of her lover, is said to be as beautiful as the
flowers of the candleberry tree. This is the most exact portrait
in the collection. But the beautiful Mêng Chiang is not
an individual. The name occurs frequently and, although it
is a name, it is only a generic name, which means no more
than *the beautiful princess*.

These impersonal lovers express only impersonal sentiments.
Indeed, the songs contain not so much sentiments as
sentimental themes, such, for instance, as meetings, betrothals,
quarrels, and separations. These events are common to all, and
all, men and women, react to them in the same way. No heart
feels any individual emotion, no case is peculiar, no one loves

[1] Cf. X, 3 ; LV, 3. [2] Cf. LVI, 3.
[3] Cf. XXXIX, 1. [4] Cf. XXIX, 3.
[5] Cf. XXXVI, 12, and LX, 4 ; cf. LX, 10. [6] XXV.
[7] Strictly speaking, it is the beauty of her arched brows that is praised.
[8] XXIII, 8. [9] XXVI.

or suffers in a fashion all his own. All individuality is absent and there is no attempt at any individuality of expression.

The scenery itself is varied as little as possible. This is provided by rustic themes, which, although they are entirely realistic, are yet no more than themes, formulæ to be introduced ready-made into the songs. They constitute a sort of stereotyped landscape, and, if they are connected with the sentiments expressed, it is not for the purpose of particularizing them, but rather, as we have seen, to connect them with general customs.[1]

No regard is directed to the particular. This accounts at once for the fact that the songs borrow lines or whole stanzas from each other.[2] It further explains how it was so easy to invest the poems with meanings at will. But, above all, it proves that it is vain to try to discover the personality of the author in individual poems. These impersonal lovers, all experiencing precisely the same impersonal emotions of love in a purely formal background, are not the creation of poets. The lack of individuality in the poems necessitates the assumption that they are of impersonal origin.

The odes reveal none of those literary processes which mark the art of the author. Their art is entirely spontaneous. No tricks of language are employed. Metaphor and simile are, one may say, almost entirely wanting.[3] Things are expressed in direct terms. Without doubt the charm of the poems is due to the combining of simple pictures and of feelings ingenuously expressed, in which there is no suggestion of art ; they are apparently not intentional but are the outcome of the facts themselves. *The correspondences between things reappear in the poems.* There is nothing to show the hidden threads which link the terms combined ; the close connection between the things is suggested by the turn of a phrase, the

[1] See *Rustic Themes.*
[2] Cf. *Hsiao ya*, i, 8 ; Couvreur, 187, strophes 5 and 6, and LVIII and XXI.
[3] Here are three isolated examples : XXIII, 2, the girls *seem like* clouds (of white flowers) ; LXIV, 8, the girl *is like* jade ; LXIII, you seem to me *like* the mallow.

arrangement of the words, the repetition of an expression. There is no suggestion that the phrases have been arranged with this result in view. Sometimes, by repetition, certain " empty " words draw attention to a parallel : this is the nearest thing to artifice. Is it artifice ? Do not the correspondences, being natural, occur naturally in the lines ? It is inevitable that the evolution of twin ideas should recur in the form of the phrases used to express them. Similarity in things gives spontaneous rise to balance of phraseology : the combining of images interprets itself perforce in symmetrical expressions. No doubt such abstention on the part of a writer is often a mark of the most delicate art, but there is already too much evidence against the scholarly authorship of the odes to admit the belief that this art is other than entirely primitive. It is even earlier than the use of metaphor. Ideas are combined with the minimum of art. They are the outcome of a natural relation revealed by the most elementary of processes, symmetry.

Symmetry is also the fundamental process in the composition of the odes. Their form as a rule is very simple, each poem comprising usually three or four stanzas, each of which contains normally four or six lines. In some instances each stanza is followed by identical lines, but really the refrain is contained in the stanzas themselves. In all of them indeed, certain lines, often unrhymed,[1] remain unchanged, while in others the change is often so slight that it is impossible in translating to indicate the difference. Sometimes, however, there seems to be an advance in the development and a cadenced march of the idea. Some poems are more complex in form, certain of them approaching very closely to the narrative style, but in the internal arrangement of the stanzas at least, symmetry still persists. Obviously such compositions are not literary. The almost total absence of development, the repetition of phrase and line, tend to prove, not only that these are popular

---

[1] The couplets are, in fact, distiches, the odd lines forming the first hemistich of each complete line : cf. p. 210.

songs, but also that they were sung in chorus, and most probably antiphonally. Thus it happened that the song of the girls alternated with that of the boys [1] :

> Now Sirs. Now Sirs.
> Sing, and we will follow you.

Is it necessary to assume that the details of these songs were carefully arranged beforehand ? The theme was fixed,[2] the tune familiar, and in the rendering there must have been some improvisation. The responses to the fixed lines which represented the theme were made to vary. In this way new couplets were composed. How were these finds made ? What was the source of their inspiration ? Perhaps they sprang out of the rhythm itself. In these simple poems, whose sole method of expression is symmetry, it is evident that rhythm is all-important. Certainly it was not entirely dependent upon the voice but was assisted by gesture. Evidence of this is found in the songs themselves. If it frequently happens that it proves impossible in translating to indicate the difference between one couplet and another, it is because the ONLY *line in which they differ contains no variation except a repeated word often inserted for the sake of the rhyme.* When the commentators wish to explain these repeated expressions it is evident that they are at a loss. They appear hardly to understand them and give only the vaguest and most general account of them, from which it appears that they depict vividly some aspect of things, that they are in the nature of intensive or adverbial particles, or, to find a better expression, *descriptive auxiliaries.* Sometimes they may be regarded as onomatopœic words. Such, for instance, are those which are joined with the name of a bird whose cry they are supposed to represent. But the commentators inform us that even these convey a deeper meaning. The descriptive auxiliaries applied to quails, to partridges, to wild geese,

---

[1] XV. [2] Probably the odd line, the first hemistich.

and to ospreys are not, so they say, intended to convey merely the voices of these birds, but are meant to represent their cries of calling and answering, and even the appearance of their flight when they go in bands or in pairs. Thus by these reduplicated expressions the human voice strives not only to imitate noises, but also to represent movements. The expressions are used to represent vocally all kinds of sense impressions. There are those which describe the young vigour of a bush, the profusion of its flowers, the luxuriance of its leaves. There are others which depict various appearances of rain or wind; still others which express the impulses of the heart. It is noteworthy that those belonging to the last class have of themselves a moral meaning. In the same way the word used to form a reduplicated expression to depict a colour also indicates that colour in ordinary speech. Is it possible that the meaning of these words comes to them from their use as descriptive auxiliaries? However that may be, it is beyond doubt that, in the poetry of the *Shih ching*, all kinds of impressions were associated with the sounds of words, especially impressions of movement. How is this to be explained except by the fact that the voices of the singers were assisted by gesture, and that *pantomime presented to the eye what the song was describing to the ear*?[1] But in that case must it not be that these songs were the offspring of the rhythm of the dance?

From their rural themes and rustic subjects, from the lack of individuality of their sentiments, from their simple, direct art, their symmetrical form, their marching gait; from the fact that they appear to have been sung in alternating choruses and from the pantomime which their brief verbal descriptions seem to demand, the songs of the *Shih ching* give the impression of being products of a rural improvization. What was the occasion of their improvization by these country lads and lasses?

---

[1] On the language of gesture, vocal, and other, see Lévy-Bruhl, *Les Fonctions mentales dans les sociétés inférieures*, pp. 183 sqq.

SONGS OF THE RIVERS AND MOUNTAINS

XLIV. *At Sang-chung (Among the Mulberries) (Yung fêng 4
—C. 55—L. 78)*

1. Where does one pick the dodder ?
2. In the country of Mei.
3. Know you of whom I am thinking ?
4. The beautiful Mêng Chiang.
5. She waits for me at Sang-chung ;
6. She yearns for me at Shang-Kung ;
7. She follows me on the Ch'i !

8. Where does one pick the wheat ?
9. On the north side of Mei.
10. Know you of whom I am thinking ?
11. The beautiful Mêng I.
12. She waits for me . . . etc.

15. Where does one pick the turnip ?
16. On the east side of Mei.
17. Know you of whom I am thinking ?
18. The beautiful Mêng Yung.
19. She . . . etc.

XLIV. *Preface* : *At Sang-chung* : A satire upon irregular unions.
Disorder and licence prevailed in the ruling house of Wei. Among
the boys and girls (of the people) illicit connections were common.
(Evil customs) spread even to the families of high public officials,
who seduced each other's wives and concubines, making assignations
with them in distant and secluded spots. The power of the govern-
ment being lost, the people became demoralized and (disorder) could
not be checked.

Chêng explains that the period in question was that of the reigns
of Dukes Hsüan (718–699) and Hui (699–668). (Cf. *SMC.*, iv,
pp. 194–8, especially p. 196, and the story there told of the infatuated
father-in-law). Unmarried men and women formed irregular unions
without waiting for the order of the intermediary (given in the
second month of spring) to come together according to the rites.

LOVE SONGS OF THE SHIH CHING

Observe that for Chêng the reference in the preface to official families is justified by the names Mêng Chiang, Mêng I, Mêng Yung. (These are really generic terms: the beautiful lady, the beautiful princess; cf. XXXVI, note.)

5. A special assignation as opposed to the gathering sanctioned by the rites. At Sang-chung: Among the mulberry trees. Cf. *Wei fêng*, 5; Couvreur, p. 117. The themes are the picking of the mulberry leaves and invitation. Mao notes, with regard to the second line: Boys and girls disregard the rules for the separation of the sexes.

7. The Ch'i: a river of Wei. On its banks gathered the young people of the three states of Pei, Yung, and Wei, which formed a traditional group: cf. XLV and XLVI, 5, 6; see also *Pei fêng*, 14; *Wei fêng*, 1, and particularly 9.

Themes: assignations by the rivers; harvestings.

XLIVB. *Wei fêng*, 9; Couvreur, p. 74: *The Solitary Fox*.

    1. There is a solitary fox
    2. On the dam across the Ch'i.
    3. My heart is full of sadness.
    4. That man is half-naked.

1. Cf. *Ch'i fêng*, 6; Couvreur, p. 107.
4. Literally: This lord has no skirt (lower garment, which completes the costume), i.e. is not married, has no mate. (Mao.) Cf. L, 3–4, and LI: crossing rivers with the skirts help up.

Themes: assignations by the rivers, and invitation.

Preface: *The Solitary Fox*: Criticism directed against the manners of the time. The unmarried men and women of Wei ignored the marriage-season, (or) lost their mistresses or lovers. In olden times, when misfortune overtook a state, the necessity for ceremonies (and ceremonial presents) was waived (cf. LXIV, preface) and marriages were many. Assemblies of the unmarried men and women were held and, by this means, the continuance of the population was assured. (Cf. *Chou li, Ti kuan*, v, *Mei shih*.)

XLV. *The Bamboo Stalks* (*Wei fêng* 5—C. 70—L. 101)

    1. The slender bamboo stalks
    2. Are for fishing in the Ch'i!
    3. Do I not think of thee?
    4. But afar one cannot go.

91

5. The Ch'uan spring is on the left,
6. On the right the river Ch'i !
7. A girl, when she goes to be married
8. Leaves afar her brothers and parents.

9. The river Ch'i is on the right,
10. The Ch'uan spring on the left.
11. A smile shows the flash of teeth . . .
12. The charms tinkle on the way . . .

13. The river Ch'i flows on, flows on.
14. Oars of cedar . . . boats of pine . . .
15. In my chariot I roam
16. To dissipate my sorrow . . .

XLV. *Preface*: A girl of Wei thinks of her marriage (when she must leave her native country).
1 and 2. Metaphor. As the thinned stems may be used for fishing so the woman who fulfils the rites may be married.
4. Refers to distance between places; one phase of the law of exogamy. Cf. XVI, 4, 8.
5 and 6. A simile: The smaller river merged and lost in the larger is a symbol of a woman who gets married. (Chêng.) See LII.
15. A chariot-drive. Cf. LVIII.
Cf. *Pei fêng*, 14; Couvreur, p. 45.
Themes: excursions by chariot, on the banks of the river, by boat; fishing; separation necessitated by exogamic marriage.

XLVI. *The Han (Chou nan 9—C. 13—L. 15)*

1. In the South are lofty trees ;
2. None can rest beneath them.
3. By the Han are strolling girls ;
4. But no one may solicit them.

5. So great is the breadth of the Han
6. It cannot be crossed by wading.
7. So vaſt is the river Chiang,
8. It cannot be crossed in a boat.

9. High on the top of the thicket,
10. I should like to gather the reeds.
11. This girl who is going to marry,
12. I should like to feed her horses.

13. So great is . . .

17. High on the top of the thicket,
18. I should like to gather the artemisia.
19. This girl who is going to marry
20. I should like to feed her colts.

21. So great is . . .

XLVI. *Preface*: *The Han*: (The expanse of) the Han (shows) the far-reaching effeċt of great Virtue. The regulating power of King Wên (the Civilizing King) made itself felt even in the ſtates of the South. His good influence with its civilizing power was effeċtive in the countries of the Han and the (Yang-tzŭ) Chiang. It did not occur to anyone to disobey the rites. It was vain to solicit any girl. (Cf. line 9 of LVI: Ask for her. . . Useless queſt . . .)

Chêng explains that everywhere else the evil influence of the laſt ruler of the Yin dynaſty was resulting in manners and songs of debased charaċter. The influence of Wên Wang was firſt felt in the South.

Observe that in the South the ancient sexual cuſtoms have been, as a matter of faċt, more commonly maintained than in the North. Cf. *BEFEO.*, viii, 348. App. III.

1–4. Mao. Simile: Chêng explains that the tall trees (giving no shade) on account of the height of their branches, no one goes to reſt beneath them. In the same way, if modeſt women go out to walk on the banks of the rivers, men have no desire to infringe the rites by approaching them. Still more they are modeſt and pure at home. (K'ung Ying-ta.)

These laſt refleċtions are the result of a wish to deprecate the idea of an actual walk. The *Li chi*, *Nei tsê*, ii, Couvreur, i, p. 675, having enacted that girls must not go out of doors after the age of ten, but must live in an inner apartment, carefully guarded, id., p. 660 : the excursion needs explanation in a country rendered virtuous by the influence of King Wên. Some commentators make a distinction between the daughters of noble families and girls of the people, the latter going out to attend to the work which women were supposed to do.

3. The *Han shih* has preserved a tradition according to which these girls walking are water-sprites, goddesses of the river Han. These water-sprites are called elves of childish appearance. Cf. *HCCCHP.*, 348, p. 40.

4. The *Han shih wai chuan*, chap. i, explains the song by an adventure of Confucius when travelling in the South.

5–8. Chêng explains that the purity of the girls is compared to the breadth of the river.

9–10. Mao explains the allusion to the purity of the girls by saying that when the men expressed a wish to cut the highest branches they implied that it was the most inaccessible and therefore the most virtuous whom they desired. Not daring to ask directly for them in marriage, they contented themselves with expressing simply the wish to provide, as a ceremonial gift, the fodder for the horses at the marriage procession.

9. A descriptive auxiliary represents the appearance of the boughs (Mao) ; for Chêng, it means that which is at the very highest point.

The artemisia has various ceremonial uses. It is believed that when the plant is burnt its scent will attract the spirits. (Cf. *Hsiao ya*, vi, 6, 5th str., comments.) The room used by a woman in childbirth is called by the extraordinary name of artemisia room. LXVIIB refers to another kind of artemisia.

The themes are walks beside rivers, the crossing, the thicket, gathering fuel, the marriage procession, and masculine diffidence.

Observe the refrain.

Since there is artemisia in the bundles of firewood, it is probable that they were intended for ceremonial fires : bonfires. Cf. the Lolo custom described by Crabouillet, *Missions catholiques*, v, p. 106. See App. III.

LOVE SONGS OF THE SHIH CHING

XLVII. *The Banks of the Ju (Chou nan* 10—C. 14—L. 17)

1. Along the banks of the Ju
2. I cut branches and briars.
3. Until I see my lord,
4. My pain is like morning hunger.

XLVII. A poem which may have a political meaning, but which has still the manner and some of the themes belonging to the songs inspired by the meetings beside the rivers. Only the first stanza is given here.

Preface : *The Banks of the Ju* (shows) that the civilizing influence of the regulating power is taking effect. The civilizing influence of King Wên extending to the states on the banks of the river Ju, the women (of these states) are able to grieve over (the absence of) their husbands and yet urge them to do their duty to the state.

10, 11. Chêng thinks that the period referred to is still during the reign of the tyrant Chou (1154–1122 B.C.), the last sovereign of the Yin. The husband, carrying out his duties in the midst of the disorder of the times, his wife, speaking allegorically, pictures herself cutting wood along the banks of a river, which she would not, as a woman, be expected to do in a well-ordered state.

The themes are the walk beside the river, the bundles of fuel, separation and the restlessness of love.

Observe that the vividness of the picture gives the impression of pain and loss.

XLVIII. *The River (Wei fêng* 7—C. 72—L. 104)

1. Who says that the river is wide?
2. On some reeds I could cross it.
3. Who says that Sung is far off?
4. Raised on tip-toe I could see it.

5. Who says that the river is wide?
6. Not too wide for a boat.

95

7. Who says that Sung is far off?
8. Not farther than a morning.

XLVIII. *Preface*: Historical interpretation without interest. The themes are crossing the river and the separation consequent upon exogamic marriages.

XLIX. *Wind from the East (Pei fêng* 10—C. 39—L. 55)

33. We cross when the water is deep,
34. On a raft, or in a boat.
35. We cross when the water is shallow,
36. By the ford, or by swimming.

XLIX. 33–6. Lines from the lament of a woman unhappily married, in which they appear as a sentimental recollection of the time of the betrothal feasts.
Cf. LXVI, lines 5, 35, 36, 53, 54.
Theme : passage of the river.

L. *The Gourd (Pei fêng* 9—C. 38—L. 53)

1. The gourd has bitter leaves :
2. The waters of the ford are deep.
3. In deep waters tuck up the skirt :
4. In shallow, hold them up.

5. 'Tis flood at the ford when the waters rise.
6. 'Tis the cry of the partridge calling !
7. The waters rise and the axle is not wet.
8. The partridge cries, calling her mate.

9. The cry of the wild-goose is heard,
10. At day-break, when dawn appears.
11. The man sets out to seek a wife,
12. When the ice has not yet melted.

13. Call, call, man in the boat.
14. Let others cross ! . . . Not I . . .
15. Let others cross ! . . . Not I . . .
16. I will await my friend.

L. *Preface*: *The Gourd*: Satire directed against Duke Hsüan of Wei (718–699; cf. *SMC.*, iv, p. 194 sqq.). The duke and the princess (his wife) both lived in vice and disorder. (The reference is to the first wife of Hsüan, I Chiang.)

1. The gourd. Mao. Simile: As the bitter leaves should not be eaten, so (comment of K'ung Ying-ta) the rites should not be transgressed. There is a tradition which says that scooped out calabashes were used to cross rivers. Note the importance of the common gourd in the Lolo myth of the deluge. *BEFEO.*, viii, 551.

The calabash figures in the marriage ceremonial. Divided into two parts it is used for the libations of the bride and bridegroom. (Cf. *I li*, Marriage. Comment of Chêng.)

2. Deep waters. Mao: A simile which according to K'ung Ying-ta means: As the ford must not be crossed when the river is in flood, so the rites must not be transgressed.

For Chêng there is an indication of date. The eighth month (second month of autumn, equinox). The Yin and the Yang meet and combine. Now the marriage rites may be begun. The choice is announced. The (personal) name (of the bride) is asked. Cf. *I li*: Marriage. For Chêng, the final rites (the marriage rites and the consummation of the marriage) take place at the spring equinox.

3 and 4. Mao. Simile: As, in order to cross water, it is necessary to conform to the natural order and lift the clothes more or less, so in the (matrimonial) gatherings of the sexes, it is essential to conform to the rites.

Chêng: In the same way natural order is obeyed in the arranging of marriages. Sages are not married to women who lack virtue nor are old mated with young; each should seek for a mate in a manner in keeping with the rules of propriety.

5. Deep waters, dangerous to cross. (Mao.)
6. The partridge (or pheasant) with its cries typifies I Chiang,

the princess, with her heart set on dissipation and excess, entering into relations of an intimate nature with men, deceiving them by her words without considering the misfortune which lies in wait for those who disregard the rites and the laws (as for those who cross flooded rivers).

7. The axles could not avoid being wet if the water was high. (Chêng.) To say that the water does not wet the axles is a figurative allusion to the princess who transgresses the rites without realizing (the misfortune which awaits her). (See Couvreur, 39, a modern development of the same interpretation : The water is overflowing its banks and they aspire to cross without even the wheel-tracks getting wet.) Cf. LXVI, 36.

8. By her cries the partridge desires to attract her mate and instead she attracts a quadruped, just as that which the princess in fact attracts (misfortune) is not what she invites (pleasure). Or again : the duke, her husband, is not a suitable mate for her. (Comments taken from the Commentary of Chêng to 3, 4.)

8. The girl calls her lover by singing as the partridge by singing summons a mate. This interpretation is supported by a new dictionary, *Hsin tzŭ tien*, Shanghai, 1st Year of the Republic— a republican publication destined to replace the *Dictionary* of K'ang Hsi, which *quotes this identical line.*

9. A descriptive auxiliary represents the cry of the wild-geese calling and answering in harmony. (Mao.) The female is supposed to respond to the male. (Cf. XV, 4.) Conjugal harmony is depicted and the compliance of the wife. Joined with modesty it forms a compound expression used in classical style to describe the feminine virtues of submission. (Cf. V, 3.)

10. The wild-goose, as a ceremonial present, is used especially in the marriage ritual (*I li* : Marriage). The explanation of this use lies chiefly in the fact that the wild-goose is migratory and goes always to warm places ; that is to say, it follows the *Yang* (male). In the same way, a woman must follow her husband. (Chêng.) Cf. Comment of Chêng on the *I li*, Marriage ; the female nevermore leaves the male and follows a little behind him (faithfulness, submission and modesty). (Cf. *Shih Ching, Chêng fêng*, 4 ; Couvreur, p. 88. See the note.)

In all the earlier rites of marriage (cf. Chêng's note on line 2) the wild goose is presented at dawn ; it is presented in the evening only at the final rite, the marriage ceremony itself. Cf. *I li*, Marriage. —This note is of importance in deciding the meaning of line 11.

11. Chêng : Cause the woman to come to his home. The expression here used usually refers to the marriage rite (cf. IX, 3,

and XLVI, 11); this use of it in line 11 refers it to the preliminary rites (cf. note on line 2) in which the bird is presented at dawn. Cf. 10 and note.

12. Mao. *Melted Ice*: a term used in the calendar; the ice melts in the first month (cf. *Yüeh ling*). All the rites connected with marriage must take place before the second month, with the exception of the last one, the marriage procession, which, according to Chêng, is held in the second month.—See a different interpretation in the *Chia yü*.—Chêng says that the rite here referred to is the penultimate one, the request to fix a date. This would be performed before the middle of the first month.

13. According to both Mao and Chêng the boatman is a ferry-man.

This explanation may be accepted although another, more subtle, might be offered. It might be maintained that the young people in the boats are performing the *calling ceremony*, that is, recalling the superior soul to unite with the inferior. See the comment of the *Han shih* on LII.

According to Mao, the call of the ferryman indicates the order of the intermediary officially mating the unmarried boys and girls, in order to prevent the arranging of individual assignations. Cf. XI, preface and notes.

16. Chêng: All respond to the call of the ferryman: all marry according to the order of the intermediary. I, a modest maiden, will not cross the water, I will not marry; for the man who should be my mate, who should be my husband, is not here; that is to say that when the rites and rules of marriage (cf. 3, 4) are not observed the marriage may not lawfully be completed.

The themes are: crossing the river, invitation, and the song of birds. Various marriage customs are recalled.

LI. *Tucked-up Skirts (Chêng fêng* 13—C. 96—L. 140)

1. If thou hast loving thoughts of me,
2. I will tuck up my skirts and cross the Chên.
3. But if thou hast no thoughts for me,
4. Are there, then, no other men?
5. Oh maddest of mad youths, in truth.

99

6. If thou haſt loving thoughts of me,
7. I will tuck up my skirts and cross the Wei.
8. But if thou haſt no thoughts for me,
9. Are there, then, no other boys?
10. O maddeſt of mad youths, in truth.

LI. *Preface*: *Tucked-up Skirts*: Longing for the appearance of a good miniſter. A wild young fellow was leading a disorderly life. The people of the ſtate (of Chêng) wished that a great ſtate would give them a worthy miniſter.

The poem appears to be an allusion to the disorder which prevailed in Chêng as the result of the quarrels between Duke Chao (696–695) and his brother Tu. See *SMC.*, iv, p. 458 sqq.

Chu Hsi: Spoken by a licentious girl to her lover.

According to Chêng the person addressed is a miniſter of a great ſtate.

4. Chêng says that firſt the miniſters of Chin, Ch'i Sung, and Wei were invited, and afterwards those of Ch'ing and Ch'u.

5. The maddeſt of mad youths refers to prince Tu. The laſt line shows the reason for appealing to the great ſtates. (Chêng.)

The Chên and the Wei: rivers of Chêng. Cf. LII.

The themes are: crossing the river, the skirts tucked up, and satirical invitation.

Mad youth: Cf. XXX and XXXI.

LII. *The Chên (Chêng fêng* 21—C. 101—L. 148)

1. The Chên and the Wei
2. Have overflowed their banks.
3. The youths and maidens
4. Come to the orchids.
5. The girls invite the boys:
. . . . Suppose we go over?
6. And the lads reply:
. . . . Have we not been?
7. Even so, yet suppose
. . . we go over again.

8. For over the Wei
9. A fair green-sward lies.
10. Then the lads and the girls
11. Take their pleasure together ;
12. And the girls are then given
    . . . a flower as a token.

13. The Chên and the Wei
14. Are full of clear water.
15. The lads and the girls
16. In crowds are assembled.
17. The girls invite . . .

LII. *Preface* : Satire directed against disorder (for Chêng, disorder between the sexes). Wars did not cease. Boys and girls were faithless to each other. Immoral practices spread rapidly. There was no hope of any influence to put an end to them. (Cf. LI, Preface.)

Chu Hsi : A song in which licentious persons express their own feelings.

2. A descriptive auxiliary depicts the flooded waters. (Chêng.) A term used in the calendar ; second month of spring ; thaw.

3 and 4. Boys and girls entice each other, none having a mate. Stirred by the spring, they go out together, picking fragrant flowers and giving themselves up to licence. (Chêng.)

6. The boys refuse to follow the girls on the pretext that they have already been to see the festival.

9. It may be supposed either that the festival itself was attractive or that it was held in a delightful spot. The second meaning is given by Chêng.

12. They perform the sexual act. When they part, the boys present the girls with the fragrant flower to bind their friendship. (Chêng.)

4. K'ang Hsi's *Dictionary* : In the sub-prefecture of Tu-liang is a mountain ; at the foot of the mountain is a clear river ; orchis grows in the midst of the water and is called the perfume of Tu-liang after the name of the mountain. Its essence is an antidote to venom and expels evil influences. For this reason the people of Chêng, in the springtime, in the third month, used to haunt the banks of the Chên and the Wei ; boys and girls helped one another to pick the orchis and make a purification.

There has persisted in various forms (cf. *HCCCHP.*, 1153, 17 rᵒ sqq.)

an important comment of the *Han shih*, in which it is said : The rising of the rivers is the one which occurs at the time when the peach flowers and the rains of the third month fall : That is the time when the orchis is gathered. Crowds of people go to pick the orchis in order to drive out evil influences. It was a custom in the State of Chêng, at the period marked by the first *Ssŭ*-day of the third month, on (or on the banks of) these two rivers (Chên and Wei) to call the superior souls to rejoin the inferior souls, and a ceremony of purifying was performed to drive out evil influences. (From the *T'ai ping Yü lan*.)

Variants : On these two rivers, Chên and Wei, the superior souls were called to unite with the inferior souls and a ceremony of purification was performed, the participants carrying orchis in their hands, in order to drive out evil influences. (*Sung shu.*)—By purification the evil humours were expelled from the air—or from the season (year).

On the orchis see the *Calendar of Hsia*, fifth month : " Orchis Gathering." See also *Chin shu*, chap. LXXX (ed. Shanghai, p. 2 sqq.) in the biography of Wang I-chih, the use of the orchis in the ceremonies of purification in spring. Cf. *Chou li, Ch'un kuan* v⁰ *Nü wu* : Female sorcerers have charge of the annual ceremonies of purification and cleansing. Cf. the comment of Chêng.

Concerning the plant given as a token, the character employed might suggest that it is a *fragrant* variety of the peony. I have an idea that the twelfth line refers to another variety of orchis, the perfume of Tu-liang. It is necessary to understand : the flower which is used as a token.

12. The ' flower given as a token ' is a medicinal plant used in magical pharmacy : See in *Chin Shu*, chap. xciv (ed. Shanghai, p. 2 v⁰, Biography of Hsia T'ung), reference to a medicine market on the occasion of a festival on the banks of the river on the first *ssŭ*-day of the third month.

In translating I have been obliged, in the case of several of the lines of the refrain, to divide them because they are so full of meaning The theme is the crossing of the river. Indication of antiphonal singing. Other themes are the spring floods, a subject connected with the calendar ; the invitation of the girls and the half-refusal of the boys ; harvestings and love-tokens (flower). Observe the use of the orchis in the Lolo myth of the Deluge. *BEFEO.*, viii, p. 551. Cf. Vial, *Lolos*, p. 9.

LOVE SONGS OF THE SHIH CHING

LIII. *The Fair, Fair Artemisia (Hsiao ya iii, 2—C. 199—
L. 279)*

   1. O the fair, fair artemisia,
   2. Which is in the midst of the hill.
   3. As soon as I see my lord,
   4. What joy and what respect.

   5. O the fair, fair artemisia,
   6. Which is in the midst of the isle.
   7. As soon as I see my lord,
   8. My heart is gay.

   9. O the fair, fair artemisia,
 10. Which is in the midst of the bank.
 11. As soon as I see my lord, .
 12. He gives me a hundred shells.

 13. Sail, sail, oh poplar boat !
 14. Now dipping, now riding the waves.
 15. As soon as I see my lord,
 16. My heart is at rest !

LIII. *Preface*: In praise of princes who attract and employ talent.
The theme is the excursion on the bank of the river and in a boat.

LIV. *The Rushes (Ch'in fêng 4—C. 137—L. 195)*

   1. The reeds and the rushes grow green ;
   2. The dew is changed to rime.
   3. That person of whom I think
   4. Is on the water somewhere . . .

5. Againſt the ſtream I go to him :
6. The way is hard and long.
7. Down the ſtream I go to him :
8. He is here in the midſt of the water.

9. The reeds and the rushes grow green ;
10. The dew is not yet dry.
11. That person of whom I think
12. Is on the water, near the banks . . .
13. Againſt the ſtream I go to him :
14. The way is rough and hard.
15. Down the ſtream I go to him :
16. He is here, on a ledge, in the water.

17. The reeds and the rushes grow green ;
18. The dew has not yet gone.
19. That person of whom I think
20. Is on the water, near the dam . . .
21. Againſt the ſtream I go to him :
22. The way is hard and ſteep.
23. Down the ſtream I go to him :
24. He is here, on a rock, in the water !

LIV. *Preface* : Hiſtorical interpretation without intereſt.
2. The changing of dew into hoar-froſt is a term used in the calendar to mark the time of the year when work terminates. Cf. XII, 2, 3 ; cf. *Li chi, Yüeh ling*, second month of autumn, Couvreur, i, p. 386.
7. Cf. App. III, the cuſtoms of Nan Chao. Su Hsing and his ladies used to go down the ſtream before the battle of flowers.
The theme is the search for the lover on the banks of the river and in the river.
Cf. *T'ang fêng*, 3 ; Couvreur, p. 123. (LIVʙ.)

LIVʙ. In the placid river
This white rock, how high.
Robe of white and collar red,
I follow thee right to Chiu. (Cf. LXVI, 5.)
As soon as I see my lord
Ah, am I not glad.

In the placid river,
This white rock, how bright.
Robe of white and collar red,
I follow thee right to Kao !
As soon as I see my lord
Ah, how should I be sad ?

In the placid river,
This white rock, how clear.
I know there is an order
And do not dare to tell.

Transposition of the theme of LIV with geographical allusions.
(Chiu, Kao.)

LV. *The Bank (Ch'ên fêng* 10—C. 151—L. 213)

1. On the bank of that lagoon
2. Grow reeds and nenuphars.
3. He is a handsome fellow . . .
4. In my sadness what shall I do ?
5. Day or night I can do nothing . . .
6. From eyes and nose my tears ſtream down . . .

7. By the bank of that lagoon
8. Grow reeds and orchises.
9. He is a handsome fellow :
10. In ſtature tall, of noble mien.
11. Day or night I can do nothing . . .
12. In my heart how grieved am I . . .

13. On the banks of that lagoon
14. Grow reeds and nenuphars in flower.
15. He is a handsome fellow :
16. In ſtature tall, of lofty mien.
17. Day or night I can do nothing . . .
18. This way and that I turn on my pillow . . .

LV. *Preface*: An allusion to an historical incident, cf. *SMC.*, iv, 233–5, the hero being an ancestor of Confucius, who gives evidence of licentious manners. In consequence of such a happening, boys and girls amused themselves together.

    5. Cf. LIV, 8.
    8. Cf. LII, 4.

The themes are meetings on the water and gathering water-plants— the torment and sleeplessness caused by love.

LVI. *The Ospreys (Chou nan 1—C. 5—L. 1)*

  1. In harmony the ospreys cry
  2. In the river, on the rocks.
  3. The maiden goes into retirement,
  4. A fit mate for the Prince.

  5. Long or short the duckweed :
  6. To left and right let us seek it.
  7. The maiden goes into retirement,
  8. Day and night let us ask for her.
  9. Ask for her . . . Useless quest . . .
10. Day and night let us think of her . . .
11. Ah ! what pain ! . . . Ah ! what pain ! . . .
12. This way and that we toss and turn . . .

13. Long or short the duck-weed :
14. To left and right let us take it.
15. The maiden goes into retirement,
16. Guitars and lutes should welcome her.

17. Long or short the duck-weed :
18. To left and right let us gather it.
19. The maiden goes into retirement,
20. Bells and drums should welcome her.

LVI. *The Ospreys* (show) the virtue of the queen. . . . In this poem (the queen) expresses her delight that she has found a pure maiden to mate with her (own) lord. She regrets that she must send (to the prince) (this girl) who is a model of the virtues (instead of going herself). (But) she does not wish to debase her (own) beauty. She regrets her (enforced) retirement, she thinks (enviously) of (the girl), perfect in virtue and talent (who is to take her place), but she has no wish to bring harm upon the good (that is, the girl). Such is the meaning of the Ospreys.

(Another version : A song of the women's apartments. The song of a virtuous wife who has lost the favour of her lord but is not jealous. Observe that, whereas the maiden is supposed to be the rival, it is the queen who is said to go into retirement.)

1 and 2. According to Mao these lines are a simile. A descriptive auxiliary represents the call of the male and female ospreys which answer each other. These birds, even though their desire to mate is at its keenest, still have regard for the rules for the separation of the sexes. This is shown by their hiding during their love-making on the rocky ledges in the midst of the water. (Note of K'ung Ying-ta : they do not fly side by side, but following (the female being behind the male). Just as the queen who esteems the virtue of her lord obeys (his will) in all things, and, in not using her beauty for unworthy purposes, respects the rules of the retired life (of the inner apartments), so, in the same way, the ospreys respect them (on the islets). In this way her good influence can extend through the world. When husbands and wives have regard for the separation of the sexes, fathers and sons fulfil the duties of their relationship ; when fathers and sons fulfil the duties of their relationship, lords and vassals observe the respect due to authority. When lords and vassals observe the respect due to authority, the audiences of the court are held regularly. When these are held regularly, the good influence of the king reaches its height.

3 and 4. The meaning is that the queen, possessing the virtue of the ospreys which call in harmony, the virtuous girls who live in retirement (in the women's apartments) in perfect chastity, become, as is proper, fit companions for the lord. (Mao.) That is to say, adds Chêng, that all wives of secondary rank who have ceased to enjoy the favours of their lord, being under the good influence of the queen, are free from jealousy (and therefore do not prevent those among them who are fitted for it, from having access to the prince).

Observe that the object of these complicated explanations given by Mao and Chêng is to show why, since the wife and the maiden are not the same person, and the former, being possessed of the virtue of the ospreys, is obliged to live in retirement, it should still be the maiden who is said (3) to go into retirement. She emulates the virtues of the queen, as do all the other wives.

5 and 6. Because she is possessed of the virtue of the ospreys who call and answer in harmony, the queen is qualified to gather the duck-weed and to prepare all the objects necessary for the service of the ancestral temple. (Mao.)

The left and right (shows that they) vied in helping one another. The meaning is that the three wives of the second rank, the nine wives of the third rank, and all the others are delighted to serve the queen. (Chêng.)

Observe that this gathering made with such emulation is supposed to have a ceremonial purpose. Duck-weed: a water-plant liked by ducks and ospreys.

8. The meaning is that the queen, whether waking or sleeping, does not cease from her search for this virtuous girl, with whose help she wishes to fulfil the duties of her position. (Chêng.)

8. Ask for her. The exact meaning of ' to ask for ', decided by comparison with XLVI, 4, and XXII, 3, is *to solicit a girl, to try to win her favour*.

Not yet having found the girl who is to help her, the queen thinks of fulfilling the duties of her position (by finding her). (Chêng.)

12. Cf. LV, 18. Depicts the restlessness of insomnia.

16. ' Welcome her '—the translation does not convey the full meaning; literally: make her *friendly* to us. To be of the same mind is called being *friends* (Chêng). The music causes all to share the same feelings.

19. Virtue being at its height, the music of bells and drums is necessary. (Mao.)

The classical interpretation may be summed up thus: T'ai Ssŭ, the virtuous wife of the civilizing king (Wên Wang) knew not jealousy. She was able to submit to living in retirement and to send to the king in her stead the virtuous girls from the women's quarters. In the women's apartments, which reflect her virtues, none of the inhabitants is jealous, and all live in retirement. They spend their time in seeking out the most suitable of their number to be the partner of their common lord and in carrying out with perfect accord the service of the king and of the temple.

A very different explanation is given in *HCCCHP.*, ch. 1423, pp. 17 sqq. There this poem is compared with LIX and LXVIIʙ (and also with No. 4 of the *Shao nan*). These poems appear to be connected with the offerings of vegetables made in the third month following the marriage. According to one theory the marriage was only consummated after this period of three months probation had passed: hence the references in lines 3, 7, 8, 9. The ceremony (in which music was played) marked the removal of the post-nuptial prohibition: hence the third stanza. This very interesting theory serves to show the passing over of popular customs to customs of the nobility. The prohibition of betrothal and the songs connected therewith correspond to the post-nuptial prohibition to which the songs were consequently referred. (Cf. How to Read a Classic, No. 15.) (Cf. Granet, *Cout. Matrim.*, *T'oung Pao*, xiii, p. 553 sqq.)

A text of the *Han shih wai chuan* (opening of chap. v) records, in a dialogue between Confucius and Tzǔ Hsia, the reasons why *The Ospreys* should be put at the beginning of the *Shih ching*. The reasons there given are the same as those given by Mao (1 and 2), but they are expressed in metaphysical terms. The conjugal virtues are the foundations of the social order and of the natural order, the props of heaven and earth, Tzǔ Hsia says.

The *Han shih wai chuan* agress with Mao's interpretation of the simile in 1 and 2. It is when the prince has retired from the court to his private apartments that the queen goes to seek him. (Cf. *Han shih (HCCCHP.,* 1150, p. 2 vo). The same book suggests that the poem could therefore be used as a satire directed against undue love of pleasure. Cf. *Hou Han shu*, Annals of the Emperor Ming, eighth year, Shanghai edition, chap. ii, p. 5 vo. Formerly the Ying gate (i.e. the prince who dealt with public affairs at this gate) having failed in his duties (in reference to sexual matters), *The Ospreys* censured the morals of the period.

The themes are the meeting by the rivers; the assembly for the gathering of plants; misgivings; separation and the retirement of the girl; sleeplessness; harmony and music. Observe the repetition of lines and the concatenation which give the poem almost the air of a mime. See Skeat, *Malay Magic*, p. 483.

(Professor Granet's 'Mouette' has been rendered 'osprey' in deference to the generally accepted meaning of Chü—*Tr.*)

LVII.   *The Hawk (Ch'in fêng 7—C. 141—L. 200)*

1.   Swift flies the hawk.
2.   Dense is the northern forest.
3.   Until I see my lord,
4.   My anxious heart is tortured.
5.   What shall I do? What shall I do?
6.   He forgets me, indeed, too often. . . .

7. On the hill are groves of oaks ;
8. The vale is dotted with elms.
9. Until I see my lord,
10. My anxious heart is joyless.
11. What shall. . . .

13. On the hill are plum tree groves ;
14. In the vale are tall wild pears.
15. Until I see my lord,
16. My anxious heart is drunken.
17. What shall I. . . .

LVII. *Preface* : Satire directed against a prince who neglects
worthy ministers.
The themes are separation, and the wooded hills and dales.

LVIII. *The Burdock (Chou nan 3—C. 8—L. 8)*

1. I gather, gather the burdock,
2. But cannot fill even one basket,
3. With longing I dream of that man
4. And relinquish it there on the pathway.

5. I climb up that rock-strewn height ;
6. My horses are worn out. . . .
7. I pour myself drink from this vessel of gold
8. That I may not continue to grieve. . . .

9. I climb up that lofty hill ;
10. My horses have lost their sheen . . .
11. I pour myself drink from this horn of rhinoceros
12. That I may not continue to suffer. . . .

13. I climb up that sandy height ;
14. My horses are all quite lame. . . .
15. My driver also is disabled . . .
16. Alas, alas, how I suffer !

LVIII. *Preface*: *The Burdock* shows the feelings of the queen. In addition (to her other wishes formulated in *Chou nan* 1 and 2) she desired to assist the prince, and, by seeking out worthy men and controlling the nominations (to office), to see to it that the vassals devoted all their energies (to the service of their lord). In the women's quarters her aim was to see that the most worthy among the women had access to the prince, and (in the same way, outside the women's quarters) she had no desire to make any selfish demands, contrary to benevolence or right (on behalf of her kindred or friends). Morning and evening she thought upon these things, until she was weary and sorrowful.

1 and 2. A simile indicating sadness. (Mao.)

3 and 4. According to Mao and Chêng this is a figure of speech meaning to appoint to office men of worth according to their merits.

7. Vessels of gold were the privilege of the prince.

The themes are the chase on the mountains ; harvestings ; misgivings ; drinkings. Observe the rhinoceros horn. Cf. *Pin fêng*, 1. A horse-race may be indicated.

In the symbolic interpretation the pursuit of the lover is explained as the search for men of worth. Being included in the *Chou nan* which is supposed to be in praise of T'ai Ssŭ, it is admitted that this song is sung by a woman.

LIX. *Grasshoppers of the Meadows (Shao nan* 3—C. 18—L. 23)

1. The meadow grasshopper chirps
2. And the hillside grasshopper leaps.
3. Until I have seen my lord,
4. My anxious heart is disturbed.
5. But as soon as I shall see him,
6. As soon as I shall join him,
7. My heart will have peace.

8. I climb that southern hill
9. There to gather the ferns.
10. Until I have seen my lord,
11. My anxious heart is tortured.
12. But as soon as I shall see him,
13. As soon as I shall join him,
14. My heart will be gay.

15. I climb that southern hill
16. There to gather the fern.
17. Until I have seen my lord,
18. My heart is troubled and sad.
19. But as soon as I shall see him,
20. As soon as I shall join him,
21. My heart will be soothed.

LIX. *Preface*: *The Grasshoppers of the Meadows* (shows) the wife of a great officer, capable of controlling her emotions in accordance with the rites.

1 and 2. The chirp of the insects and their leaping are depicted by descriptive auxiliaries.

Simile showing the wife of a great officer accompanying her husband to fulfil the rites. (Mao.)

The grasshopper in the meadows chirps, and the one in the woods leaps to rejoin it. They are different varieties of the same insect. So boys and girls at the time of the festivals, in obedience to the rites, seek and call one another. (Chêng.)

Observe this reference to the law of exogamy.

On the subject of the grasshoppers and of sexual relations see VI.

Although married, the wife thinks of the family to which she will be readmitted (her own family which she has left, and to which she will return, it may be on a visit, or divorced, or a childless widow). (Mao.)

'Until I have seen my lord' shows that the time of the journey (marriage procession) has arrived. She is sad at the thought of not suiting her lord, and of not paying the visit (for the purpose of) setting the hearts of her parents at rest. (Chêng.) Cf. Shao nan, 2 ; Couvreur, p. 7, lines 1, 18. (Being a married woman) therefore her heart is sad, for she does not cease to think with affection of her family.

6. Chêng, following the *I ching*, gives the meaning of sexual

union. Cf. LX, 24, 29, and X, 5 var.: As soon as I see my lord =
When the communal feast takes place on the evening of the marriage.
As soon as I shall join him = When the marriage shall be
consummated. At first she was sad at the idea of being unsuited
(to her husband) but now that her lord has behaved in accordance
with the rites, she hopes to be able to go to pay the visit which shall
set the hearts of her parents at rest. Moreover, her heart is relieved
of its anxiety.

9. Cf. *Yung fêng*, 10, st. 3; Couvreur, 62.
On the marriage journey she sees people picking ferns. Those
who harvest the ferns get what they seek and so she who is travelling
hopes to find (on arrival) (a husband who will fulfil) the rites.
(Chêng.)

18 ends with two separate words depicting sadness; not, as lines 4
and 11, with a duplicated word.

Mao quotes in explanation a formula attributed to Confucius by
the *Tsêng Tzŭ wên*, *Li chi*, Couvreur, p. 429. "In the home of
a girl who is getting married the lights are not extinguished for three
days; the thoughts are of separation." (Note that in this same
passage of the *Li chi* is found evidence of the sacrifice offered by the
wife in the third month.)

Lines 1–7 occur again in No. 8 of the *Hsiao ya*, i (Couvreur,
p. 189), lines 33–8.

One school connects this poem with LIV, LXVIIB, and *Shao nan*, 4.
(Cf. *HCCCHP.*, p. 12 vᵒ sqq.) This school refers it to the offering
of vegetables made in the third month after the ceremony, the
marriage being consummated only after the sacrifice has been offered.
The harvesting refers to the gathering of the plants to be offered.
The woman, who had arrived three months earlier, has not yet seen
her husband, and is not yet united to him. This school, unlike Chêng,
does not think that the lines refer to the marriage ceremony; that
makes the explanation of the harvesting too complicated. Like Chêng,
however, it explains the woman's sadness by the custom of the visit to
her parents. This visit is taken in the same sense as the corresponding
rite of the release of the girl in the third month. (Cf. *Tso chuan*, Chêng,
9th year, Legge, p. 369.) (Compare the visit of the husband to his
parents-in-law, which was made in the third month in some cases.
The account in the chapter on Marriage in the *I li*.)

This tradition is important as explaining the development of popular
customs into rules to be followed by persons of rank. It will be
noted that, in the meetings of the grasshoppers, Chêng sees a symbol
of the sexual festivals. On the other hand, he believes in the
rule of marriages in the spring. But he himself states that the chirp

of the grasshopper denotes the end of autumn. Comment on the *Shih ching, Hsiao ya,* i, 8, lines 36–8, in which the first couplet of LIX occurs again. But there is nothing to show that Chêng was unaware of the festivals of the sexes held in autumn. See his comment on L, 1 and 2.

The themes are: the excursions on the heights; the mating of animals; harvestings; the restlessness of love; and its satisfaction.

LX. *The Chariot Axles (Hsiao ya* VII, 4—C. 293—L. 391)

1. With heavy blows I have made fast the axles of my chariot.
2. I go to find the fair young girl, the substance of my dreams.
3. What can hunger mean to me? What care I for thirst?
4. With her charm she is coming to me.
5. Although I have no good friends,
6. Yet come, let us feast and be merry.

7. In that thick forest on the plain,
8. The pheasants meet together.
9. At the proper time this noble girl
10. With her great virtue comes to help me.
11. Come then, let us feast and sing her praises.
12. I will love thee and never tire.

13. Although I lack delicate spirits,
14. Yet come, let us drink, I invite.
15. Although I have no dainty dishes,
16. Yet come, let us eat, I entreat.
17. Although my virtue does not equal yours,
18. Yet come, let us sing and then dance.

19. I climbed that lofty height
20. And there cut down branches of oak.
21. And there cut down branches of oak.

22. Their leafage how fresh and green.
23. What luck for me to unite with thee.
24. Ah, my heart, what comfort it knows.

25. The lofty heights may be admired ;
26. The high roads may be travelled.
27. My four horses how docile they are.
28. Their six reins suggest a lute.
29. I am joined with thee, my new-made bride,
30. And thus I set peace in my heart.

LX. *Preface* : A satire against King Yu and his favourite Pao Ssŭ. Cf. *SMC.*, Chavannes, i, 280 sqq. Pao Ssŭ was jealous and lacking in virtue (*tao*). The people of Chou desired to find a virtuous girl to mate with their king, wherefore they made this song.

The themes are the chariot ; charm ; the communal feast ; birds, festival seasons, songs and dances ; climbing ; bundles of firewood ; and union of husband and wife.

LXI. *The Bundles of Firewood (T'ang fêng 5—C. 124—L. 179)*

1. I have bound in bundles the branches.
2. The three stars are in the sky.
3. Ah, what an evening is this one
4. On which I see thee my wife.
5. Alas for thee ! Alas for thee !
6. With my wife, what shall I do ?

LXI. *Preface* : Satire directed against times of disorder. The disturbances in which the people were involved prevented the making of marriages at the proper seasons.

1. The theme is the faggot of firewood bound up. Symbolizes the effect of the rites upon men and women. (Mao.)

2. The three stars are the stars of the constellation Scorpio. From the fact of their visibility at evening the commentators deduce a date which proves that marriages were not being made at the proper seasons. According to Chêng, from the end of the third to the middle of the fourth month.

3 and 4. From the appearance of the night it is evident that the month is one in which marriages should not take place. (Chêng.)

8. The position of the ſtars indicates the end of the fourth and the middle of the fifth month. (Chêng.)

10. Meeting, the woman met at the feſtivals. Cf. X, 5.

14. The position of the ſtars indicates the end of the fifth and the beginning of the sixth month. (Chêng.) The middle of the firſt month. (Mao.)

16. A great officer has one wife and two secondary wives. (Mao.) Cf. *Kuo yu, Chou yü*, ii, and *SMC.*, Chavannes, i, 265 and 266, No. 2.

The themes are bundles of firewood ; marital perturbation ; meetings.

(Notes 8 to 16 refer to the remainder of the poem of which only one verse is here translated.—Tr.)

LXII. *The Hill of Yüan (Ch'ên fêng* 1—C. 145—L. 205)
  1. Oh you who go to disport yourselves
  2. On the top of the Hill of Yüan,
  3. Truly you are full of life,
  4. It is not a sight to be looked at.

  5. To the sound of drums that are beaten
  6. At the foot of the hill of Yüan,
  7. What matter, Winter ? Summer, what matter ?
  8. You hold the egret plumes.

  9. To the sound of the drums of clay
  10. On the road up the hill of Yüan,
  11. What matter, Winter ? Summer, what matter ?
  12. You hold the egret fan.

LXII. *Preface* : A satire upon Duke Yu of Ch'ên (854–832). Unlimited dissipations ; irregular marriages ; excursions and amusements indulged in without reſtraint.

3. The lords referred to being licentious in their feelings, their manners are not pleasant to watch. (Chêng.) Cf. *Chou li*, Biot, i, 266–9.

Themes : heights, excursions, pantomimic dances.

LOVE SONGS OF THE SHIH CHING

LXIII. *The Young Elms (Ch'ên fêng 2—C. 145—L. 206)*

1. At the Eastern Gate, the young elms ;
2. On the hill of Yüan, the oaks :
3. It is the daughter of Tzŭ Chung
4. Who dances beneath their shade.

5. On a beautiful morning they seek each other
6. Out on the southern plain.
7. Let no one tarry to spin the hemp.
8. To the market, go, dance, dance !

9. On a beautiful morning they take a walk
10. And go out together in bands.
11. I look at thee, thou art like the mallow.
12. Give me those fragrant herbs !

LXIII. *Preface* : Poem reprobating disorder. The licentious and profligate conduct of Duke Yu was the cause of the decay of good manners. Boys and girls abandoned their traditional occupations, held great assemblies in the roads and streets, and sang and danced in the market and by the wells.

1. The place indicated was the meeting-place for the state, the place where the boys and girls met. (Mao.)

3. Tzŭ Chung is the family name of a great officer of Ch'ih. (Mao.) Refers to a boy. (Chêng.) According to the moderns ; girls of good family.

5. Cf. 9. Modern scholastic interpretation—*HCCCHP*. 428, p. 42. A cry to call down rain, used in the rain sacrifice.

6. Yüan is the name of a great officer. (Mao.) The daughter of the Yüan family living in the south. (Chêng.) For the moderns *yüan* is not a name but has its ordinary meaning of level ground.

7. The end of the work of spinning and weaving.

11 and 12. The boys and girls meet and talk, and the gift of fragrant herbs is to cement their friendship. (Chêng.) Cf. LII, 12. Line 11 is spoken by the boy and line 12 by the girl.

12. Concerning the aromatic seeds and their uses, see Couvreur, *Shih ching*, pp. 420 and 124. Cf. *HCCCHP*., 428, 5 v°. The sorcerers use them in the service of the gods.

12. Lit. : Give me a handful of fragrant herbs.

117

Themes : excursions on the wooded heights ; the pursuit ; the
termination of work ; the dance ; gifts of flowers. Evidence of
antiphonal songs.

LXIV. *The Dead Hind (Shao nan 12—C. 26—L. 34)*

1. On the plain there is the dead hind ;
2. With white grass wrap it round.
3. There is a girl dreaming of spring.
4. Good fellow, solicit her.

5. In the forest there are bushes ;
6. On the plain there is the dead fawn.
7. With white grass wrap it round.
8. The girl is like a diamond.

9. Gently, gently ; press me not.
10. Do not touch my girdle !
11. Whatever you do, do nothing
12. To cause my dog to bark.

LXIV. *Preface* : *The Dead Hind* (shows) abhorrence of the failure
to observe the rites. The kingdom was in a state of great disorder (at
the end of the Yin dynasty). Ruffianism prevailed and manners
became demoralized. When the civilizing influence of King Wên
made itself felt, although the period was still one of disorder, yet
the absence of rites was deplored.

Failure to observe the rites : no intermediary employed and no
ceremonial presents sent (wild geese and lengths of silk), marriages
consummated by force. (Chêng.)

In times of distress ceremonial presents decreased in value.
(Instead of the deer-skin which should have been sent), (*I li*, Marriage),
the girl hopes that some of the flesh of a deer that has been killed
and divided by the hunters may be sent to her wrapped in couch-
grass. (Mao and Chêng.) (*Chou li*, Biot, i, 208.) Presents of food
must be presented on a bed of herbs. (*Li chi, Chüeh li*, Couvreur,
i, 45.) The couch-grass, being white, was used because of its purity.
(Mao.) Cf. *I ching*.

3 and 4. The young girl thinks longingly of the spring because it is not lawful for her to await the autumn. (Mao.) Mao thinks that the girl had reached 20, the limit of the marriage age. She cannot wait for the autumn-winter season, (according to Mao, the proper marriage season), but thinks longingly of the spring, the time when marriages could take place summarily, in which rites and ceremonial presents are not essential.

Chêng is of opinion that the second month of spring was the recognized time for the completion of marriages. The girl thinks of the time when, in accordance with the rites, it will be permissible for her to unite with the boy. It was necessary for the boy first of all to send an intermediary to ask for her hand (line 4). Chêng believes that the preliminary betrothal ceremonies took place in autumn. Cf. L, 1 and 2.

5 and 6. A bundle of firewood wrapped in white grass like the deer-flesh, also served as a ceremonial present (again the theory of the decreased value of the ritual gifts during times of disorder. (Chêng.)

8. Virtue like jade. Owing to its whiteness and its strength jade is symbolic of the girl's virtue. An equivalent is used in the translation.

9. A descriptive auxiliary is here used to depict an attitude in which there is no violence.

10. A kerchief attached to the girdle. (Mao.) This kerchief is an important item of feminine dress. On the birth of a girl such a kerchief was hung at the door. *Li chi, Nei tsê*, Couvreur, i, 663. When the girl set out on the wedding journey (*Shih ching, Pin fêng*, 4 ; Couvreur, 167), her mother fastened a kerchief to her girdle when she gave her parting instructions (*I li*, Marriage, note). On the marriage night the matron in charge of the girl presented it to her after she had undressed (*I li*, Marriage). She used it to cleanse herself (Chêng, note on *I li*, Marriage). To touch the kerchief denotes the consummation of the marriage.

11. More particularly a large hound in the grass. (Mao.) The dogs bark when violence is offered to anyone in defiance of the rites. (Mao.)

Regarding this detail, compare Hakka, No. XII, App. III.

Themes : invitation and half-refusal; bundles of firewood; hunting.

FESTIVALS AND SONGS OF ANCIENT CHINA

LXV. *The Axe Handle (Pin fêng 5—C. 170—L. 240)*

1. How is an axe-handle made?
2. With no axe it cannot be done.
3. How is a wife to be taken?
4. With no match-maker none can be had.

LXV shows the virtue of the Duke of Chou—powerful enough to make men good—by means of argument. Like obtains like.

3 and 4. It is the intermediary who carries out the rites. (Mao.)

The intermediary can carry messages between the two families (which are being united by the marriage). (Chêng.)

The first stanza of *Pin fêng*, 5, is given in order to show the traditional linking of the ideas of the intermediary and the axe used to cut the firewood.

Cf. *Ch'i fêng*, 6; Couvreur, 107, lines 13–15 and 19–22, LXVB.

13. How is the hemp to be grown?
14. The furrows must be crossed (E. to W. and N. to S.)
15. How is a wife to be taken?
16. Her parents must be informed.
19. How are the boughs to be cut?
20. With no axe it cannot be done.
21. How is a wife to be taken?
22. With no match-maker none can be had.

16. The living are consulted, and divination is employed (by means of the tortoise) beside the tombs of the dead. (Chêng.) The relation between the ideas is comprehensible if the gathering of the bundles of firewood plays an important part in autumn, the period at which it was usual to set up housekeeping and to conduct negotiations between families (cf. LX, 20, 21; LXI; LXVI, 7, 10; and also XXII and LXVI, 4). LXIV shows that the bundles of firewood were ceremonial presents. Cf. XLVI, 9–12, and 17–20. I fancy that the crossing of the furrows N.-S. and E.-W. typifies the crossing of two different families (exogamy). Compare the comparison drawn from the junction of two rivers. LII and XLV.

LXVI. *The Peasant (Wei feng 4—C. 67—L. 97)*

1. Oh, peasant who seemed quite simple,
2. Exchanging thy cloth for silken thread,
3. Thou cameſt not to get the silken thread :
4. Thou cameſt to inveigle me.
5. I followed thee over the Ch'i,
6. As far as the hill of Tuan . . .
7. " — 'Tis not I would poſtpone the time ;
8. Thou haſt no good go-between."
9. . . . " I pray thee be not angry.
10. Let autumn be the time."

11. I climbed upon that ruined wall
12. To look towards Fu Kuan . . .
13. Nothing in sight towards Fu Kuan . . .
14. My tears fell down like rain . . .
15. When I saw thee towards Fu Kuan
16. Ah, then I laughed and talked.
17. . . . " The tortoise and the milfoil
18. Foretell no ill for me."
19. . . . " Come then and bring thy carriage
20. My trousseau to convey."

21. When the mulberry sheds its leaves
22. They are tender to the touch. . . .
23. Alas, alas, O turtle-dove,
24. Eat not the mulberry fruits.
25. Alas, alas, O gentle girl,
26. With boys take not thy pleasure.
27. When a young man takes his pleasure,
28. He may be excused.
29. But when a girl takes pleasure,
30. There is no excuse.

31. When the mulberry sheds its leaves,
32. They fall, already yellow . . .
33. Since I came to live with you,
34. Three years have passed in poverty . . .
35. How high is the river Ch'i,
36. Wetting the carriage hangings . . .
37. The girl has never been forsworn.
38. The boy has played a double game.
39. The boy, t'is true, has been unjuſt
40. Twice, thrice, he changed his mind.

41. For three years I have been thy wife,
42. Of toil I never wearied ;
43. Early to rise and late to reſt,
44. I never had a morning.
45. And as long as that endured
46. Thou didſt treat me harshly . . .
47. My brothers, they shall never know.
48. They would laugh and mock me . . .
49. Quietly I ponder it
50. And hug my grief in secret !

51. Along with thee I would grow old,
52. And, old, thou haſt made me suffer . . .
53. Yet the Ch'i has its banks . . .
54. Yet the valley has sides . . .
55. In my girlish head-dress thou didſt feaſt me ! . . .
56. Thy voice, thy laugh, they pleased me.
57. Thy vow was clear as the dawn.
58. I did not dream that thou wouldſt change . . .
59. That thou wouldſt change . . . I did not dream . . .
60. Now, it is finished . . . alas . . .

LXVI. *Preface* : A satire upon the times. In the reign of Duke Hsüan (718–700 B.C.) rites and duty had fallen into decay. Loose manners were prevalent. Boys and girls did not (keep the rule of) separation, but went together into the fields and solicited favours of one another. Flowers fallen and beauty faded, they turned away from each other. There were those who suffered much in consequence and felt remorseful, and having lost their partners, made known their situation in order that it might have an effect upon the manners of the state. This return to the right way is admired and licentious ways are reprobated.

2. At the end of spring the breeding of silkworms begins, and, at the beginning of autumn, the silk thread is sold. (Chêng.) Cf. LXIII, 7.

7 and 8. The girl speaks.

9 and 10. The boy speaks.

17 and 18. The boy speaks.

19 and 20. The girl speaks.

21. The middle of autumn. (Chêng.)

24. For fear of becoming intoxicated.

29. The woman, says Chêng, has never any business which should take her outside the inner apartments. Her only moral principle is the maintaining of absolute chastity.

31. The last month of autumn. (Chêng.)

36. Hangings (curtains) peculiar to the carriages of women. Cf. LV, 7.

41. Thy wife, or, more accurately, daughter-in-law to thy parents.

55. Bound hair; the style of hair-dressing of girls who have not yet been given the hair-pin, being still under age. Cf. *Li chi, Nei tsê*, Couvreur, i, 624.

Song of a woman unhappily married. Cf. *Pei fêng*, 10; Couvreur, 39.

Themes: markets; meetings; excursions on the heights and beside the rivers; antiphonal lines; the intermediary; hill climbs in autumn; divinatory practices; carriage; the custom of trousseaux for women; crossing rivers; and the young men's wooing.

He who has not the virtue of the legitimate ruler is likely to keep his subjects too long under arms; homes are thereby broken up and there are too many unmarried people. Such are the results of an extended term of service, and the causes of licence: "Licence passed beyond all bounds; marriages were made without regard to propriety; excursions and amusements were enjoyed without restraint." [1] In all seasons—what matter,

---

[1] LXII, preface.

winter? summer, what matter?[1]—girls and boys sang and danced in the fields ; undeterred by rules, whenever possible, they took their pleasures.   But in the golden age of the *Great Peace*,[2] were there not times ordained for excursions and festivals, when enjoyment was authorized ?

I would willingly believe, on the evidence of the odes, that at stated times, and in places set apart, custom required the holding of great rural gatherings.

These gatherings were held on the banks of a river or on the mountains.   It might be a sea or a lake ; a ford or a spring ; the junction of two rivers or a high hill ; a wooded eminence or the depths of a valley, which attracted the revellers.   In the case of certain states the sites of these gatherings can be determined.   In the states of the South[3] the girls strolled beneath the tall trees on the banks of the Han, not far from the place at which it flows into the (Yang-tzŭ) Chiang.   In Chêng it was on the fine stretches of grassland across the Wei river where it met the Chên that the girls met the foolish young fellows of the countryside.[4]   From Ch'ên[5] they went to disport themselves under the oaks which grew on the hill of Yüan to the east of the town.

In Wei, the beautiful Mêng Chiang and the beautiful Mêng I and the beautiful Mêng Yung,[6] as also the woman who was enticed by the country-lad,[7] went with their lovers along the banks of the Ch'i, to where, at a bend of the river, there grew a clump of fine bamboos.[8]   Nearby was the hill of Tuan which they visited at the same time.[9]   From the fact that the songs often refer to mountains and rivers together it would appear that it was usual to meet near a hill overlooking

---

[1] LXII, 7.

[2] *T'ai P'ing.* Cf. *Han wei tsung shu* in the *Han shih wai chuan,* a long and weighty exposition on the period of the *Great Peace* and the good morals of that golden age.

[3] XLVI, 1–2, notes and C. and App. III, references to *BEFEO.,* viii, 348.

[4] LI, LII.   [5] LXII, LXIII.   [6] XLIV.   [7] LXVI.

[8] Couvreur, p. 63 ; see also p. 74. For the states of Wei, Pei, and Yung this one place beside the Wei seems to have been the only resort. These states anciently formed one group. Cf. *SMC.,* iv, 8, n. 2.

[9] See *Ch'ien Han shu,* geog. monog. Shanghai ed., ch. 28*b*, p. 15, v. 4. LXVI, 6.

the river, or beside a stretch of water or a spring situated on the side of a hill, and, most probably, always on the grassy meadows near the foot of the hill, or beneath fine groves of trees—in those places, in short, where the vegetation was beautiful.

When were these excursions made ? The rustic themes themselves indicate the time ; it is not necessary to attempt to fix it accurately as do the commentators when referring these themes to the rural calendars of which they were the basis. It is probable, indeed, that the dates differed in different states. It seems evident that the favoured months were those of autumn and spring, since it is at these seasons that the springs are full and the rivers rise. Between the dry, rigorous cold of winter and the moist heat of summer there are in China two wonderful seasons. In the vast plains of eastern Asia the seasons change abruptly. In winter the earth seems dead : no blade of grass in the dusty-yellow expanse, no cry of beasts, no sound of running water, no work possible. The east wind comes and the longer days. Suddenly the snow disappears ; the ice melts, the springs awaken, the grass pushes its way up through the more yielding clods of earth, animal life stirs, the first rains fall : the season of agricultural work has begun.[1] From the bounteous and too circumscribed earth the greatest possible number of crops is hurriedly gathered. Then the wind begins to blow from the west. The oppressive, breathless atmosphere of summer is succeeded by cool, changeable, delightful weather ; the last rains fall, allowing the final labours of the season to be carried out and filling again the springs and rivers. Finally, all life, vegetable, animal, and human, disappears abruptly from the countryside. The bursting of leaf-buds, sudden blossomings, the swift fall of leaves, the arrival and departure of migratory birds, the awakening and the disappearance of insects, the mating of animals, the roll of thunder, the rainbow,

[1] See the calendrical terms of the *Yüeh ling*. Cf. *Song of Solomon*, ii, 10 sqq.: " For, lo, the winter is past, the rain is over and gone ; the flowers appear on the earth ; the time of the singing of birds is come, and the voice of the turtle is heard in our land."

dew and frost, whatever begins and ends the wet season, everything that opens and closes the agricultural year—with these the rustic themes concern themselves, and it is this fact that would seem to justify the belief that the assemblies in the fields were held at the beginning and at the end of the long winter interlude. " In the second month of spring " says the *Calendar of the Hsia*, " the boys and girls, in great numbers, made merry together." In the calendar preserved by Kuan Tzŭ, the festival is referred to the end of spring when it occupied three periods of twelve days each. In the autumn, likewise, thirty-six days were set apart for a similar festival.[1] In his notes on the *Shih ching*, Chêng K'ang-ch'êng refers on several occasions to festivals in which boys and girls, in conformity with the rites, sought and found one another. Stirred by the springtime, he says, they went out together.[2] Chêng belongs to a school which maintains that marriages were made in the spring, his authority being the *Chou li*, a collection of elaborate works tricked out in the form of an Utopia by archæologists versed in feudal matters.[3] In this reference is made to an official whose duty it was to regulate the matrimonial gatherings in the second month of the year. By some other writers [4] the beginning of the marriage season is referred to the fall of the hoar-frost in the second month of autumn, but they admit that marriages also take place at the period of the thaw. Chêng, on the contrary, refers to the autumn the second series of ceremonies connected with betrothal.[5]

The divergences between these different archæological theories may be adequately explained by the fact that sometimes one and sometimes another of the complicated marriage rites was considered the essential one. At one time it was the

[1] Time limits, appointed times.
[2] Comments on LIX and LXIV, and also LII.
[3] *Chou li, Ti kuan*, v. *Mei shih* : Biot, i, 307.
[4] E.g. the *Chia yü* and the Commentaries of Wang Su (ch. *Pên ming chieh*). When the hoar-frost falls, women's work is ended and marriages may be made. When the ice melts, the field work begins and the gathering of mulberry leaves, and it is then that the marriage rites approach completion.
[5] Cf. comments on L.

betrothal and at another the marriage ceremony. All agree that spring and autumn were the favourable seasons for these gatherings of the sexes. A philosophical explanation is also forthcoming [1] : the girls (who are *yin*), stirred by the spring (which is *yang*), think of boys (also *yang*). Inversely, in autumn (*yin*) boys (*yang*) are influenced by the appeal of girls (*yin*). Lastly, the songs themselves are quite explicit, and it is evident from them that the gatherings were held at stated times.[2]

> " The man sets out to seek a wife
> When the ice has not yet melted," [3]

says one. Another depicts a young girl dreaming of the spring,[4] and *The Peasant* describes two young people who meet in the spring and, when autumn comes, set up house together.[5] What took place at these spring and autumn festivals by the rivers and on the heights ? The young people gathered from the various villages and hamlets, there being, it would seem, only one such meeting-place in each state.[6] They went to find one another and then set out together.[7] Some offered the use of their carriages, and others secured invitations.[8] When they reached their destination a scene of great animation presented itself.[9] No doubt there was a temporary settlement, with travelling merchants,[10] a crowd of carriages and boats, and ferry-men calling for passengers.[11] Numbers of people strolled about on the banks of the river or on the slopes of the hills, happy, laughing gaily,[12] admiring the scene, the beauty of the trees, the magnificence of the mountain,[12] the splendour of the cedar boats. . . . Then followed the contests : the crossing of the river, the climbing of the hill.

The ford was crossed with skirts held or tucked up,[13] or by swimming,[14] perhaps with the help of hollowed calabashes.[15]

---

[1] Notes on XXI.   [2] Cf. LX, 9.   [3] L, 11, 12.   [4] LXIV, 3.
[5] LXVI, 1st and 2nd stanzas.
[6] In the states of Yung, Pei, and Wei, which in ancient times formed one group, the only meeting-place seems to have been the banks of the Wei.
[7] LXIII, 5 and 9.   [8] XLV, 15 ; XXXV, XXXVI, and XII, 16.
[9] LXII, 3.   [10] LXIII, 8, and LXVI, 2–3.   [11] L, 13 ; XLV, 14.
[12] XLV.   [13] LX, 25, 11, 12, 14.   [14] L, 3, 4 ; LI, 2.
[15] XLIX, and L, 1 and 2.

When the water was too deep, or the river too swift, those who had carriages [1] used them, feeling rather uneasy if the water reached the axles or the hangings. Sometimes a boat was hired and the excitement of rising and sinking with the waves was experienced.[2] They pursued each other along the riverside, the embankment, and the dam, and even in the water, as far as the sandbanks and the reefs [3] in the middle of the river. They passed the time fishing [4] but chiefly in gathering the flowers and plants which grew in damp nooks or in the water—rushes, water-lilies, orchids, artemisia, duckweed, mallow, and fragrant herbs.[5]

They climbed the hills, often at racing speed, in their carriages, until their horses were worn out.[6] In the woods and meadows they gathered flowers [7] and possibly hunted.[8] Above all, they collected bundles of firewood, cutting down oak boughs [9] with axes and gathering brushwood and ferns.[10]

There must have been great rivalry in all these sports. Crossing the river, climbing the hill, pursuing one other, gathering flowers and firewood, afforded many opportunities for contests and competitions ; invitations and challenges were flung from one to another.[11] It is certain that, in the joyful tumult of this youthful assembly, there was never any irregularity. Except in the contests there was no jostling ; save for the challenges, no shouting. Actions and voice were guided by the sound of music. Drums were beaten and clay tabors sounded,[12] and, to the rhythm which they set, along the edge of the river, on the side of the hill, the dancers wound their way in procession, singing.[13]

On the occasion of festivals as old as the instruments played at them, on ceremonial occasions when the field-work was

[1] L, 7, and LXVI, 35–6.   [2] LIII, 13–16.   [3] LIV, LV, LIVв.
[4] XLV ; cf. XX.   [5] XLVI, LII, LIII, LV, LVI, LVIII, LXIII,
[6] LX, 1, 19, and 25–7 ; LIX, 8 ; LVIII. Cf. *Ch'i fêng*, 2. Couvreur, 104.
and *T'ang fêng*, 2 ; Couvreur, 123.
[7] Cf. XLII.   [8] Observe in the songs the themes of hunting and fishing.
[9] LX, 19–21 ; LIX, 9.   [10] LXI. Cf. LXV and LXVв.
[11] The challenge is clear in LII, LI, and L.   [12] LXII.   [13] See p. 151.

inaugurated or the harvest garnered, in beautiful places hallowed
by tradition, youths and girls, who at other times were kept
apart,[1] met with those of neighbouring villages.[2]   On these
unique occasions the girls saw men who were not related to
them, and boys saw girls who were not their sisters or cousins,
girls of the neighbourhood whom they could marry, while
the girls saw the men for whom they would leave behind
parents and brothers.[3]

Then, in addition to other contests and competitions [4]
which must have taken place, groups of boys and girls vied
with each other in contests of song and dance which brought
poetry into being at the same time as love.

While the groups dancing in procession to the sound of the
drums were crossing the river or climbing the hill, from one
company to the other were flung rhythmical challenges and
provocative songs.   In antiphonal lines or songs [5] a duel of
impromptu verse was indulged in, often beginning with raillery,
a fact which explains the mocking tone of many of the songs.
Were they worth troubling about, these young fools, these
artful fellows of the neighbourhood ? [6]   Choice was not
lacking ; was there not plenty of time to await a partner
worthy of one's self ? [7]   As the boys, overcome by the charms
of the girls, hardly dared to make advances, and addressed them
humbly, so the girls became increasingly disdainful.[8]   When
challenge passed to invitation, it was the girls who took the
lead and the boys who did not dare to yield immediately.[9]
As the extemporizing progressed, the strangers of a short time
before, brought closer by their poetical contests, though mocking

---

[1] See again XLIII and XXXVIII.
[2] Cf. LXVI and XL. The various villages of a state were enclosed places in which
the members of one clan gathered during the winter.
[3] Cf. XVI and XIV ; see also XXIII, 3. The reference to distance suggests the
territorial aspect of the law relating to exogamy.   Cf. The complaint of the Lolo
bride. App. III, p. 274.
[4] See p. 190.
[5] Evidenced by XV. Examples in XLII and particularly LII, LXIII, 11 and 12 ;
LXVI, 7–10 and 17–20 and XI. Cf. App. I.
[6] LI. Cf. XXXI and XXX.   [7] L. Cf. XXXV.
[8] LXIV. Cf. XV and XXII.   [9] LII.

only a moment ago, felt themselves drawn by friendly feelings and proceeded to pair off,[1] after which declarations of love and gifts of flowers brought the contest to a courteous end.[2]

But to the couples thus formed, neither this declaration of love nor the flower of betrothal was enough to satisfy the desire for union which they now experienced. As the water-birds fly away in pairs to hide on the islets in the river,[3] as the woodland birds in couples take refuge in the depths of the forest,[4] so these young people withdrew to the low grassy meadows or beneath the great trees and the tall ferns on the hills and there came together.[5] Vows, love-tokens, gathered flowers, trinkets, bought no doubt at the neighbouring fair, and drinking and eating together terminated the fellowship in which their new love declared itself.[6] The festival ended with a feast in which the ancient rhinoceros horn figured, for these celebrations were of an imposing character.[7]

Such, judging from the songs, appear to have been the festivals of the mountains and rivers ; such, at any rate, were their general characteristics. I believe that the crossing of the rivers and the gathering of flowers played an important part in the spring festival, and the hill-climbing and the collection of faggots in the autumn one. But these ceremonies were not confined to one festival. The themes corresponding to them are scattered indiscriminately throughout the songs. A more evident difference is that the spring seems to have been the time of betrothal and autumn the season of marriage. The girls chose a mate in the contest of dance and song at the season when the partridges summon their mates by singing.[8] The lovers then made appointments for the autumn,[9] and, after the autumn festival was over, they went away to live together, husband and wife. Elsewhere the spring and autumn festivals

[1] LII.   [2] LII, LXIII, 11 and 12.   [3] LVI.
[4] LX, 8.   [5] LIX, 6 ; LX, 23, and LII, 10–11.
[6] LII, 12 ; XXXIX, 9–12. Cf. XLIII, 13–18 ; XXVII, 12 ; XXVIII, LXIII, 11–12.
[7] LXII, and particularly LVIII, 10.   [8] L, 6, 8, 16 ; LXII, 7–10.
[9] Cf. LXII, stanzas 1 and 2.

do not seem to have had the same importance ; the spring being, without question, the season of greatest rejoicing.

During the progress of seasonal festivals which marked decisive periods in the lives of the country-people, in contests which brought the boys and girls of neighbouring villages into collision with one another, love was born in the midst of rural gatherings, in the songs and dances. It is not necessary to see in either the songs or the dances a mime devised for the purpose of expressing the emotions by means of voice and gesture. The feelings and their expression presented themselves together and sprang into being simultaneously ; moreover, the songs express primitive emotions with the minimum of artistic device.

What constituted love at the time of the songs is quite clear. It was first experienced in the heart as a pain so severe as to amount almost to actual physical suffering. Seldom is the joy of loving remarked ; it is the sickness of love that is presented, something in the nature of a primitive animal need,[1] a contraction of the heart comparable to the feeling of being famished, of morning hunger.[2] Genuine agony, inability to work or to sleep and fits of weeping are the result of the disturbance caused by love which the sufferers desired to throw off by taking walks.[3] But when, at the rural festivals, the young couples met and were united, they were immediately conscious of peace and a relief which restored them to happiness.[4] By the commentators the agony of love is expressed in terms of philosophy. In spring, they say, when the power of the *yang* is on the increase, girls feel its influence, which is opposed to their real nature, while in autumn boys are affected by the opposing *yin* influence.[5]

---

[1] LV, 5–6, 11–12, 17–18 ; LVI, 8–12 ; LVII, 4–7 ; LVIII, 12 ; LIX, 3–4 ; XXI, 21, etc. Cf. XVII, 16.

[2] XLVII, 4.　　[3] XLV, 16. Cf. LV, 5–6, 11, 12, 17, 18, and LVI, 9–12.

[4] LIX, and LX, 23–4, 29–30.

[5] Cf. comments on XXI, 21 (Chêng). In spring girls feel the *Yang* influence and think of boys. In autumn boys feel the *Yin* influence and think of girls. They undergo a physical change (under the influence of the contrary principle), and are in agony. At the times of the assemblies, of the festivals, the *Yang* and the *Yin* are united, like the boys and girls (equinoctial festivals). Cf. Chêng ; comment on LXIV, 3 ; cf. comments on LIX, 2.

Thus the alternating attraction between the sexes consists in a feeling of loss and bereavement, of regret for the incompleteness of their nature. When, therefore, during the intervals between these seasons, the *Yang* and the *Yin* combine in the world, the boys and girls, by uniting, reach the full development of their natures. This theory needs only to be expressed in concrete terms : if at the outset there is agony followed later by a consciousness of peace and fulfilment it is because love is a communion. It brings together two persons who by sex, family and country are strangers. It begins with a kind of duel in which the opponents are full of apprehension : this unknown girl who is to be taken into his home, this strange youth to whom she will go—each is a sealed book to the other. Face to face, in a contest, they put one another to the test. Each is aware of the difference between their virtues and each yields to the other's attraction. They are stirred by the contrast between their respective qualities and they feel dimly that antagonism might be changed into affection. Their personalities are opposed and they feel the need to bring them into harmony. In order to understand how powerful these complex feelings were it is only necessary to consider the life of the peasants of feudal China. They were firmly attached to the soil [1] ; they tilled the family fields with the assistance of their relatives ; men and women had different occupations and lived their lives apart. This opposition of family groups and of the sexes was the fundamental principle of social organization,[2] and the rule of separation was relaxed only on the eventful occasions when the people of the whole state assembled to hold a general festival.

Then, and in the orgy during which they forgot for a time all the rules of their barren and narrow existence, they became aware of their affinities, betrothals were arranged and marriages concluded, and the agony of apprehension which had possessed the lovers suddenly gave place to profound peace ; the violence

---

[1] *Chou sung*, iii, 5. Couvreur, 439.
[2] The principle of the separation of the sexes.

of their former feeling exacting a powerful reaction. No mere declarations and tokens of love sufficed to bind hearts which demanded nothing less than that complete union which would give them eternal possession of each other. It is not to be wondered at that, in songs in which Chinese commentators see only licentiousness, foreigners find traces of an ancient morality, preferable to the existing one. This is due to the fact that, in the lavish protestations of faithfulness made by the lovers, they see an ancient monogamy. As a matter of fact, from the time of their union in the festival of general harmony the lovers considered themselves bound irrevocably, and their apprehensions and agony gave place to security and peace of mind.

Like the emotions of love, the process of the love-poetry is explained by the ceremonies of the seasonal festivals. Arising out of the extempore compositions in the contests of song and dance, the odes retained, even when they portrayed love in the village, or the love between husband and wife, the form which was suited to the antiphonal chorus, a rhythm which presumed the accompaniment of a dance, verbal descriptions which demanded a mime for their elucidation, and rustic themes deliberately designed to stir the feelings. I shall emphasize only this last feature, which is important. In the *Shih ching* there are poems more scholarly than those I have translated, but, curiously enough, they contain lines which are identical with lines found in the love-songs. One poem [1]

---

[1] Cf. Couvreur, p. 189 :—

> The meadow grasshopper chirps,
> And the hill-side grasshopper leaps.
> Until I have seen my lord
> My anxious heart is disturbed.
> But as soon as I shall see him,
> My heart will have peace.—LIX, 1–6.

Cf. XXI, 19–20.
> Redoubtable is Nan Chung,
> He comes from routing the Hsi fêng.
> { *In spring when the days draw out.*
> And the plants grow thick and strong,
> When *the oriole* sings his song,
> *And in crowds they gather the artemisia*!

which describes the labours of a general, in presenting a picture of his self-denial in carrying out his duties separated from his wife, interpolates, one after the other, without warning and without any alteration, two well-known themes. How is this to be explained unless these themes are regarded as the exact counterparts of the sentiments with which they were originally associated ? Chinese poetry has subsisted on the poetic material wrought upon by the original improvization, and it is clear from the *Shih ching* how an inventive genius could make use of it in its own way. I have translated *The Peasant*,[1] the lengthy plaint of an unhappy wife, who tells the story of her desertion in six declamatory stanzas of ten lines each. The story is commonplace, the heroes no one in particular, yet there is a personal touch in this long tale which grows gradually more incensed and excited until it ends in a passionate wail. Now this pathetic song is composed of known themes and sayings, but these themes and sayings recall immediately the state of mind which is their natural concomitant. In order to call to mind as a reproach the happy hours of their former love certain ready-made formulæ suffice :

" How high is the river Ch'i
Wetting the carriage hangings."

or again :

" Yet the Ch'i has its banks . . .
Yet the valley has sides . . ."

There seems to be scarcely even an attempt to make the poetic material fit the present case.

The mention of fresh young leaves recalls the first meeting in spring, and faded leaves the reunion in autumn. The connection between newly-opened leaves of the mulberry tree and the turtle-dove [2] is also made beforehand, but, in this

---

[1] LXVI.
[2] Cf. XXI, XV, and *Chao fêng*, 3. Couvreur, 157, and *Yüeh ling*, third month, *Li chi*, Couvreur, 350.

instance, there may be personal association, a device, which is indicated also by the rhythm alone :

" Alas, alas, O turtle-dove,
Eat not the mulberry fruits.
Alas, alas, O gentle girl,
With boys take not thy pleasure."

It seems to me that, in these lines, it is possible to comprehend the process by which poetic imagery was able to seize upon and turn to its own uses the matter to which it was limited by tradition. But there exists in the poems the inverse process also, which inserts new poetic matter into the traditional framework of the odes in such a way as artificially to create *correspondences*. One example will suffice to make this clear. Here is a poem in which it is desired to state in poetic language the difference between the condition of a princess who goes alone and in state to the apartments of the prince, and that of his secondary wives, who visit him stealthily during the hours of darkness, carrying their bedding, and, since they wait upon him two at a time, curtains also.

LXVII. *The Little Stars (Shao nan* 10—C. 25—L. 31)

1. O humble little stars.
2. *Hsin* and *Liu* shine in the East . . .
3. Modestly, passing through the dark,
4. Morning or night we go to the palace . . .
5. For our rank is not equal (to hers).

6. O, humble, lesser stars.
7. Only Shen and Mao are seen . . .
8. Modestly passing in the dark,
9. We carry our covers and curtains . . .
10. For our rank is not equal (to hers).

LXVII. *Preface : The Little Stars* (shows) the (princely) kindness reaching the lowly. The princess displaying no jealousy in her conduct, her kindness extended to the lesser wives of secondary rank and permitted their approach to the prince's couch, and they, recognizing the inferiority of their rank (the number of insignia embroidered on their clothes) were able to devote their whole mind (to the service of the princess).

Chêng says that the jealousy is of two kinds, that caused by beauty and that inspired by actions. Just as numerous small nameless stars accompany *Hsin* (the constellation of three stars) (Scorpion) and *Liu* (constellation of five stars) (Hydra) in the heavens, so all the wives of second rank obey the princess by conforming to the order fixed for their attendance on the prince. (Chêng.) (The influence of the virtue of the princess is such that they are not jealous, but are content with their share of love.) Cf. LXI, 2.

The word used to express submission is a term applied formally to women. Cf. V, 3.

3, 4, 5. The wives of secondary rank go, with modest bearing, during the dark hours, in the early morning or when evening falls, to the apartments of the prince. . . . As a rule they may not pass the (whole) night there. (Chêng.) (This expression, used differently, occurs in the *Li chi, Nei tsê*; Couvreur, i, p. 661.)

7. Orion and the Pleiades.

8, 9, 10. When the women of secondary rank visit the prince they take with them their bedding and curtains. (Chêng.) One comment explains that the latter are necessary as they attend the prince two at a time.

A palace song. Astronomical correspondences. Cf. *SMC.*, iii, 348. Comp. LXVIIB.

LXVIIB. *The Artemisia (Shao nan 2—C.17)*

1. I will gather artemisia
2. On the pond and on the rock.
3. Thereafter I will use it
4. In the service of the prince.

5. I will gather artemisia
6. In the middle of the dale.
7. Thereafter I will use it
8. In the palace of the prince.

9. How modest is my head-dress
10. In the palace, morn and eve.
11. How splendid is my head-dress
12. When I return again.

LOVE SONGS OF THE SHIH CHING

LXVIIB. *The Artemisia* (shows that) the princess was not remiss in her duties. The princess was able (since she went to gather artemisia) to offer the sacrifices and was therefore not remiss in her duties.

Chêng explains "not remiss in her duties" by line 10, "In the palace, morn and eve."

2. The wives of princes take the artemisia to use in the sacrifices. (Mao.) K'ung Ying-ta associates this gathering with that of the cresses in LVI.

4. In the service of the prince = in the service of the prince's temple. (Mao.)

8. Palace = temple. (Mao.)

9. Refers to a ceremonial form of hair-dressing.

9. A descriptive auxiliary is used to depict a modest and respectful bearing. Morning and evening in the palace shows that at all hours of day and night the princess was superintending the preparations for the sacrifice. (Chêng.)

11. This line contains a descriptive auxiliary depicting a quiet and suitable bearing. Cf. (*Pin fêng*, i), XXI, v, 20. The same descriptive auxiliary is said to depict a crowd in a line which also refers to gathering of artemisia. Cf. *Hsiao ya*, iii, 7, st. 4 (evidence of the uselessness of comments on the descriptive auxiliaries).

12. To return from the temple to her apartment. (Chêng.)

This song is one of four used in *HCCCHP.*, 1423 (p. 17, vᵒ) in defence of the theory that marriages were consummated only in the third month after the sacrifice of vegetable offerings to the ancestors. Cf. LVI and LIX (and *Shao nan*, 4).

The theme of the gathering (of plants) on the river, 2, 5 (cf. LVI, 5, 6), the association with XXI, 20, on the one hand, and the exact likeness between line 10 and LXVII, 4, on the other, suggest the connection of this palace song with the women's sacrifices in the princely worship and the relations between husband and wife, and that it is derived from the harvesting songs sung at the spring contests. Observe the description of the dress. Comp. *Li chi, Nei tsê*, Couvreur, i, 661, the description of the night attire of a woman.

This poem is important as showing the transforming of the popular poetry and customs into poetry and customs of the court. Cf. *Hsi ching tsa chi*, chap. iii.

A court song. Theme: gathering plants on the river.

Neither the personal art of the writer of *The Peasant*, nor the more subtle art of the author of *Little Stars* would be comprehensible without a knowledge of the natural art of the love-songs. A study of Chinese poetry would readily prove the importance of the two methods of construction to which I have referred. The art of the *symmetrical sentence* is an academic method corresponding to the spontaneous measure of the early improvisation.[1] The *literary allusion* is simply the repetition of an old theme. This use of such themes is something more than mere pedantry, for the mention of a theme calls forth in its original intensity, and with all its wealth of traditional meaning, the emotion first associated with it. Parallel sentences, in which the rhythm, while giving no clue to the writer, sets up a parallel between things and words, and literary allusions, in which personal feeling is concealed beneath the depth of ancient emotions, combine to give to Chinese poetry that characteristic air of impersonality which, in the early stages of the art, was the result of the actual circumstances in which poetry was improvised. But it is no part of the purpose of this present study to trace the development of a literary form whose beginnings we have discovered ; all that is required is to show how great an influence these beginnings had upon its development.

Our researches into the love-songs of the *Shih ching* are ended. The texts, and the texts alone, have been the subject of our study and to them alone are we indebted. Studies such as these, being inductive, assume part of the hypothesis which it is desired to prove, but the conclusions which have been drawn may be verified by comparison.

Among most of the aboriginal peoples of South-West China and Tonkin the holding of contests of love-songs is a common practice. They are also held in Tibet and were common in old Japan. All that is known of them confirms our inductions.

(1) *The songs have their origin in antiphonal choirs composed, one of boys and the other of girls.*

---

[1] These artificial correspondences consist in a personal remark linking a natural fact and a moral fact. This association, essentially a device of art, is made by a flight of fancy similar to that which, in the west, gives rise to simile and metaphor. But the very existence of traditional lists of terms which it is permissible to combine is evidence that freedom to devise metaphors at will has been very limited in China.

LOVE SONGS OF THE SHIH CHING

Among the *Hakka* people there are songs which Eitel calls *responsoria*. "One stanza is sung by a man and the response must be sung by a woman."[1]   The *Man* of Tonkin form choirs of girls and boys who take it in turns "to sing quatrains."[2]   "The *Laqua* are very fond of songs which take the form of dialogue between lasses and lads."[3]   Among the *T'u jên* of Kuang-hsi the young men and girls like to walk in couples singing.[4] "They gather together to sing songs in alternate couplets." Among the *Miao* "the young men and women, holding hands and standing face to face in two rows, dance to the sound of the small drum and the *lou-sen* (pan-pipe).   Each side having challenged the other, the couples which have paired off proceed to respond to each other in improvised songs."[5]   "The young people (of the *Lolo*) of both sexes form lines facing one another and cut fern to the accompaniment of improvised songs".[6] In Tibet "they are fond of double choruses, of men and women, standing opposite each other and answering each other verse by verse, advancing or retiring, in time to the music".[7] In ancient Japan there existed the practice of the *Uta-gaki*, walls of song, or *Kagai*, antiphonal singing.   Two groups assembled in the market place, and, taking up their positions face to face, sang alternately . . . The young men took advantage of this method to declare their love to the girls of their choice, who, in turn, replied in song. . . .[8]

(2) *The choruses were varied by extempore songs in which the young men and girls challenged each other or declared their love.*

We have seen that this was so among the *Miao*. It was so also in old Japan : "a member of one group stepped forward and improvised a song to which a member of the opposite group extemporised a response in the same manner."[9]   In Tibet, marriages were concluded " by joint songs executed

---

[1] App. III, p. 280.   [2] Bonifacy, id., p. 271.   [3] Bonifacy, id., p. 272.
[4] Beauvais, id., p. 271.   [5] Deblenne, id., p. 263.   [6] Crabouillet, id., p. 263.
[7] Grenard, id., p. 261.   [8] Florenz, id., p. 259.
[9] Ibid., cf. Kojiki, Chamberlain's translation, ibid., p. 260.

alternately by maidens and youths : he who is found wanting
when his turn comes to improvise his distich or quatrain is
made to pay a forfeit ".[1] "The young man and the girl,
facing each other, make love by means of these songs in
alternate couplets . . . It is a kind of contest."   There exist
among the *Chung-chia-tzŭ* of Kuei-chou also gatherings of
the two sexes on the mountain at which contests in
eloquence and poetry are still held.[3] " When a couple (*Mo-so*) [4]
have sung in harmony they go off into the valleys or into the
woods, and there unite."

(3) *The love-song contests take place, among other competitions,
on the occasion of seasonal festivals at which the attendance is
large. These festivals, which include sexual observances, are
regarded as betrothal or marriage festivals.*

In the spring the Tibetans indulge in singing performances.
" A certain air of solemnity envelops them.   The time is
settled in advance ; the males and females who take part must
have performed their ablutions and be dressed in clean clothing
as for a religious ceremony.   To dance casually for amusement
and not in accordance with prescribed regulations would be
considered immodest." [5]   On the occasion of the new year
the *Lolo* of Yünnan assemble and make an excursion to the
mountain to cut wood or dried grass to make a bonfire.[6]   Among
those of Tonkin this festival is called *con-ci*.[7]   " The whole
of the first month is devoted to love-making."   " The *Thos* [8]
of the region of Cao-bang celebrate a festival of youth a few
days after the new year.   On the appointed day the boys and
girls, dressed in their best, assemble on a wide plain, generally
in the neighbourhood of a pagoda, under the protection of
which they disport themselves.   In the vicinity are gathered
traders selling food, fruit, cakes and sweetmeats. . . . In

[1] Grenard, id., p. 261.   [2] Beauvais, id., p. 271.
[3] Roux, in Vial, ibid., p. 274.
[4] Barbarians under the rule of Yünnan, id., p. 269.
[5] Grenard, ibid., p. 261.   [6] Crabouillet, ibid., p. 263.
[7] Bonifacy, ibid., p. 272.   [8] Billet, ibid., p. 265.

the case of the Cao-bang region the festival is held on the great
peninsula of Pho-yen, near a pagoda containing the well-
preserved images of many gods, and a great crowd of young
people and sight-seers is annually attracted to the festival from
many villages in the region from Cao-bang to Nuoc-Hai and
Mo-Xat, and even from the groves of Luc-khu and Tap-Na
. . . Soon the young folk have selected their partners . . .
the various couples disperse about the country-side, in the shade
of the bamboos, the pomelo trees and the banyans. The boys,
back-to-back with their fair partners . . . strike up a series
of realistic lamentations. . . . About noon the couples
reassemble, this time face-to-face in two ranks about fifty
paces distant. . . . Each boy holds a ball attached to a long
string which he throws in the direction of the girl of his choice.
If she catches the ball or picks it up it is a sign that she approves
of the thrower and, for the remainder of the festival, she
becomes his ' conquest '. If, on the contrary, the girl returns
the ball to the thrower, it indicated that he has not yet captivated
her. The rejected suitor then begins his song anew and the
game of ball continues until the girl declares herself satisfied,
which usually happens quite soon. In most villages this is
really a betrothal festival, but in certain places it would be a
pretext for a variety of excesses which it would be quite wrong
to think of atoning for by marriage." Among the *Miao*
of Kuang-hsi this festival is known as *Hoi-gnam*, a term whose
meaning, according to Colquhoun,[1] is indecent. " On the first
day of the year men and women assemble in a narrow valley,
the men on one side and the women on the other. They
proceed to sing, and when a boy has pleased a girl by his singing
she throws him a coloured ball. Nearby is a fair where the
lover may purchase a variety of gifts for his mistress." Among
the *Miao-tzŭ* of Yünnan the festival is held in the first month
of spring. " They indulge," says a Chinese observer,[2] " in
dancing by moonlight . . . and singing in chorus. . . . They
indulge in mimes. . . . They make balls of coloured silk,

---

[1] Colquhoun, ibid., p. 267.   [2] In Sainson, ibid., p. 268.

select the girl who attracts them, and amuse themselves by
throwing the ball (to her). In the evening they assemble to
vie with each other in skill and high spirits and do not separate
until the morning. Then follow discussions on the question
of the conditions and date of marriage. They beat the bronze
drum, blow the trumpet, offer sacrifices of thanksgiving and
draw up the contracts." "About the time of the new year,
the young men and girls (*Miao*) . . . dressed in their best
. . . assemble at an appointed place . . . this often constitutes
a betrothal festival." [1] In Kuang-hsi,[2] "every year, during
the third or fourth moon, the young people of both sexes
(*T'u jên*) from different villages assemble . . . the inhabitants
of the neighbouring villages, bringing their provisions, come
to look on at the competitions. Every such gathering is attended
by not less than a thousand persons of about twenty years
of age. The natives pretend that if these assemblies were
hindered or prohibited for any reason, the harvests would
fail to ripen and the people would be punished by many
epidemics." "These ceremonies are often supposed to be
held for the purpose of settling the preliminaries of marriage
. . . frequently those couples who are mutually attracted
ramble in the neighbouring thickets and in the undergrowth
of the jungle, there to exchange pledges of future marriage."
Su Hsing, King of Nan Ch'ai (Yünnan) (A.D. 1041–4)
"during the months of spring used to go to bathe supported
by the ladies of his court; thus he travelled down stream
from the three springs Yu-An as far as the pool of Chiao-chiu-liu.
The men and women seated themselves and battled with
flowers, putting them in their hair, and day and night they
gave themselves up to pleasure.[3] "In the same country
in spring the rivers are warm, springs rise everywhere . . .
everywhere wine is sold, and everywhere hairpins and bracelets
are displayed. The fragrant blossom is sought and in the

[1] Deblenne, ibid., p. 263.
[2] Beauvais, ibid., p. 270.
[3] Sainson, ibid., p. 268.

142

newly-decorated rest-pavilions are held contests ; song follows song beneath the jujube trees and elegant verses are composed . . . (in the third month) they sing songs and are answered." [1]

(4) *The song-contests are held between boys and girls of different villages.*

Among the *La-qua* [2] "the young unmarried people . . . sing in the mountain, but the boys must not belong to the same village as the girls ". This, according to Colonel Bonifacy, is a survival of early exogamy. Indeed, in their songs, the *La-qua* girls look upon their partners as strangers.

> Never has stranger been seen in this land ;
> This stranger, whence comes he ?
> This charming stranger who has come
> In his honour we must sing.
> Whence then comes this charming stranger ?
> Comes he, or not, by the river ?
> How many rivers and lands has he seen ?
> How has he crossed these waters deep ?
> How kind to traverse a thousand places.

The same rule exists among the *Lolo* of Tonkin,[3] but not in all the tribes. Their songs also take it for granted.

(Boy.)   " . . . What is your country, fair lady ?
> Where do you dwell, fair lady ?
> I think now of you ;
> I have never seen you before.

(Girl.)   " . . . You speak brightly,
> You express yourself fairly.
> If you would be my husband
> Come, let me consider you.

---

[1] Id., p. 269.   [2] Bonifacy, ibid., p. 271.   [3] Ibid., 271.

We may now conclude. Our analysis of the odes of the *Shih ching*, corroborated by comparison,[1] has shown this poetry to be the outcome of the inspiration of the seasonal festivals. It was the expression of the love which was generated along with it. On other occasions love still continued to express itself by the methods which were proper to the old extempore singing of the companies of dancers, and thus there arose many songs which were collected. These songs, bearing the signs of their ritual origin, continued to preserve something of their sacred associations. They were sung at the court ceremonies, and in the collections they were placed side by side with dynastic and ritual songs. Revered by reason of their antiquity, preserving in their rustic themes traces of seasonal regulations, they became a source of material for exercises in moral rhetoric. The collections were studied by counsellors of state who turned them to account when they set up the theory that the ruler was responsible for natural and moral order, and when they desired to furnish precedents for their discourses on politics and their dissertations on history. Conjoined with edifying anecdotes, used as symbols and allegories, they seemed suited for purposes of education and, being given a learned and moral interpretation, they took on the appearance of moral and learned works. Set forth as a classic, these songs, which are a mirror of ancient manners, serve to disseminate the rules of life elaborated by their interpreters, and thus to ensure submission to social conventions. The potency of the symbolism which distorted them had its origin in their original sacred character.

Restored by critical study to their original meaning, they are important to the study of early art. They show that voice and gesture combined to express the emotions, and that the emotions did not exist before the mimic and vocal expression of them, but that songs, dances, and love arose together out of the festivals of which they formed the various ceremonial

---

[1] I have collected here the clearest passages, but the perusal of Appendix III in full will show that these are corroborated and amplified by other observations, less precise or less detailed.

phases. Thus they reveal a state in which thought is concrete and direct, in which syntax cannot be separated from rhythm, and in which metaphorical associations have not yet replaced spontaneous connections and natural correspondences.

Lastly, they throw light upon old customs hidden behind classical orthodoxy. They reveal the existence of rural and seasonal festivals which brought an element of rhythm into the life of the Chinese peasant, and the relations between the sexes. They show, in their crude state, the feelings which stirred the young people during these periodic gatherings, and during times of separation. They also provide us with concrete examples of the emotions which constituted love and the relation of these emotions to social customs and a definite social organization. Thus they deserve to be more than an excuse for a study in literary history. These songs will indeed enable us to determine the significance of the agricultural festivals, the functions of a ritual based upon the seasons, and so to comprehend the social realities which facilitated their own development.

II

THE ANCIENT FESTIVALS

From the love-songs of the *Shih ching* it is possible to determine the general character of the seasonal festivals of mountains and rivers, and we shall now proceed to the study of some local festivals.

LOCAL FESTIVALS

The Spring Festivals of Chêng (Ho-nan).—In the state of Chêng the youths and girls gathered in large numbers at the junction of the Chên and Wei rivers. They came there in companies to gather the orchis, they challenged one another in antiphonal songs and then, with skirts tucked up, they crossed the Wei. When the couples were united the new lovers presented each other at parting with a flower as a love-token and symbol of betrothal.[1]

The festival was held when the Chên and the Wei were full, that is to say, we are told, at the time when the thaw caused the spring floods.[2] It was during the first month of spring that the east wind brought the thaw.[3] Yet another tradition refers the festival to the period when the peach tree blossomed and the first rains fell,[4] two events of the agricultural year which are both referred by the calendars to the second month.[5] This fact, however, does not forbid the festival being assigned to the first cyclic *ssŭ* day of the third month.[6]

---

[1] Cf. *Chêng fêng*, LI and LII.   [2] LII, 1–2.
[3] *Yüeh ling*, first month. Couvreur, i, 332. 'The east wind loosened the frost.'
[4] Notes of the *Han shih*.
[5] *Yüeh ling*, second month. Couv., i, 340 : 'The rains began. The peach tree began to flower.'
[6] *Han shih*.

It is evident that the festival, connected in the first place with the spring awakening, was later assigned to a definite date fixed by the calendar.

We have further evidence as to the site. The assembly was held at the foot of a mountain in the sub-prefecture of Tu-liang. From the mountain issued a very clear spring where grew the orchis known as the 'Fragrance of Tu-liang'. The festivities which were attended by the young people of the narrow mountain-country of Chêng, were held on the bank of the river and at the foot of the mountain.[1]

The orchis-gathering is the feature of the festival concerning which most information is available. It was, we are told,[2] a method of warding off evil influences, of making oneself impervious to poisons, and it was a rite of purification. We are told further that it was on the river that the youths and girls of Chêng, carrying orchis in their hands, drove away evil influences, ill fortune, and the impurities in the air, or in the year. At the same time they summoned the souls, or, more exactly, they summoned the superior souls (spiritual souls) to rejoin the inferior souls (material souls, ghosts, passion souls.)

In Chêng, propitiations, various purifications, flower-gathering, crossing the water, singing-contests, sexual rites, betrothals, were all combined in the spring festivals of rivers and mountains.

The Spring Festivals of Lu (Shan-tung).—One day, while talking with four of his disciples, Confucius questioned them as to their ambitions : how would they use their ability if, perchance, some prince should recognize it and employ their services ? One expressed a wish to strengthen a state enfeebled by famine and war ; another would give instruction in music and the rites ; and a third would assist in the ceremonies of the temple or the palace. But the fourth, laying down the stringed-instrument which he had been playing, replied (if the Chinese interpreters and the European translators are not

[1] Cf. Geogr. Monograph of the *Ch'ien Han shu*. Ed. Shanghai, K. 28*b*, p. 12 *recto*.
[2] See the traditions of the *Han shih* in the notes on LII.

148

mistaken) that he, for his part, would like " in the third month of spring, dressed in every particular in the costume proper to the season, and in company with five or six grown men and six or seven young lads, to go and bathe in the river I, enjoy the breeze at the foot of the altar of rain, and having sung (or, singing), to return home. And Confucius approved.

This approval is surprising. Would the Sage prefer the pleasures of a country excursion to the higher affairs of state ? Had he determined, under the influence of Lao Tzǔ, to concern himself no longer with the guidance of men ? Or did the answer imply a subtle flattery by which he was affected ? This is the impression to be gained from the commentator. According to him the ingenious disciple wished to imply that he could have no other wishes, after enjoying for a space the pleasures of the spring, and singing, as was proper, the praises of the ancient rulers, than to return immediately to the presence of the Master.[1]

Innocent pleasures ! Touching affection ! This bland explanation is hardly satisfactory, for why should he specify the dress proper to the spring, the company of a definite number of youths and men and a definite position at the foot of the rain-altars, if all that he really desired was to enjoy himself for a while ?

It is highly probable, judging from the text alone, that the wishes to which Confucius gave preference were not really different from the others. No doubt this disciple, like the others, desired, in his own way, to be of service to the state. Now rain is a matter which is the concern of the state. It is part of the duty of a good government to see that rain falls in due season. The fall of such seasonable rain is a much greater evidence of merit than material progress, regulation of the rites and ceremonial observance. It is very possible that Confucius was of this opinion ; it is certain that this passage from the *Analects* has been so interpreted in China. Wang

---

[1] Legge : *Lun Yü*, xi, 25. See a somewhat confused but very full discussion of this passage in *Lun yü chêng i*, HCCCHP., 1064 inf.

Ch'ung, in his *Lun hêng*,[1] believes it to be a description of the spring rain-festivals as they were conducted in Lu, the native state of Confucius.

Wang Ch'ung has preserved various commentaries on the passage, as well as one variant. The word which is translated '*to return*', and which allowed the classical interpretation to pay such a delicate compliment to the Sage, is homophonous with another word which means '*a meal*', and may well be applied to the feast which follows a sacrifice. Wang Ch'ung gives this character and explains that after the singing in the ceremony a feast was given.

The other notes are also interesting. It is objected that the date cannot be in the third month, because the spring clothes are finished in the second month, and are donned for the ceremony. Those who took part were dancers and musicians, to whom were entrusted the ceremonies connected with rain. They consisted of two companies, one comprising six or seven youths and the other an equal number of grown men, for the disciple of Confucius who wished to take part in and superintend the festival must be added to the number of the men. They forded the river in a band and sang upon the hillock consecrated to the dances and songs which were employed to attract rain. It is unbelievable that they should have bathed or dried themselves in the wind, for in the second month of spring it was still too cold. Instead of " enjoy the breeze among the rain-altars " or " dry the body in the wind on the rain-altars ", he would read " sing by the rain-altars ", a rendering which changes the

---

[1] *Lun hêng*, 15, chap. *Ming Yü*. According to Wang the people of Lu made the sacrifice for rain on the river I in the fourth month of the year, i.e. the second month of spring, when the spring clothes were ready. The persons mentioned in the *Lun yü*, grown men and youths, are musicians connected with the conduct of the sacrifice. ' They (the persons wading across the river) represent the dragon coming up out of the midst of the I.' Instead of ' to return ' read ' the communal banquet at the sacrifice.' In accordance with these explanations the passage must be translated : One evening in (the second month of) spring, when the spring clothes are ready (and are donned) I should like to go with five or six grown men (myself being the sixth or seventh), and six or seven youths (an equal number of youths) to wade across the I (imitating the dragon which came out of the water), sing by the rain-altars, and after repeating some lines, take part in the sacrificial feast.

ordinary meaning of the word *wind* to that of *singing* or *song*, which it has, for example, in the first part of the *Shih ching*. Lastly, and this is very instructive, in the fording of the river I he sees a kind of processional dance representing the dragon coming up out of the water.

There was then in Lu, in the springtime, at a date which may have varied but which at any rate corresponds with the time when the weaving of light clothing was finished,[1] a festival on the banks of the river, in consequence of which rain was expected. Two groups of actors danced and sang, and a sacrifice and a banquet brought to an end the ceremonies of which an essential feature was the crossing of the river.

It seems clear that there is connection between this festival and those of Chêng which are held at the same period of the year, and in which an essential rite is also the crossing of thn river. There is reason to think that in Chêng also, when they crossed the river they did so in imitation of the dragon. In 523 B.C. ' there were (in this state) heavy rains ; dragons fought in the marsh of the Wei. The people wished to sacrifice to them '.[2] The chief minister, a philosopher, was opposed to the idea, but, although he did not believe it necessary to appease the dragons which control the rain, the common people did, and it may be supposed that, when they crossed the Wei, the young people were representing the dragons issuing from the waters, so that rain could not but result.

Were there in Lu no flower-gathering and no sexual rites ? Apparently the latter were not included because the participants were only a few couples of officials and youths.[3] The Chou

---

[1] Cf. *Shih ching*, seventh month. Couvreur, p. 162, the weaving of hemp is the work of the winter-time.

[2] *Tso Chuan*, Chao, nineteenth year Legge, p. 675. Tzŭ Ch'an (a disciple of Confucius and minister of Chêng) opposed the suggestion on the ground that as the dragons did not interfere in the battles of men, men should not concern themselves in the quarrels of dragons. In his opinion they should be left alone in their abode in the marsh of the Wei.

[3] Observe the balancing of a number of youths with an equal number of grown men.

according to their *Rites,* employed sorcerers of both sexes[1] to bring rain. In Lu, however, only men took part, and in this official rain-festival Confucius found nothing to censure.

The Festivals of Ch'ên (Ho-nan).—According to the *Kuo yü,*[2] Ch'ên owed its fortune to T'ai Chi. The commentators upon the *Shih ching* hold T'ai Chi responsible for the evil manners prevalent in the state. Ta'i Chi was a princess of the blood-royal of China who had come from the capital of the Chou to marry the prince of Ch'ên. She had no children and she delighted in the dances of the sorcerers and sorceresses, and this was the reason why, long afterwards, the people of Ch'ên sang and danced without restraint under the oaks on the hill of Yüan.[3]

To dance thus without cause was a scandal,[4] but a still greater scandal was the intermingling of the sexes in the dances. Even the children of great families appeared in places where it was not fitting that they should be present. It is possible that they did dance too much and too frequently : " What matter winter ! Summer, what matter ! "[5] says one song with perhaps a hint of censure. It is certain that the sexes intermingled ; antiphonal songs were sung, declarations of love were made and flowers presented,[6] but that the best families were disgraced thereby is the decision of the commentators who have recorded the names of Tzŭ Chung and Yüan, two of the families thus compromised.

With reference to Tzŭ Chung, the ode mentions a child of his[7] who danced in the market-place. He was, we are told, a great officer. To find a name as common as that of Tzŭ Chung in the annals of Ch'ên presented no great difficulty. In the case of Yüan more credit was due. Yüan is found

---

[1] *Chou li, Ssŭ wu, Nan wu, Nü wu,* Biot, ii, p. 102. When there is a great drought the chief of the sorcerers, leading the sorcerers, calls down rain by executing dances. P. 104, sorceresses also take part in these dances.

[2] *Kuo yü, Chou yü,* 1st disc.

[3] *Ch'ên fêng.* See Comments of the preface. Cf. *Ch'ien Han shu.* Geog. Monogr. Ed. Shanghai, K. 28*b*, p. 12 v°.

[4] See LXII, LXIII, and comments.   [5] LXII.   [6] LXIII.

[7] I take the child to be a girl, in accordance with the opinion of modern commentators.

in the text where he (or rather his daughter), appears in the lines which I have translated :—

"On a beautiful morning they seek each other
Out on the southern plain."

The interpretation I have adopted is perfectly simple and clear. It is that of the moderns, who, in this passage, give to *Yüan* its ordinary meaning of *a plain*.

The ancients, whose good fortune it was to find a *Yüan* family in the state of Ch'ên, ingeniously read the lines as implying :—

"On a beautiful morning they go to seek
(the daughter of the) Yüan (family) which lives in the South."

As it was unquestionably a girl that they found thus between the lines, it was clear that she had been seduced by the child of Tzŭ Chung who was, therefore, obviously a boy.

Such ingenuity ought not to be forgotten. The determination of the interpreters to find in this poem the names of officials is instructive. For the commentators it describes a rain festival, of course official. The son of Tzŭ Chung, who there appears, is a leader of the dancers, so that it is his duty to dance beneath the young elms. Why then the outcry? Because he brings with him female dancers. But is it not stated in the *Chou li* that the leaders of the sorcerers led the dances of the sorceresses? [1] The point is that these cannot be professional dancers ; they are evidently girls whose ordinary occupation is weaving,[2] and whose participation in such a display is indeed disgraceful. It is obvious that the classical interpretation is inconsistent and the commentators do not escape from their dilemma because of their determination to see in the popular festival described by the ode an official ceremony analogous to that of Lu.

The festival of Ch'ên took place at the time when the work of weaving was finished [3] (thus it was possible to don light

[1] Cf. p. 152, note 1.   [2] LXIII, 7.
[3] Weaving lasted throughout the cold period. Cf. together LXIII, 7 ; Couvreur, p. 162, and *Chia yü*, already quoted, p. 132. Add LXVI, 2-3.

clothes of linen). Ancient instruments were played,[1] and
fans and egret feathers waved in time to the singing. Up and
down the rising ground of Yüan the companies of dancers
moved praying for rain. Did they cross a river for this
purpose ? Did they represent a dragon coming up out of the
water ? The commentators of all schools are so sure that a
rain festival is in question that some of them understand the
last two characters of lines 5 and 9 of *The Elms* to indicate
the special cries [2] used to call down rain.[3]

Singers and dancers were of both sexes. As in Chêng on
the banks of the Wei, so, on the hill of Yüan, boys and girls
hailed each other in song, offering flowers and declaring their
love. Sexual rites had their place in the festival, the reputation
of T'ai Chi being responsible for their inclusion.

T'ai Chi was childless and T'ai Chi loved these festivals.
Was she anxious merely that the rainfall might be assured ?
And would those who made offerings of fragrant seeds be
satisfied with the fertility of the soil ? As a matter of fact,
the seeds were one of the symbols of fecundity and it was
as a token of fecundity as well as of love that the gift of a handful
of fragrant herbs was made. Their fragrance, it is said, was
capable of bringing down the divine powers ; thus on the Wei
the souls were summoned by means of the 'Fragrance of
Tu-liang'. At the spring festival in Ch'ên, girls followed

[1] LXII, 5, 9. Cf. *Chou li, Yüeh Chang*, Biot, ii, 66. As in the Cha festival a
the end of the year (see p. 168), earthen drums were beaten to call the aged to rest
so also in the festival when a prosperous year is asked for.

[2] LXII, 8, 12. Cf. *Shih ching, Pèi fêng*, 13 ; Couvreur, p. 44, and particularly
Wang fêng, 3 ; Couvreur, p. 78.
> My lord, oh, what happiness :
> His left hand holds his flute ;
> His right calls me out of the house!
> Ah, what joy is not mine !
>
> My lord, oh, what pleasure.
> His left hand holds the egret fan ;
> His right calls me to the pageant.
> Ah, what is not my joy !

Cf. *Chou li*, Biot, ii, 65.

[3] *HCCCHP.*, 428, p. 4, i.

the example of T'ai Chi and prayed for children. So also, no doubt, did the girls in Chêng when they gathered the orchis, for was it not a Count of Chêng who was miraculously conceived when his mother was presented with an orchis ? [1]

Festivals of rain, of birth, of betrothal, with singing and dancing contests, flower-gathering and sexual rites, such were the festivals held on the hill Yüan.

The royal spring festival.—Neither on the banks of a river nor at the foot of a mountain, but in the southern suburb of the capital, on the day of the spring equinox (the official day of the return of the swallows) ' an ox, a sheep, and a pig were sacrificed to the Supreme Intermediary (Kao Mei). The ruler attended in person and the queen conducted thither the nine wives of the second rank and all the other royal ladies. A ceremonial gift (a cup of wine) was presented to those who had shared the King's couch, and cases of bows were brought, and bows and arrows presented (to these women) before Kao Mei.' [2] At first sight, this ceremony seems perfectly clear. The bows and arrows betokened male children [3] : thus it appears that Kao Mei was petitioned for sons. But who was Kao Mei that this alone of all the festivals in the classical ritual should bring men and women in company into the open country ?

Chinese divinities are often the functionaries of an earlier time deified. There used to be an official who was called the Intermediary. According to the *Chou li*, it was his duty, in the second month (the month of the spring equinox), to organize the assembly of boys and girls. His office dated back to the institution of marriage, and he was responsible for the carrying out of certain rites of purification at marriage ceremonies.

The royal ceremony held at the time of the return of the

[1] *Tso chuan*, Hsüan, fourth year, Legge, p. 294. See the analysis of the passage on pp. 188–9.
[2] *Li chi, Yüeh ling*, second month, Couvreur, p. 341.
[3] *Li chi, Nei tsê*, Couvreur, p. 662. Commentary of Chêng on the *Yüeh ling*.

swallows had no connection with marriage. What then was the part played therein by the Supreme Intermediary? It is interesting to note that he is identified not with any past holder of the office of intermediary, but with an emperor. *Kao Mei*, it is said, is the Emperor *Kao* Hsin,[3] from whom the royal house of Chou, like its predecessor, Yin, claimed descent. It is pointed out by others that sometimes the term used is *Chiao Mei* : the Sacrifice to the Intermediary in the *suburb* and not the Sacrifice to the *Supreme* Intermediary. It is impossible to say more of this vague deity whose feast was celebrated in the middle of spring than that he appears to be connected with certain marriage purifications, and that excursions into the country were made for the purpose of praying to him for children.

The Yin and the Chou were both descended from Kao Hsin, that is to say, they were descended from two of that Emperor's wives who both miraculously conceived their noble sons.

The mother of the Chou was Chiang Yüan. She conceived while offering a *Yin* sacrifice, that is, a sacrifice with pure intent, or for the purpose of purifying herself. " She removed thereby the misfortune of her childlessness " or, according to the note, " she cleansed herself thereby from the impurity of barrenness." What form did this purification take?

All that is known is that Chiang Yüan [4] trod in the print of a great toe and became pregnant.[5] Whether it was the imprint of a giant or of the Emperor of the worlds above, or that of her husband, Kao Hsin, is a disputed question. The general opinion is that the miracle occurred at the festival

---

[1] *Chou li*, Biot, i, 306.   [2] *Lieh nü chuan*, 6 (biogr. of Tsou ching nü chüan).
[3] The tradition concerning Kao Hsin related by Chêng K'ang-ch'êng.
[4] *Shih ching*, *Ta ya*, ii ; Couvreur, p. 347, and *Lu sung*, 4 ; Couvreur, p. 452. *Taya*, ii.
[5] *SMC.*, i, 209. (Chiang Yüan) went into the country and there saw the footprints of a giant. Her heart was moved thereby and she was seized with a desire to walk in them. When she had done so she felt the thrill of a woman who becomes pregnant.

156

of Kao Mei and in the southern suburb. Ssŭ-ma Ch'ien relates simply that Chiang Yüan was walking in the country.

Chien Ti,[1] ancestress of the Yin, conceived while bathing. ' As she was going to bathe in the company of two other women (her attendants), she saw a black bird (a swallow) drop an egg which she swallowed and became pregnant.' This account given by Ssŭ-ma Ch'ien is completed by the annotator of the Bamboo Annals [2] : " At the time of the spring equinox, on the day of the return of the swallows, Chien Ti went in the train of the Emperor (her husband, Kao Hsin), to sacrifice to the Intermediary in the suburb (*Chiao Mei*). In company with her younger sister she bathed in the river by the rising ground of Yüan, and a swallow dropped an egg which it held in its mouth. The egg was of five colours and very beautiful. The two women struggled [3] for possession of it, to put it under cover in a jade basket. Chien Ti obtained it first and swallowed it, whereupon she became pregnant."

A spring festival of rivers and mountains, with purifications, bathings, and contests, a festival conducive to pregnancy, was the original form of the festival of the return of the swallows, which, in the classical ritual, was reduced to a simple festival of fecundity.

FACTS AND INTERPRETATIONS

From the documents thus gathered it is possible to study four local festivals which are evidently all of one type. The few remarks interspersed in their description will have sufficed to show the relation between them. Their apparent divergencies are due less to local variations than to the condition or the character of the text.

---

[1] Cf. *Chang sung*, 3 ; Couvreur, p. 462 : ' Heaven directed a swallow to descend and cause the Shang to be born.'

[2] *SMC.*, i, 173. ' (Chien Ti) was a secondary wife of the Emperor K'u. As she was bathing with two (other) women (her attendants), she saw a black bird let fall an egg which she swallowed and became pregnant.'

[3] Cf. *Cal. of Ch'ing Ch'u*, second month, see p. 204.

Of the four festivals in question, three were held in the states and one at the court ; two are known in their official form, one through a ritual, the other through a literary document, and two are known in their popular form through documents which allow them to be examined directly. By comparing them it will be possible to gain some notion of how the official ritual grew out of the popular.

The change from one to the other was made by discarding various ancient features. The royal festival of the return of the swallows lasted only one day and that day was definitely fixed and noted in the solar calendar.[1] The official festival of Lu does not seem to have lasted longer : yet the doubt which evidently exists concerning its date suggests that the day of its celebration was only the critical stage—a variable one—of a long favourable period. Even less definitely dated is the festival of Ch'ên : so indefinite is it that, with the loosening of manners, the festivities connected with it might be unlimited in extent. The case of the festival of Chêng is striking : it is held at the time of the melting of the snows, of the spring floods, of the first rains and of the blooming of the flowers, a lengthy period extending over the three months of spring. Judged only by the odes it would not appear to have been reduced to a single day ; it is in the later texts that it is so reduced.[2] It is noteworthy that this is not a date of the solar calendar but a day in the cycle, having no fixed connection with the astronomical year.

The location of the festivals also becomes more and more definite. The young people of Chêng disported themselves in a wide stretch of country where rivers, meadows and mountains adjoined. In Ch'ên the dances take place all along the hill of Yüan. In Lu the essential part of the festival is held in a strictly defined area, upon an altar ; further, it is beside a river which also plays its part in the festival. The

---

[1] Spring equinox : note, however, that the return of the swallows, which is the symbol of the spring equinox, is connected with a saying from the calendar.
[2] The first ssŭ day of the third month.

place where the royal ceremony is held is simply to the south
of the capital, at a spot marked exclusively by the altar of Kao
Mei ; it had previously been held near the spring which issued
from a hill.[1] As with the duration of the festivals, so the location
narrows down and tends to become established at a spot chosen
arbitrarily.

The number of those participating decreases. All the
young men and girls of Chêng and Ch'ên sing and dance and
take part in the contests. In the south suburb only the royal
family appears and, in one of the prototypes of this festival,
it seems that only two of the wives of the king figure in the
contest on the water. Again, at the ceremony of the swallows,
the participants are of both sexes, whereas in Lu this is no longer
the case ; here only men take part. They are divided into
two equal groups—this being all that remains of the old contest
of dance and song—and they are officials specially trained for
the performance of these duties. The official festivals are
not shared in by all ; the performers are chosen by rule, and
the principles of their selection vary.

In the case of the ceremonies themselves, their impoverish-
ment and specialization are still more marked. It is only in
Chêng and Ch'ên that contests, betrothals, sexual rites, flower-
gatherings, etc., occur all together. In Lu the whole ceremony
seems to be reduced to a mimic rite intended to bring rain, and
in its latest form the royal festival is no more than a spell
designed to obtain male children. Thus the festivals continued
to undergo a process of simplification until they appear in the
official ritual reduced to one single custom designed for a special
purpose.

The process of impoverishment and of specialization which
changed a popular cult into an organized one is not only worth
knowing for its own sake. To those who know it, a question
arises. The festivals I have described seem to be more
comprehensible in their most recent form. The ancient
festivals are more complex, and we are tempted to interpret

[1] Legend of Chien Ti.

them by what we know of those which are simple and more obvious and most lucid. But is it wise to do so ? The festivals of Lu and Kao Mei seem to be a rain-festival and a fecundity festival derived from prototypes similar to the festivals held in Chêng and Ch'ên. May it be stated that they were established for the express purpose of ensuring at one and the same time fertility for women and moisture for the fields ?

A similar difficulty presents itself from another view-point : is it necessary to assume, because a particular practice in the official ceremonies is said to serve to bring about certain definite results, that the same practice occurring in the popular ritual was originally devised for the same purpose ? Knowing how arbitrary has been the evolution of the official ceremonies from the popular festivals, one hesitates to take later practices as a starting-point in explaining the early forms, however plain the meaning of such practices may seem to be. But what is their clearness worth ? It appears questionable when one ceases to consider them independently. It is indeed extraordinary, but one would feel more certain of understanding the official festivals if they were known quite by themselves. Anyone who had read only the classical description of the ceremony of the swallows would say confidently that it was a festival commemorating the legendary founder of the dynasty. The swallow is its protector and it is natural to thank him for the fecundity of women, wherein lies the hope of the race, and to ask him for sons to maintain its authority. The manner in which this request was made is very evident. The bow and arrows which were hung at the door of the house when a boy was born are the symbol of the virile state, and to present bows and arrows to the royal wives in the presence of Kao Mei was to bestow upon them in his name a token that they should bear sons. The festival was held in the springtime, the period of universal fecundity. In Lu it was rain that was wanted : what more natural than that they should make an incantation in water, with water, in order to obtain water ? Is it not known that the dragons control rain ? During the dry season they hide in the deeps and then ascend to the sky whence they send rain, wherefore it was imagined that the representation in springtime of the dragon coming up out of the water invited, or rather compelled, him to come forth at the proper time from his hiding-place and from his inactivity.

All this is natural, indeed, and would no doubt appear conclusive if, the attention being once awakened by what is known of the old and complicated festivals, one did not meet in the simpler ones certain features which remain unexplained by the interpretation which at first suggested itself. Why should it have been necessary, in order to obtain children from Kao Mei, to go into the country to ask them of him ? Why, in the prototypes of the festival, should princesses bathe and purify themselves in the open country ?[1] Why should the god of fertility bear the name of an official in charge of the ceremonies of purification connected with marriage, while at the same time he is supposed to be the founder of two dynasties ? Why should the mimic rites inviting rain be accompanied by songs, sacrifices and banquets ? Why should there be two opposing groups responsible for inviting the dragon to come forth from the River I ? Why must there be a young lad opposite to each man ? Why, lastly, should spring clothes be worn ?

One might say that these are merely survivals. This is an easy answer to the questions and it would be well to inquire what it involves. It assumes the complex festivals of the popular ritual to be a series of practices in conjunction, each serving its own specific purpose. In the same way, the later festival, confined to a single purpose, would comprise, in the main, one rite devoted to that purpose, the others being accessory and maintained only by force of tradition. Our interpretation certainly does not explain this added element, but it is not on that account incorrect or even incomplete, for it accounts for

---

[1] The part played by the women is undoubtedly the reason why the Chinese critics are inclined, for the sake of moral orthodoxy, to deny the authenticity of these tales.

the basis of the festival. Is this certain ? Conclusive proofs must be demanded for there are reasons to believe that the specialization of ceremonies is in some degree arbitrary. The suggested interpretation is certainly arbitrary if we can find another one, not less satisfactory, one which has also had its adherents.

The dancers of Lu array themselves in clothes appropriate to the new season : might not this change of dress be regarded as a rite to bring about a change in the season ? At once the whole festival takes on a new meaning ; we must see in it a ceremony of purification.[1] From this point of view, the bathing becomes perfectly intelligible also : What more natural than to use water for purposes of purification ? Is it not stated that the young people of Chêng rid themselves in the Wei of the impurities of the season ? Why should not the same proceeding have been carried out in the I ? More of the characteristics of the ceremony are understandable if it be regarded as a purification. What proof is there that it was originally devised for the purpose of causing rain ? It may be that this, the interpretation given by Wang Ch'ung, is of later date ; others have not observed it. It seems adequate, but so does another, and there is nothing to cause a preference for either. This result, though negative, is yet interesting. From the preceding remarks two rules of methodical criticism may be evolved :

(1) When the documents set before us a collection of customs and of representations connected therewith, care must be taken to avoid setting them all on the same plane forthwith, for what we are given as beliefs may well turn out to be the result of a work of learned or individual thought. In other words, they are not really beliefs but rather interpretations. Doubtless

---

[1] According to the traditions of the *Chêng Tzŭ T'ung* there were two series of *hsi* rites, one in the spring, comprising the rites of the river I (in Lu), the rites of the *lan t'ing* (see note on LII, traditions of the *Han shih* with reference to the purifications in the Wei), the rites of the *shang ssŭ* period ; the other in the autumn (*Hsi ching tsa chi*), the rites of the period of the 7th–14th of the 7th month. Cf. the comments of Chêng in the *Chou li, Nü wu,* Biot, ii, 104, and the *Hou Han shu,* xiv, p. 4 (Shanghai ed.).

these are not quite unconnected with the facts : the connection varies according to the worth of the interpreter, and may be more or less close ; in any case such interpretations are only indirectly informative. (2) The beliefs—and equally, the more or less arbitrary interpretations—which we find to be, at a given moment, connected with certain customs—do not necessarily explain the establishment of those customs. It may be that the spring festival which was held in Lu on the banks of the I really was a rain ceremony in the time of Confucius or of Wang Ch'ung. It does not therefore follow that the festival which was its prototype was, even in part, designed to cause rain. Thus, practices which occur in two different states of the evolution of a festival, and which, in the later stage, are said to produce certain effects, may quite possibly have been credited with this particular power only at a later date and only when the festival itself has been accredited with a special purpose. It may have been supposed, in the time of Wang Ch'ung, that crossing the river caused rain, and yet it may be that in the beginning the crossing was not devised for this purpose, if indeed, when it first originated, it had any fixed purpose.

It seems scarcely likely that from its inception a rite should have had a definite object, that it should have been a means selected in order to bring about a particular result : all the practices were regarded as efficacious whatever the purpose in view. Crossing the water serves to bring rain or to purify, and equally, it was believed, to summon the souls, not to mention the fact that, no doubt, a bath was a healthy prelude to taking part in sexual rites.[1] Fragrant flowers have many uses : efficacious purifiers, potent remedies against poisons, they serve also as love-tokens and talismans, as well as to make contracts binding and to ensure fecundity. Is it possible to say whether a girl receiving flowers is receiving them as a

---

[1] Marriage purification. *I li*, Marriage. Cf. LXIV, 10. Purification before intercourse. *Li chi, Nei tsé*, Couvreur, p. 661 and *Shih ching, Wei fêng*, 8, lines 7–8 ; Couvreur, 73 (XX B).

betrothal bouquet or as a promise of fecundity? Inversely, the most varied means are used to bring about the same result. In order to conceive, a woman might, with equal effect, swallow an egg or set her foot in a foot-print; a flower would have the same result, or a seed, and not one particular kind of flower or seed but a variety of kinds.[1] The relation between means and ends is vague, or rather one has been fixed only indirectly. It is not the flower itself which induces pregnancy or binds friendship but the fact of picking it or receiving it in a given place, at a given moment, under special conditions. In the beginning, practices had no special individual significance: a peculiar efficacy was attributed to them when the primitive practices developed into simpler ceremonial, arbitrarily reduced, and when, as the result of religious thought, a special purpose having been assigned to them, attempts were made to show the suitability of the means used to attain the desired ends. But since this work of classification and analysis was possible, and *since its effects have been so varied*, it is obvious that the material to be classified and analysed must in itself have been capable of being used for any desired end. Thus it is not the individual practices which have significance and which explain the whole; it is the festival which confers upon the practices their varied efficacy.

Accordingly, in order to understand the ancient Chinese festivals, the following rules will be applied: (1) Facts will not be explained by representations which might be suspected of being explanations deliberately thought out, or beliefs of derived formation. (2) No attempt will be made to explain the whole by the parts. This latter rule has one great advantage. It will prevent the explaining of all the practices of a festival by the one which is regarded as essential, and from which— we have seen why this would be so easy—all the others could be derived by a mental process similar to the work of classification of religious thought.

[1] Orchis (LII); mallow, fragrant herbs (LXIII); prickly ash (cf. Ch'ing Ch'u, fifth month), arum (de Groot, *Emouy*, 336), water-lily seeds (cf. LV).

THE ANCIENT FESTIVALS

Let us review the facts. We have found evidences of old festivals, common to all the states of China, best known as they were performed in Chêng and Ch'ên. Open to all, they were seasonal festivals, held in the country, near a mountain, beside a river. Crossing water and climbing hills were important features of the festival, as were the picking of flowers and the gathering of fire-wood. The attendance was large and many ceremonies were performed, the young people of the state being the principal participants. Contests of dance and song formed the essential feature of the gathering, and in these the boys and girls of different villages were set over against one another. After a contest of poetic extemporization, they paired off ; sexual rites concluded their betrothals, and the whole ended in an orgy. So intense was the emotion generated by these festivals that out of the sentiments to which they gave rise and the expression of them has grown a literary style, complete in shape and substance.

Although traces of a pastoral order are found at the time to which these festivals belong,[1] agriculture was already the chief occupation of the Chinese people. Work was divided between the sexes ; the men looked after the growing of cereals while the women were responsible for the care of silkworms and the weaving of silk. Life was ordered by a seasonal rhythm, based upon the alternation, well marked in those climates, of the period of dry cold and that of moisture and heat. During the former period the peasants remained apart in their villages and in their houses ; in the hot season they were scattered about the fields [2] ; twice a year they changed their manner of life entirely. Although a kind of national sentiment already

---

[1] The importance of the rearing of horses and oxen. References to pasturage, XXXIX, 9.

[2] This rhythm is clearly marked in the oldest of the calendars, *SMC.*, i, 44 sqq. In the middle of spring the people disperse, and continue to live dispersed through the summer. In the middle of autumn work comes to an end ; the people live a calm and peaceful life. In winter they remain in their houses and keep themselves warm. Also *Yüeh ling*; Couvreur, 343 : In the second month of spring there are few labourers in the houses ; after the autumn equinox, when the white frost falls, work ceases and everyone returns home ; Couvreur, 386.

existed,[1] their chief sentiment was that of attachment to the country.[2] During the working period relations went to work together in the family field[3]; during the cold spell they were together in the clan village.[4] So contrasted were the various units of a single local community[5] that the saddest of all feelings were those of the new bride, obliged by the law of exogamy to leave behind her own relatives and go to strangers.[6]

THE SEASONAL RHYTHM

The old Chinese festivals are seasonal and rural. Apparently those which took place in spring were the most important, but they were also held in autumn. Have they any connection with the course of the sun? The answer is in the negative : they are not connected with any solar terms.

When a fixed date is assigned to them it is by a date in the civil calendar that they are marked, and this calendar does not depend entirely upon the course of the sun. In the beginning the date was fixed only by the state of the season.

Are they connected with the cycle of vegetation? If they are, it seems difficult to understand why their content differs so little whether they belong to spring or autumn. Possibly

---

[1] This national solidarity, which in feudal times was understood to mean oneness with the ruler, could cause the entire population of a state to emigrate in a body in the train of its chief. *Shih ching, Ta ya*, ii, 6 ; Couvreur, 360, Cf. *SMC.*, i, 214.

[2] This feeling of attachment to the soil is sometimes finely expressed. See the end of *Chou Sung*, iii, 5 ; Couvreur, 439, where speaks the pride of an aboriginal people. See also *Hsiao ya*, vi, 6 ; Couvreur, 280.

[3] *Chou Sung*, iii, 5 ; Couvreur, 459 : Now the father, the eldest sons, the other lads, the assistants, the hired labourers, all eating their food noisily . . . they carefully sharpen the ploughshares and begin work in the southern fields.

[4] *Ping fêng*, i ; Couvreur, 163 : In the tenth month the cricket finds its way under the beds. They fill up the cracks ; they smoke out the rats ; they shut the windows on the north ; they coat the doors with clay. Come, my wife and my children, the year is at the change. Let us return into our house . . . 164 (in the tenth month) : Come my workmen, the grain is piled up, let us assemble ; let us climb up and go home again (to the village built on a height), and let us take care of our houses." (Cf. ibid., p. 168.)

[5] A state or local community is divided into clan villages, separated from one another and surrounded by walls or hedges. Cf. XL.

[6] See the complaint of the Lolo bride. App. III.

the crossing of the river was the more important rite in the spring and the ascent of the mountain in the autumn, but this specialization, if it had ever existed, was very vague, and we find it hard to believe ; moreover that it could have arisen from a distinction between the festivals of spring and that of the death of vegetation.

Are they connected with the cycle of agriculture ? Judging by their uniformity, it would hardly seem that some are festivals connected with sowing, for example, and others with harvesting, or with tillage, or with weaving. The theory that they are dependent upon the rhythm of peasant life is more plausible.

Actually, it is certain that there is a link between these festivals and the ritual of marriage.[1] Now, it appears from the disputes of scholars that, in the opinion of the Chinese, spring and autumn were regarded as the favourable periods for the celebration of marriages—or rather those times during the spring and autumn when the peasants changed from one manner of life to another quite different. A tradition is set forth thus : "When the white frost falls, women's work is finished ; then marriages may be made. When the ice melts, the work of the field begins and the gathering of mulberry leaves : at this time marriage rites approach their end."[2] The women's work to which reference is made is that connected with the production of silk, which comes to an end at the same time as the work in the fields. "When the white frost begins to fall all work stops."[3] The men no longer remain scattered through the fields, but—after a great celebration— "all return to their homes".[4] During the dead season they spend their time in indoor occupations such as twisting rope[5] while the women work at weaving hemp[6] : when the cloth is woven and ready for sale,[7] when the spring clothes are finished and ready to be worn at the spring rites[8]—then

1. Cf. p. 126 sqq.
2 See *Chia yü.*
3 *Yüeh ling*, ninth month ; Couvreur, i, 386.
4 Ibid. Cf. *Pin fêng*, i ; Couv., 163.
5 *Pin fêng*, i ; Couv., 164–5.
6 Ibid., p. 162 ; cf. LXIII, 7.
7 LXVI, 2–3.
8 Cf. p. 150.

167

is the time that girls, ceasing to spin, follow the youths of the neighbourhood [1] to the festivals, the time when the ice melts [2]—and the peasants begin to give up living in their villages. [3]

The times when individuals changed their occupations and their dwelling, and formed themselves into new groups were doubtless pathetic times, and social activities must then have taken on a new solemnity. The festivals which correspond to these momentous periods may, perhaps, mark the time of the rhythm of the life of the peasants. How far this theory is able to take us we are able to judge from a fortunate example.

The termination of work in the fields and the return to the village were the occasion of festivities with which we are acquainted in their official form, the festival of the *Pa Cha*. [4]

The *Yüeh ling* refers this festival to the tenth month, and to the midst of a group of ceremonies which is clearly the most important mentioned by this text. [5] The *Chiao tê chêng* refers it to the twelfth month and describes it by itself. [6] The dates differ. The festival described by the *Yüeh ling* is assigned to the first month of winter, that is to say, to the end of the agricultural year ; the other is referred to the twelfth month, the end of the civil year. Native scholars say that the date of the festival was changed in the Ch'in dynasty, to which period they attribute the *Yüeh ling*. The cosmological principles adopted by this dynasty resulted in the coincidence of the agricultural year and the civil year, and the festival was moved

---

[1] See LXIII, 7, and LXVI, 1–2.   [2] See L and LII.

[3] Cf. *Yüeh ling*, second month ; Couvreur, i, p. 343, and *SMC.*, i, 44.

[4] Concerning this festival we have only scattered information, of varied age and origin and very unequal in value. It would be almost impossible to say what constituted this *Pa Cha* festival at any given period, say, for instance, at the time when Confucius witnessed it. On the other hand, all the texts we possess throw light upon certain characteristic facts which prove to be of the utmost importance for this work. It is with these facts that I propose to deal. It is not my intention to attempt a reconstruction of the festival. This would be impossible.

[5] *Yüeh ling*, tenth month ; Couvreur, i, 395–6.

[6] *Chiao tê chêng, Li chi* ; Couvreur, i, 594–8.

forward and placed in the tenth month (which in the new calendar became the twelfth month), that it might always indicate the close of the civil year. But would not the original time of a festival of general thanksgiving be after the harvest ? As a matter of fact—and this decides the question—the *Shih ching* [1] like the *Yüeh ling*, assigns it to the tenth month. This, then, is the old date which was later set back. At first the festival marked the close of the actual year, the end of the cycle of production, and, later, that of the civil year, the arbitrary conclusion of the astronomic cycle. [2]

The celebration had all the characteristics of an orgy [3] ; Those who took part in it ate and drank to repletion. In olden times sexual rites were a feature. Later, by a deliberate misinterpretation, both the deer and the women whom the Sovereign was entitled to receive, among other gifts, were struck out of the list of offerings because, at that time, such gifts were regarded as immoral. [4]

[1] *Pin fêng*, i ; Couvreur, p. 165 : The last couplet which describes the festival says explicitly " in the tenth month " ; a corresponding saying from the calendar is " the cricket steals under the beds ". It has been used as the chief theme of another poem of the *Shih ching*, *T'ang fêng*, i ; Couvreur, 120, which describes the same festival. Both these poems show that in the tenth month the year *is drawing to an end*. From this remark it appears that, as a matter of fact, the different calendars which are attributed by the Chinese to successive dynasties were employed concurrently (*Pin fêng*, i, 1, proves it conclusively), one as the civil, and the other as the agricultural and religious calendar.

[2] The last couplet of *Pin fêng*, 1, shows clearly that the tenth month festival, the festivities connected with the close of the year, the harvest, and rest, was related to an agricultural period, the fall of the white frost, when it begins to freeze, and that thus it corresponds to the spring festivals at the thaw and the flooding of the rivers (cf. LII). This fact will be compared with that proved by *SMC.*, iii, 440–7, 442, 453–4, that sacrifices were offered to the mountains and rivers at the time of freezing and thaw. Cf. Worship of ancestors at the times of the hoar-frost and of the dew ; *Chi i*, *Li chi*, Couvreur, ii, p. 271.

[3] *Yüeh ling* ; Couvreur, i, 393 : ' great drinking.' Cf. *Pin fêng*, 1 inf. ; *T'ang fêng*, 1.

[4] *Chiao t'e chêng* ; Couvreur, i, 597. The superintendent of snares presented the deer and the women. This official is mentioned in the *Chou li*. Cf. Biot, ii, 30, where it is said that for the festival of the Pa Cha he prepared snares (to catch deer), and short tunics (women's garments). Chêng Ssŭ-nung believes that the snares were provided to catch quadrupeds. Why were they prepared in conjunction with short garments appropriate for women's wear ? Chinese commentators, analysing the text of the *Chiao t'e cheng*, point out that it was the duty of the superintendent of snares to issue to the envoys of the feudal princes a warning, cautioning their masters against the dangers of an immoderate love of hunting and women. Thus

During the feftivities " the people of the whole country were as if mad ".[1]   There were dances and music [2];   the weapon dance and the banner dance were accompanied by the clay drum.   There were even kinds of ceremonial masquerades in which people represented, for example, cats and leopards.[3] There was a shooting match in which the targets were painted

they find means of reading into a passage which seemed, regrettably, to refer to gifts of women, a meaning conforming with orthodox morals. But this reading necessitates a grievous miftranslation of the word which I have translated ' to present ', a word which is a ritual term applied to presents.

The same word is used to designate the laft, culminating rite of marriage, the embassy which, three months after the marriage, marks the final delivery of the bride, being described as the presentation of the girl. Finally, the exact value of the word is specifically defined by its use in a very important passage of the *Kuo yü* (*Chou yü*, i, 2nd discourse ; cf. *SMC.*, i, 265). For the analysis of this very detailed passage, see Granet : *la Polygynie sororale et le sororat*, Texts. The mother of Duke K'ang of Mi advised her son who, in an access of feudal arrogance had taken to wife three sifters (the rites ordained, indeed, the taking of three women of the same family, but only two should be sifters, the third being a niece of the others) to *present* his wives to the emperor. Thus it is certain that at the ancient Pa Cha ceremonies all kinds of tribute were entrufted to the superintendent of snares (particularly animals of the chase sent by the princes), and these included deer and women to be presented to the son of heaven as tribute to their liege. There should be nothing surprising in the association of deer and women. With the idea of marriage is bound up the idea of a gift of deer flesh or skin (cf. LXIV and *I li* : Marriage, where the presentation of ceremonial deer-skins is described). This gift is associated in the mind of the Chinese with the very inftitution of marriage ceremonies. Cf. the *Annals of the Three Rulers* in *SMC.*, i, 7 : " (Fu Hsi) was the firft to order the marriage of women and of men and he made the gift of two skins a rite." It will be observed (and here is the fact which explains the possibility of misinterpretation by the Chinese commentators) that with the idea of gifts, of offerings which the feudal princes were bound by their oath to make to their lord, is associated the idea of moderation. This is why, at a ceremony which originally consifted in the exchange of women and animals caught in hunting, it was considered advisable to make solemn declarations againft excessive love of hunting and of women. On this point see *T'ang fêng*, i ; Couvreur, 120, and note that this ritual ode of the Pa Cha feftival is quoted in the passage of the *Kuo lieh nü chuan* which refers to the mother of Duke K'ang of Mi. See p. 176.

   [1] *Li chi* ; Couvreur, ii, 190.
   [2] *Chou li*, Biot, i, 266 (officers of the drums). In all the sacrifices offered to the spirits of all things (lit. the hundred things) they accompany with drums the weapon dance and the dances performed with wands tufted with silk (ibid., 260 (dance mafters)). They direct the weapon dance and are dance-leaders at the sacrifices offered to the spirits of mountains and rivers. They direct the dance performed with wands tufted with silk and are dance-leaders at the sacrifices offered to the spirits of earth and cereals. They direct the feather dance and are dance-leaders at the sacrifices offered to the spirits of the four regions (cf. LXII). They direct the variegated feather dance and are dance-leaders at the ceremonies in times of drought (cf. LXII).
   [3] *Chiao t'ê chêng* ; *Li chi* ; Couvreur, p. 595, and the note of Su Mei-shan : Men represented animals.

figures of animals,[1] and success therein paved the way to feudal honours. This complex, lively, dramatic festival, which seems at first to be connected with the harvest and the chase, has two main features upon which I propose to lay stress. This is a concluding festival, it is a festival of thanksgiving.

In it a general thanksgiving was made. The ceremonies described by the *Yüeh ling* include [2] prayers for the year (harvest) to come, offered to the celestial Tsung ; the offering of many victims in sacrifice to the god of the public fields, as well as the *La* sacrifice (offering of venison) made at the gates of the villages and towns to the Ancestors and to the five spirits of the house. The catalogue of the *Chiao t'ê chêng* [3]—none too lucid as regards detail—mentions first eight (*pa*) varieties of sacrifices (*cha*) offered mainly to the first husbandman (men ?) (Shên Nung ?) [4] ; then to the minister (s ?) of agriculture (Hou Chi ?), to the hundred seeds, to the workers in the fields, to the bounds (or the guard-huts built on the edges of the fields), to all the animals (birds and beasts). The list is completed by comment inserted in the text : " They presented themselves (for the purpose of sacrificing to them) before (persons representing) cats and leopards " because the former eat field-mice and the latter boars. From the invocation used it is evident that the ceremony also had reference to the earth, water, insects, plants and trees. According to the *Chou li*,[5] the music which was played was meant for feathered creatures and the spirits of rivers and lakes ; hairless creatures and the spirits of mountains and forests (or of mountain forests) ; scaly creatures and the spirits of mounds and hills (or of cliffs and shores) ; to hairy creatures and the spirits of plains and uplands ; horned creatures and the spirits of the earth ; to stellar beings and heavenly gods (*shên*). Thus thanksgiving

[1] *Chou li*, Biot, ii, 547, and note. [2] *Li chi*, Couvreur, i, 396. [3] Id., i, 594–5.
[4] Cf. *SMC.*, i, 13. Shen Nung established the Cha Sacrifice. With a red whip he beat the grass and plants. (Cf. the invocation to the Pa Cha in *Chiao t'ê chêng*, *Li chi* ; Couvreur, i, 596.) He was the first to examine all the varieties of plants and the first to discover healing medicines. (Cf. the gathering of herbs and simples at the festivals of rivers and mountains.)
[5] Cf. Biot, ii, 33.

was made to all classes of beings, animate and inanimate, imaginary and real, in groups and separated. Also, to *Cha*, the etymology of which was obscure, was given the meaning of " to seek ". " Throughout the whole country search was made for the *Kuei* and the *Shên* and sacrifices and offerings were made to them ".[1] It is also said that sacrifices were offered to the hundred things, that is to say, to all things.[2]

With the help of all things thanksgiving was made to all things. " In the twelfth month of the year, they gathered together all things (lit., the ten-thousand things), and seeking them, they offered them."[3] At the *Cha* festival of the son of heaven, the superintendent of the nets was entrusted with the animals (birds and quadrupeds) which formed part of the vassals ; the produce of the harvest was also included.[4]

In the same way, everyone contributed to the sacrifices and everyone took part in them. The people of the whole state gave in proportion to the yield of the harvest[5] ; the vassals sent their gifts to the emperor by envoys.[6] The envoys took part in the ceremonies ; the sovereign prepared a grand drinking bout for his adherents, the flesh of the sacrificial victims being set out on tables. " The field-workers were rewarded (for their toil) in such a way as to give them rest."[7] The heads of districts collected all the people in the arena.[8] All the basic rules of the social order[9] were displayed during the ceremony : filial piety, respect for elders, respect for rank, a spirit of deference, a desire for purity, feelings of reverence. Those present were divided into two groups, one group taking the side of the Master of the Ceremony, the other that of the guests.[10]

[1] *Chiao t'ê chêng, Li chi* ; Couvreur, i, 594 ; cf. *Chou li, Ti kuan*, section of *T'ang chêng*, Biot, i, 250.

[2] Cf. Biot, i, 267. [3] *Kiao t'ê chêng, Li chi*, Couvreur, i, 594. [4] Ibid., 597.

[5] Ibid., 598. [6] Ibid., 597. [7] *Yüeh ling, Li chi* ; Couvreur, 394–5.

[8] *Chou li*, Biot, i, 251 : " When, throughout the state united prayers are offered to the spirits and sacrifices made, then the head of the district gathers all the people together and drinks wine in the public arena (cf. the drinking in the royal court referred to in the *Yüeh ling*). Thus he sets them in order in accordance with their respective ages."

[9] See *Li chi* ; Couvreur, 652 sqq. ; see note on p. 653.

[10] Confucius appeared as a guest in the festivals of Lu. Cf. *Li chi* ; Couvreur, ii, 190, and i, 496.

THE ANCIENT FESTIVALS

The position of the guests was fixed by an orientation whose
influence, it was believed, connected each group with the
opposing forces of the universe [1]—heaven and earth, sun and
moon, *yang* and *yin*—which decide the rotation and the
opposition of the seasons. The leaders of the two groups
and their assistants offered goblets to one another in turn.
Two companies of musicians played one after the other and
then together.[2] The effect of this festival was general
harmony ; it was said to mark the highest point of Benevolence
(*jên*, the virtue of man in his social state), the perfection
of justice (*i*, the law of human relationships).[3]

From all that is known of this thanksgiving festival it is
evident that it made obvious the unity of the All, the world
of matter and the world of men, and that the consciousness
of this unity was the result of setting over against each other
things arranged according to opposites. Sacrifice was offered
to everything, and everything was used in the sacrifice ; all
were bound to serve as offerings and all shared in the offerings.
While they took part in the offerings, the members of the human
group were divided into two groups, just as the things in nature
were divided into two categories.

From another point of view, the *Pa Cha* are a concluding
festival. This brings the agricultural year to an end.
Mourning is worn for it, and this is the reason why white
clothes are donned with a girdle of hemp and a staff of hazel-
wood.[4] It is thus that the ageing year is conducted to its end.

This festival of the old year is also a festival of old people [5] ;
it teaches that they should be reverenced ; to them is given
the most honourable seats at the banquet, at which they drink
the spirit mixed with fragrant herbs which "sustains the strength
of the old men with long eyebrows ",[6] and their companions
drink to their long life : "Eternal years ! Life unending ! "[7]

As the purpose of the festival is to give back vigour to things

[1] *Li chi* ; Couvreur, ii, 654 sqq.   [2] Id., 662.   [3] Id., i, 595.
[4] Id., 596.   [5] *Chou li*, Biot, i, 251 ; *Li chi*, ii, 659.
[6] *Shih ching*, Couvreur, 440, and 163 ; cf. 450.
[7] Ibid., 165 ; cf. 183 and 285.

173

that have grown old, weary with producing,[1] so to men, as the reward of their toil, is given rest. One invocation ran : " May the Earth return to its place ! May the Waters withdraw into their channels ! May summer Insects not bestir themselves ! May Trees and Plants return into the lakes ! "—mysterious phrases, of which a perfectly intelligible explanation may be found elsewhere.

The *Yüeh ling* shows how the winter becomes a double process of shutting up : Men shut themselves up in their houses and dwell there in retirement ; creatures withdraw each into its own sphere and have no further communication with each other. In the last month of autumn " the white frost begins to lie ; all works cease [2] . . . the cold becomes intense, beyond human endurance, and everyone retires into his house [3] . . . hibernating animals hang their heads and remain in the depths of their lairs, the mouths of which they block up."[4] In the tenth month, says the *Shih ching*,[5] " the cricket finds its way under the beds, crevices are stopped up, rats are smoked out, windows facing north are closed up, and doors are coated with clay. Come, my wife and my children ! the year is at the turn ! Let us go back into our house ! . . . Come, my workmen, our grain is gathered, let us go up again, let us return home, let us mend our houses ! " And in another place : " (When I returned home in the autumn) my wife had sprinkled and swept the ground and stopped up the cracks." Reverting to the *Yüeh ling* we find : " (In the first month of winter) water begins to turn to ice, the earth begins to freeze ; the pheasant plunges into the great river (Huai) and turns into a shell-fish ; the rainbow hides itself and is seen no more [6] . . . The emanations from the heavens have re-ascended to the heights [7] ; the emanations from the earth have gone down into the depths ; heaven and earth are no longer in communication ; the shutting up is finished

---

[1] *Chou li*, Biot, ii, 66.   *Li chi*, Couvreur, 386.
[3] Ibid.   [4] Ibid., 389.
[5] *Pin fêng*, i ; Couvreur, 163–4. Cf. *T'ang fêng*, I ; Couvreur, 120.
[6] *Li chi*, Couvreur, 391.   [7] Ibid., 393. Cf. inversely first month ; ibid., 336.

and it is winter . . . (They) protect the storehouses. . . .
There is nothing that remains dispersed. They mend the double
walls ; they keep guard at the doors of the villages and towns ;
they repair the bolts and fastenings ; they take care of the keys ;
they strengthen the earthen embankments on their boundaries ;
they furnish the frontiers with defences ; they keep a look-out
on the barriers and bridges ; they close up the roads and the
footpaths.[1] . . . (In the second month of winter) the ice
thickens, the ground begins to crack [2] . . . Work in the fields
must not be begun ! Take care that nothing be uncovered
which is covered ! Let neither house nor room be opened !
Let there be no gathering in crowds ! Let all remain shut in !
Let all remain closed up ! (otherwise) the emanations of the
earth would make their escape and be dispersed ! This would
be as if the dwellings of heaven and earth were opened !
Hibernating animals would die thereof ! The people would
not evade pestilences ! [3] . . . Everything must be completely
shut up. . . . If a peasant has failed to gather in and shut
up his crops, if a horse or an ox or a domestic animal be left
unprotected, anyone taking possession thereof commits no
crime.[4] . . ." They coat the doors with plaster . . . in order
to help in the shutting up of heaven and earth.[5] . . ."

When men take their rest they give rest also to things, and
they conceive this rest of nature in the likeness of their own.
Because they live during the winter snug in their homes,
shut up in their clan village, they look upon the dead season
as a period of universal confinement, during which all things
return to their original dwellings, live there shut up with their
own kind, and have no further dealings one with the other.
Each species, now shut in, is beyond the reach of any other,
remote from all outside contact, placed under an interdict :
The earth, dedicated, no longer yields to human toil ; exclusive
rights of ownership no longer hold good at a distance ; there
are no longer any ties save between beings in close proximity
and of the same nature. While men are reviving their powers

[1] Ibid., 395. [2] Ibid., 398. [3] Ibid., 399. [4] Ibid., 401. [5] Ibid., 403.

in the intimacy of their family circle, and, in contact with their own people, are restoring in themselves the genius of their race, they believe that in the same way the various classes of beings, also dwelling among their intimates, regain their particular attributes, and that their revived nature is being prepared for the spring. Thus the formula of the *Pa Cha* which effected universal separation, effected also universal revival.

We have studied the festival under two principal aspects ; we may endeavour to understand its deep meaning. As a festival of universal thanksgiving it makes manifest universal harmony ; as the concluding festival of the rural year it ushers in the dead season during which each goes to live in a narrow and homogeneous circle. As a preliminary to this domestic isolation, all the inhabitants of a particular district meet together in order to strengthen in themselves the consciousness of their mutual relationships.

It is in an orgy that the social covenant is renewed, but a definitely regulated orgy wherein the respective worth of the contracting parties is proved. Competitions give opportunity for the display of their abilities ; they take their places according to their standing ; they contribute in proportion to their means. The contributions being the measure of that standing which each believes he may claim ; whoever would keep all for himself would annul his own claim. Is it not a principle of the feudal law of the times that, if the ruler desires to establish his authority on a firm basis,[1] he must keep practically nothing under his immediate control ? A true lord must never lay up treasure ; he was reminded of this during the ceremony : " He who loves hunting, he who loves women (this means : he who makes too great a display of the most striking outward signs of fortune) loses his lordship. The Son of Heaven cultivates cucumbers and fruits (which are eaten forthwith) ; he does not accumulate or hoard up grain." [2] The festival

---

[1] Cf. *Chang sung*, 3. *Shih ching* ; Couvreur, 463, fourth strophe.
[2] *Li chi* ; Couvreur, p. 597. Cf. *Kuo yü, Chou yü*, i, 2nd discourse: ' What virtue have you that you should deserve this thing of value which has been committed

thus taught that *Wealth must not be monopolized* [1]; it made clear the value of moderation in prosperity. " Love pleasure without folly . . . The worthy man is cautious." Out of arrogance springs misfortune. On the other hand, it is essential for a man to know how to *make his wealth accessible to others* and " distribute it all down the scale of beings ", thus by his liberality affecting " not only men, but sacred powers and all things *in such a manner that each*

to you ? Even a king would not be worthy of it, and how much less you, mean fellow . . . A mean fellow who hoards shall surely end by being lost.'
In his note on the *Kuo yü*, Wei Chao refers to the moderation enjoined upon the princes in matters connected with the chase. Cf. *Ku lieh nü chuan*, section *jên chih chuan*, and note the reference there made to the first poem of the *T'ang fêng, Shih ching* ; Couvreur, 120.

> The cricket is in the hall
> And the year draws near its end.
> Why then no feasting ? . . .
> The days and months flee past,
> Yet let us be restrained,
> And think of our estate,
> Love pleasure without folly . . .
> The worthy man is cautious.
>
> The cricket is in the hall
> And the year is at its end.
> Why then no feasting ? . . .
> The days and months roll on,
> Yet let us be restrained,
> And think of the unforeseen,
> Love pleasure without folly, . . .
> The worthy man is reasonable.
>
> The cricket is in the hall,
> The carriages put away.
> Why then no feasting ? . . .
> The days and months fly on,
> Yet let us be restrained,
> And think of days of toil, . . .
> Love pleasure without folly.
> The worthy man is moderate.

Cf. *T'ang fêng*, 2 ; Couvreur, 122.

[1] Cf. *Kuo yü, Chou yü*, 4th discourse and *SMC.*, i, 269 : " The royal house rushes to its doom. The Duke of Ying loves to monopolize Wealth, and has no consciousness of misfortune. Wealth is that which springs from all beings (lit. the hundred things). (It is) that which depends upon heaven and earth, and, if there are people who monopolize it, they do injury to many. It is the duty of the ruler to share out wealth and spread it high and low throughout the scale of beings, so as to cause the holy powers, men and all things to reach their highest possible development." Cf. *SMC.*, i, 160, a legendary example of this universal benevolence.

attains its highest development ". Thus, when the harvest, as soon as it was gathered, was used with liberality, the social order grew in strength to the great benefit of the universe. The feelings of gladness and proportion which then filled men's hearts gave them reason to anticipate the further welfare of Nature and to understand its order. At once the efficacy of human festivals reached beyond the sphere of human society.

In the same way, the natural laws conceived by the Chinese upon the model of the rules governing their own life, appeared to them to be constant when they themselves remained subject to the laws appropriate to men. The rhythm of their life decided the alternation of the seasons ; their festival of rest gave nature authority to rest ; their winter seclusion assured the independence of species for the season ; irregularity in their customs would have thrown the universe into disorder. If, during the slack season, they had not remained shut up in their houses with all the cracks stopped " the frost would not have closed up the outlets in the earth, and the emanations of the earth would have been scattered through the heights ".[1] If, on the other hand, holding firm the sense of order which had been developed in their minds during the festival which marked their transition from one mode of life to another, they submitted to the new manner of existence ; the emanations of the earth, shut in like themselves, would no longer be able to mingle with the emanations of the heavens and so cause rain to fall. In order to initiate the dry season, it was enough solemnly to invoke the Water and tell it to withdraw into its channels.[2] Chinese peasants did not shut themselves up in the winter with any magical purpose in view or anticipate that the effect of their action would be to shut up unseasonable rain and prevent it from falling, but, being accustomed to remain in seclusion in their homes during this season, when it never rained, they therefore assumed that the practices of nature were identical

[1] *Li chi* ; Couvreur, i, p. 397.
[2] See the invocation formula of the *Pa Cha.*

178

with those of men. From this standpoint their various customs were so many rules of practice whose influence extended to the material world. The regular rhythm of their life was, as a matter of fact, an exact copy of the regular progress of things ; but this regularity in nature was made intelligible to them by the uniform course of their own lives, and because of that same course they judged regularity to be incumbent upon the whole universe. In the same way, their faith in the efficacy of their observances was due to the confidence and the respect inspired in them by their customs. It is therefore not surprising that the seasonal festivals, which mark first of all the emotional moments in the life of the community, should also have had an effect upon Nature, nor that the means by which this effect is brought about, far from having been devised and adapted for such a purpose, merely arise from customs instituted for the purpose of providing for human needs.

There is nothing unjustifiable in maintaining that the more general conclusions to which our study of the *Pa Cha* [1] has brought us may be true of other seasonal festivals. Held at the critical moments in the rhythmical existence of the Chinese peasants, they correspond to the times at which individuals and small groups, secluded for the remainder of the year, gather together to constitute once more the community in which they

[1] In fact, a study of the texts relating to the *Pa Cha* gives the impression that this festival had its origin in the popular festivals which the ancient Chinese held in autumn on the banks of sacred rivers. This is especially so if the following facts are taken into account :—

1. The original festival is a festival of the autumn equinox connected with the fall of the frost and opposed to a festival of the spring equinox connected with the thaw (*Pin fêng*, i). It is therefore connected with the worship of mountains and, more particularly, of rivers, and consequently related to the autumn festivals of mountains and waters.

2. The festival is an orgy in which sex rites obviously played an important part. [The women whom Duke K‘ang of Mi refused to present in tribute to King Kung had been mated with him (the same term is used to denote the unions at the festivals of the Rivers and Mountains) on the banks of a river.]

Once the *Pa Cha* had become an official ceremony it was not long before the orgy of food became the predominating feature of the festival, while the orgy of sex, by reason of the moral principles current among the noble classes, declined in importance.

are associated. Speaking generally, they are festivals of union, in which people become aware of the bonds which unite them and, at the same time, of their oneness with their natural environment. To crown all, they also serve to guarantee, along with the prosperity of men and things, the regular working of Nature.

THE HOLY PLACES

The royal ceremony of the *Pa Cha* was not held in any particular spot ; the festivals usually took place on the banks of a river and at the foot of the mountains

It has long been known that Mountains and Rivers played an important part both in the official religion and in the popular beliefs of the Chinese. From the most remote antiquity, we are told, Mountains and Rivers have been objects of worship in China. This statement is liable to be misinterpreted : there is a danger that it may be understood to mean that special worship was offered to them and that individual cults sprang up in connection with this sacred mountain or that sacred river. Hence the temptation to explain their worship by analysing the figurative ideas which were suggested to Chinese minds, which may be suggested to anyone, by mountains and rivers, by the majesty of mountains and the might of rivers.

The problem presents itself to us under a different aspect. We have seen that the festivals were held, not at one place beside a river and at another at the foot of a height, but always amid a scene of rivers and mountains, where vegetation, trees and grass, was abundant. It is a significant fact that, even in those instances where at first mention is made only of the mountain or the river, one usually discovers elsewhere reference to that which appears to be omitted.[1] What has to be explained, therefore, is not the worship of mountains and rivers but the existence of holy places whose every feature, rocks, waters, and woods, was also holy.

This opinion is supported by the fact that the Chinese believe

[1] Cf. p. 124.

180

rivers, mountains, and woods to be divine forces of the same order and worship them conjointly,[1] or, if one feature of the sacred scene seems to predominate, it is evident that it does so because it is looked upon as the moſt vivid manifeſtation of the divine force incorporated in the whole. Let us see what the texts [2] say : " Mountains, foreſts, rivers, valleys, heights, hills, have the power to produce clouds, to make rain and wind, and to cause portents to appear : of all these things it is said that they are *Shên*, sacred powers." " It is the sacred powers of mountains and rivers [3] who are entreated by means of sacrifices when floods, droughts, or epidemics befall." One of these sacrifices has always been famous. It was offered by T'ang, the founder of the ancient dynaſty of Yin, on the occasion of an unusually long drought. T'ang offered his own person to the mulberry foreſt in order that deliverance might be granted.[4] Long after, in 566 B.C., when the ſtate of Chêng was experiencing a great drought,[5] several persons, including an invoker, were sent to sacrifice to a mountain of the same name. " They cut down the trees thereon ; rain did not fall." The blundering messengers were punished by a wise miniſter : " When sacrifice is offered to a mountain," he said, " it is offered in order to cause the foreſt to grow ; to cut down the trees is therefore a great crime."

It is true that the mountain-tops are wrapped in cloud, and that miſts are given to hanging over foreſts and valleys ; is it by observation that the source of rain has been discovered to lie in the places where clouds appear to form ? But is not the power to avert peſtilence also attributed to mountains and rivers ? It may be affirmed that this power is dependent upon the others. The spread of infeaction is due to too much or too little moiſture. In faact, the power of mountains and rivers

---

[1] *SMC.*, iii, 443, 448, evidence that in the holy places numerous sacrifices were offered to deities of all kinds.

[2] *Li Chi* ; Couvreur, ii, 260.

[3] *Tso chuan*, Chao, 1ſt year ; Legge, 580 ; cf. *SMC.*, iv, 479.

[4] Cf. *Chu chu chi nien*, T'ang, 24th year.

[5] *Tso chuan*, Chao, 16th year ; Legge, 665.

is not as specialized as it would be if it were based upon observation of the facts of nature. They are not merely storehouses of rain, they are rather controllers of the regularity of the seasons. In the natural order they occupy a position analogous to that of the ruler in human society.

It is noteworthy that they are assigned a position in the feudal hierarchy. They hold the rank of lord, and a title corresponding to their power.[1] On the other hand, their worship appertains to the chief,[2] it is a privilege of sovereignty.[3] It is still more significant that the rulers negotiate with them in the name of men, concerning the affairs of nature. The word negotiate is hardly correct, for it suggests two powers face to face. It would be incorrect to say that, when the drought was carrying off his subjects and he offered himself to the Mountain of Mulberries, T'ang went as the chief of a defeated people to put himself in the hands of a superior power. To him it was not a question of appeasing an enemy power by paying homage. Had it been hostile, he might have tried to subdue it, whereas, on the contrary, it must not be weakened ; the trees, for example, must not be cut down but must be made to grow. Nor was it a question of calling to aid a higher power. Who are most affected by public misfortune ? the chiefs. In times of drought the prince became powerless[4] : " his subjects were scattered "[5] ; "there was no longer any place to which he might withdraw ; death is at hand ; he knows not where to lift up his eyes, where to turn his head.[6] . . . ." The mountains and rivers are not less affected. " The drought,

---

[1] *Li chi* ; Couvreur, i, 289–90, and note ; cf. *SMC.*, iii, 418.
[2] *Li chi*, ibid. Cf. *Ch'ien Han shu* : Article on the *Chiao* sacrifice, ch. 25a, p. 2 r °.
[3] *SMC.*, iv, 379–380. The King of Ch'u refuses to sacrifice to the Ho, which is not in his state. He believes himself justified in sacrificing only to those rivers which belong to his domain, the Chiang and the Han. Cf. *Shih ching, Lu sung*, 4 ; Couvreur, 457.

> T'ai shan is very lofty,
> The state of Lu looks out on it,
> Lu owns the mountains Kuei and Mêng ;
> Lu guards and owns Mounts Fu and I.

[4] *Shih ching, Ta ya*, iii, 4 ; *The Milky Way*, Couvreur, 391, str. 4.
[5] Ibid., str. 7 and 2.
[6] Ibid., str. 4.

how excessive it is ! Exhausted, Exhausted, are the mountains and rivers !"[1] The rivers are dried up, and vegetation disappears from the mountains. They are quite as much abased as the prince.

The fact of the matter is that their power is only another aspect of the power of the prince. When the prince lacks virtue there is no order among men ; when the mountain lacks power, rain does not fall in its appointed time.[2] But if any should propose to punish the mountain for failing in its duty, he would be holding the wrong person responsible.[3] Disorder in nature is only the result of disorder in society ; it is the prince who should hold himself to blame both when rain fails and when it rains too much.[4] He must restore his virtue and at the same time restore to its pristine vigour the efficacy of the holy place. If he fails to correct himself, punishment will surely fall ; it may be dealt him at the hands of men, but his punishment depends upon himself. The power of a wicked prince may crumble away or be dried up, and his mountains and rivers, evil like himself, crumble away and dry up. King Yu[5] (782–772 B.C.) was a disastrous ruler. In the second year of his reign an earthquake disturbed the course of three rivers ; the sages were not mistaken about it : "The Chou are about to perish . . . (for) a state must have the support of its mountains and rivers. When the mountains crumble and the rivers dry up, it portends destruction." The king's destruction was assured in less than ten years. He was killed in 772. In 780 three rivers had dried up and mount Ch'i had crumbled away.

King Yu ruined himself for love for a woman.[6] Feminine influence brought disorder in the government

---

[1] *The Milky Way*, Couvreur, 391, str. 5.
[2] See the commentaries on the *Milky Way* and the preface to the poem.
[3] Cf. p. 181.
[4] Cf. *Li chi* ; Couvreur, i, 261 ; cf. *Hsiao ya*, iv, 9 ; Couvreur, 238, str. 3.
[5] *SMC.*, i, 278. Cf. *Hsiao ya*, iv, 9 ; Couvreur, 239, str. 3. Cf. *Hsiao ya*, i, 6 ; Couvreur, 184, str. 6.
[6] *Pao Ssŭ* ; cf. *SMC.*, i, 280.

and that disorder threw nature into confusion : *the Yin oppressed the Yang* and " the earth shook ", " the springs dried up, the parched mountains crumbled away ".[1] For men the results of such calamities are inevitable : they no longer find any means of support nor any place to bury their dead, with the result that they suffer famines, plagues and untimely death.[2]

The virtue of mountains and rivers is thus entirely dependent upon the virtue of the prince. If they guarantee to the people life and health it is through no innate qualities of their own, for no such qualities are inherent in the essence of their being. In everything they are dependent upon human government ; they are worth what it is worth ; they last as long as it lasts.

Wicked princes appear at the end of dynasties. Their wickedness does not arise from themselves, but from the fact that the virtue of their house is exhausted.[3] The virtue of their mountains and rivers becomes exhausted at the same time.[4] " In olden times the I and the Lo dried up and the dynasty of the Hsia perished ; the Ho dried up and the dynasty of the Shang perished." " Now the T'ai Shan is crumbling ", Confucius sang when nearing his end,[5] foreseeing the fall of the Chou. The power of a princely house and the potency of the mountains and rivers of its state are identical.

Princely families bear the name of their state as their *cognomen*. In legendary times there were many who were distinguished by the name of a mountain or a river.[6] Undoubtedly there

---

[1] Ibid., 279–80.

[2] *Kuo yü, Chou yü*, 3. Note that the mountains are burial places. At the spring festival of *Ch'ing ming* the mountains are climbed for the purpose of visiting the tombs. Cf. de Groot, *Emouy*, 231 sqq.

[3] When the essential virtue of a family is exhausted it must come to ruin : witness the words of the king of Ch'u on feeling the end draw near. Good fortune comes not twice. *SMC.*, iv, 364.

[4] *SMC.*, i, 280.   [5] *T'an kung, Li chi* ; Couvreur, i, 144.

[6] *SMC.*, i, 14 : " Shên-nung came from Mount Lieh ; that is why Tso said : The son of Lieh shan was called Chu." Ibid., 163 : The mother of Chi was a daughter of Tu shan. (Cf. ibid., 158 : On the day *lin* and *jên* (said Yü, the father of Chi), I married Tu shan.) See particularly i, 93 : " From Huang-ti to Shun and Yü all (the emperors) had the same family name, but were distinguished by the name of their state in order that their (different) virtues might be made evident (cf. the comment : the virtue decides the family names).

184

is here not merely a simple indication of habitat but
the mark of an exceedingly close bond between the ruling
house and that which was regarded as the very core and
soul of the state. Huang Ti and Yen Ti were both
sons of Chao Tien and, apparently, of the same mother,
yet they established rival families. The reason for this lay
in the fact that they were *moulded*, that they were fashioned
under the influence of two different rivers. The Chinese
word *ch'êng* cannot be accurately translated. It suggests
the idea of perfection, of fullness ; it is used of a full-
grown man, one who is of age ; it expresses the successful
issue of anything, the accession of a dynasty. In each case the
river *made* Huang Ti and Yen Ti all that they became : *they
received their surname also from the rivers.*[1] " It was by the
river Chi that Huang Ti was fashioned (*ch'êng*) ; it was
by the river Chiang that Yen Ti was fashioned, and being
thus fashioned, their virtues were different. Thus Huang
Ti was named Chi and Yen Ti was named Chiang. The
two emperors raised armies and fought against each other
because their virtues were different : surname different,
virtue different ; virtue different, nature different." Compared
with the influence of the river, paternity does not count ;
it is the former which decides the nature (lit : kind),
the virtue and the name, the only mark of their kinship. It is
the river which engenders the destiny, the spirit, and the
dominion of the race. Is it to be wondered at that mountains
should have been regarded, literally, as the source of local
dynasties ?[2] " The holy mountains are mighty and extensive ;
their summits reach to heaven ! It is from the holy mountains
that the sacred powers came down which gave birth to
(the princes of) Fu and Shên."

Thus mountains and rivers appear to be the agents by means
of which the regulating influence of the government
made itself felt through the state.[3] Their potency arises

[1] *Kuo yü, Chin yü,* 148.   [2] *Shih ching, Ta ya,* iii, 5 ; Couvreur, 396.
[3] *Tao-tê* ; see prefaces to the odes.

not from any qualities inherent in themselves, but from a sort of delegation of this regulating power. Such authority as it possesses they also possess, and, as long as it is capable of lasting, their power lasts. So closely identified is it with that particular virtue which, in any state, serves to maintain in authority the ruling power, that it might be said of mountains and rivers that they are, as it were, the *principle of that rule made manifest.*

Such were the beliefs connected with the princely worship of mountains and rivers. Their relation with the beliefs connected with seasonal festivals is easily understood. While the princes, on whom rested the double responsibility of maintaining good order in society and in the universe, thought to make use of the potency of mountains and rivers to uphold their rule, the seasonal festivals, which brought together, close to the mountains and rivers, the members of a local community, while they served in the first place to display the ordered course of the life of the community, further assured the orderly functioning of nature. Indeed, the rhythm of the life of the community accorded with the rhythm of the seasons, and this is why, as we have seen, the festivals which mark its periods seem to be possessed of a two-fold regulative power. But how does it happen that the prince possesses this power ? If the virtue of the prince exercises the same beneficial influence as the seasonal festivals, is it not because the social order, before it was maintained by the unremitting efforts of local authority, had previously been manifested at regular intervals in these festivals and had there been immediately believed to be identical with natural order ? And if the princes regard the mountains and rivers as the source of their authority, is it not because the seasonal gatherings were held in the holy neighbourhood of mountains and rivers ? But in that case, since sacred mountains and rivers never possessed any power other than that delegated to them by the ruling authority, must it not also be true that the holy places had no virtue of their own ? Their sanctity was entirely due to the fact that the local communities which gathered there rendered effective in these places, which had witnessed their reunions from generation to generation, the principle of the sacred forces set in motion by the seasonal festivals.

Thanks to these festivals they hoped to avoid plagues, ensure rain in due season, and to be granted children. Believing their livelihood, both present and future, to be guaranteed by the favour of the hallowed place of their assemblies, the members of the local community felt themselves bound to it by a relationship teeming with benefits, which caused them to adhere to it as faithful vassals to a powerful lord. When they were gathered together to keep these festivals from which so much good resulted, each one, hoping for all these benefits, ascribed a variety of virtues to mountains, rivers, and woods, with which he was familiar and which seemed to him worthy of reverence. He endeavoured to assimilate and to woo the protecting power which, it seemed to him, invested the spot where at all times his people had attained their loftiest desires. While coming freely into contact with the holy place at these solemn festivals, wandering about in it, leaping half-naked into the river, while gathering the varied products, flowers or branches, in which its power appeared to be displayed and embodied, a feeling of reverence was generated in the minds of the faithful together with a consciousness of belonging to the land.[1]

We have seen that certain princely families bore the name of a holy place from whose influence had been derived the special virtue of their traditional ancestor. In other instances, the name of the family is explained by the miraculous circumstances which surrounded the conception of the founder. Thus the Hsia were called Ssŭ because Yü was conceived as the result of his mother swallowing a lotus seed.[2] In this case the family name is derived from the rite by which conception

[1] It is expressed in the proverb : " The dying fox turns its head towards the hill where it was born." Cf. *Li chi*; Couvreur, i, p. 131.
[2] *Chu chu Chi nien*, Book of the Hsia, Yü, 1st year, where two versions are mentioned : (1) The mother of Yü conceived through seeing, when on a walk, a falling star ; (2) through having swallowed a water-lily seed.

was brought about. This was similar to those practised at the festivals of rivers and mountains. It was at a festival of the same kind that Chien Ti,[1] through swallowing a swallow's egg (*tzŭ*) became the mother of the ancestors of the Yin, and the name of the house of Yin was Tzŭ. Thus it sometimes happens that the name, indicating the genius of the race, springs directly from the holy place, while at others it is supplied by the miscellaneous things connected with the festivals held there. Is there any very real difference between the two cases ? Should not the holy places be regarded as *ancestral centres* where the genius of the family was felt to be, and whence those belonging to that race thought to obtain, on the occasion of the festival, that which would ensure the fecundity of their women ?

In order to prove this theory, it would be necessary to cite instances in which conception, being induced exactly as in the festivals of rivers and mountains, is yet due to an ancestor. Of such instances I have met but one—a significant one, however. A certain prince of the state of Chêng had risen to power despite the fact that he was apparently of ordinary birth. A story shows that he had a right to his estate. In order to make it clear, I will draw attention to three facts : (1) In the festivals of this state of Chêng it was customary to gather orchis, and, when the lovers were united, the girl was given a flower as a token[2] ; (2) In Chêng, again, boys and girls carrying orchis summoned the souls, or rather, they called the superior soul to rejoin the inferior soul.[3] (3) Finally, so close was the relation assumed to be between the superior soul and the personal name that, at the moment of death, it was by calling the personal name that the superior soul was summoned in an attempt to persuade it to rejoin the soul of the corpse.[4] The story is as follows[5] : Duke Wên of Chêng had a wife of secondary rank named Yen Chi, who dreamed that a

---

[1] See p. 157. Cf. *Po hu t'ung*, ch. *Hsing ming*.
[2] Cf. Festivals of Chêng, and LII.   [3] Cf. Notes of the *Han Shih* on LII.
[4] *Li Chi* ; Couvreur, i, 93, and i, 756. Cf. *I li*, *Shih sang li* ; Steele, p. 145 ; cf. ibid., 95.
[5] *Tso chuan*, Hsüan, 4th year, Legge, 294 (cf. *SMC.*, iv, 463).

messenger from heaven presented her with an orchis (lan) saying,
" I am Po-yu, thy ancestor [1] : out of that make thy son. Since
the orchis has a royal fragrance, he will be recognized (as
prince) and loved." Thereupon Duke Wên paid her a visit,
presented her with an orchis, and lay with her. She,
pleading, said, 'Thy handmaiden is a person without ability.
If, by thy favour, I should bear a son, no one will believe me.
Dare I take this orchis as evidence ? ' The Duke replied,
' Yes.' She gave birth to (him who became) Duke Mu,
whose personal name was Lan (orchis). . . . When Duke
Mu was ill, he said, ' when the orchis shall wither, it is then
that I shall die, I who live by it ' (or equally correctly, who
owe my birth to it). When the orchis was cut [2] he died
(B.C. 606). The story implies that soul, personal name,
ancestral protector, external soul or token of life and kind
(plant) conjoined,[3] source of maternity, pledge of love, proof of
paternity, and title to power are equivalents. Most probably
the young women of Chêng who, by means of flowers gathered
in the neighbourhood, where the festivals took place, summoned
souls there, and [4] believed themselves assured of maternity
by the same flowers, assumed that with these products of the
holy place of their people, these gathered fragments of its
guardian power, they received into themselves the souls of
children springing from an ancestral spirit.[5]

---

[1] Observe that the being responsible for the miraculous conception is an ancestor
of the woman.

[2] In the tenth month. [3] A perfectly clear case of totemism.

[4] Note the practice of summoning the souls and of calling the personal name
at the tomb festivals of Ch'ing ming.

[5] The connection between the holy places and the burial places still awaits
investigation. We will only note at this point that, like Chiang Yen, the mother of
Confucius, who by reason of her husband's age could have had but the faintest
hope of children, offered a sacrifice with pure intent. This she offered in the family
temple of her husband, Shu-liang Ho, which was on Mount Ni (Ni Ch'iu). Cf.
SMC., v, pp. 288–90. The personal name of Confucius was Ch'iu, and his style
Chung-ni. Very probably the sacrifice made by his mother was responsible for both
these names. The commentators explain them by the shape of the sage's head, but
why should his elder brother Po-ni have been called Ni ? The name given to the
two brothers would be much more easily explained if it were conceded that both the
wives of Shu-liang Ho went to pray in his family temple and obtained children
in consequence of their pilgrimage to Mount Ni.

FESTIVALS AND SONGS OF ANCIENT CHINA

As the feudal princes looked upon their mountains and rivers as the principle of their authority made manifeſt, so the local communities realized in their holy places the genius of their race. By reason of the age of the ties which bound them to these places dedicated to their solemn assemblies they had come to regard them as anceſtral centres, while the regularity of the feſtivals held there gave them the impression that here dwelt the powers in control of nature. Diſtributors of souls, controllers of the seasons, it was from them that the indigenous groups drew alike their exiſtence and their continuance. These holy places were revered not for their rivers, their mountains, and their woods ; they maintained their venerable character through having been the traditional link of the seasonal feſtivals. They appeared as the witnesses and the protectors of the social covenant renewed at regular intervals by these assemblies. Hence their majeſty. Hence also it happened that when princely rule was set up, and to the prince, surety for the unity of the people, was ascribed a like majeſty, they supposed a sort of partnership between the holy places and the prince.

THE CONTESTS

It cannot be supposed that the seasonal feſtivals of the mountains and rivers were eſtablished either for the purpose of offering worship to the mountains and rivers or celebrating any particular occurrence in the cycle of vegetation, or in the solar cycle. They seem like feſtivals of union, gathering together in one place, hallowed by tradition, the members of a local community, at the momentous periods of the year at which they change their mode of life. Why were dancing and singing conteſts held ? Why did betrothals find a place among sexual rites ?

These feſtivals included conteſts other than that of singing love-songs : indeed, of all the cuſtoms I have been able to observe, there is none, if I may say so, concerning which there are not reasons for saying that it was the occasion of a conteſt or a competition.

190

The river was crossed by fording. Wang Ch'ung maintains that two groups of dancers facing each other in the river I imitated the movements of a dragon in order to bring down rain. Now, rain is often supposed to be induced by fights between dragons.[1] The river was also crossed in boats. There were a great number of these. It has been proved that rain festivals in China included, at a very early date, fights between dragon-boats.[2] The mountains were climbed. The actual festival of the climb gave rise to kite-flying competitions,[3] which foretold success in the field of honours, as the shooting competition of the Pa Cha gave admittance to it. Faggots and ferns were cut. The young men and women of the Lolo range themselves in lines, face to face, and cut ferns with which they make bonfires, and it is then that they improvise songs.[4] Flowers were gathered amid great rivalry. Ching Ch'u's calendar describes a festival at which there was a contest in which all kinds of plants were employed,[5] and battles of flowers took place between men and women at a springtime assembly in the kingdom of Nan Chao.[6] At the spring equinox, Chien Ti and her sister struggled for possession of an egg of five colours, which was very beautiful. At Ching Ch'u, in the second month, eggs decorated with designs and pictures were used in the contests.[7]

Thus, in our festivals, every kind of ritual activity—the substance employed in it is of little consequence—took the form of a contest, and ceremonial contests were engaged in for any reason whatever. Why then does each practice seem to be nothing more than a fresh means of bringing the participants in the festival into opposition, setting them face to face? What is the reason for this arrangement wherein the groups are regularly brought into opposition? This arrangement in opposing groups was still adhered to in the already scholarly ceremonial of the Pa Cha[8]: the division of

[1] Cf. 151 ; cf. de Groot : *Emouy*, 373 sqq.   [2] *Emouy*, 356 sqq.
[3] Ibid., 538 sqq.   [4] App. III, p. 263, in Crabouillet.
[5] Ching Ch'u, fifth day of the fifth month. Cf. *SMC.*, i, 13.
[6] App. III, p. 268, in Sainson.   [7] Ching Ch'u, second month.   [8] Cf. p. 173.

things as well as men into two categories gave rise in this festival to a perception of the unity of the All, the world of matter and the world of men. The reason why the seasonal festivals of the mountains and rivers are entirely devoted to contests and competitions seems to lie in the fact that they also are festivals of Harmony. They were the occasion of the reunion of the members of the local community who usually lived in small groups, groups which were limited, homogeneous and exclusive. Their horizon was bounded by the family field which they cultivated during the warm season, and by the clan village where they dwelt in seclusion during the season of rest.

Living entirely in the life of the family, each was imbued with the clan spirit,[1] and all the relatives, living in complete and lasting fellowship, were conscious of their homogeneity. Perfect community of feeling drew them together as the result of apparently inherent similarity. Strengthened daily, and without effort, as it were, the ties which bound together the members of one group, the ties of kinship, seemed to exist in fact and of themselves. Between relatives there were no ties which remained to be invented. On the other hand, between those who were fundamentally strangers, none could possibly be invented. But completely exclusive though these family groups might be, they did not remain always entirely isolated. Adjacent groups used to meet at intervals in the festivals.

The members of one local community found themselves, on these occasions, temporarily drawn into a close fellowship which broke down the barriers between the too exclusive groups and, for a short space, militated against family exclusivism. This periodic feeling was by no means so simple and definite as the ordinary feelings upon which family unity is based. The more complicated unity of a local community is not founded upon an abiding sense of an apparently exact likeness, nor is

[1] Cf. a similar process among animals, plants, and things which hibernate in winter. Cf. p. 174 sqq.

it of a fellowship conſtantly revived ; it is a higher unity which, in unusual circumſtances, links together elements which commonly appear to be in opposition. The transition of feelings by which, at the close of a duel in which they tried and proved each other, the young men and girls felt themselves linked by permanent ties of friendship, and seized by an overwhelming and sudden need of intercourse, assumes that, through this conteſt, their sense of their affinities, usually unperceived, overcame the more conspicuous and cuſtomary feeling of opposition. A union between usually remote and exclusive groups could not be brought about unless their rivalry were firſt awakened by their sudden bringing together. At their firſt contaſt it was inevitable that they should come into collision and confront one another.[1] Unlike the family feelings which were nourished by a conſtant flow of tranquil and habitual emotions, the exceptional feeling of general harmony came into being suddenly as the result of a violent process. The cuſtomary opposition, the solemn drawing together, the rivalry, the unity of neighbouring villages, expressed themselves in competitions and conteſts, in polite and peaceful emulation. Since, at critical periods of the year, seasonal gatherings ſtrengthened social unity, it was natural that the feſtivals of rivers and mountains should, for the moſt part, be devoted to conteſts.

The musical conteſt predominated and, no doubt, was the oral counterpart of all the others. This was a conteſt of love-songs, and, in it, the various groups were set in opposition, not only as individual againſt individual but also as sex againſt sex. If opposite partners muſt belong to different villages, it was also invariably to a girl that a young man responded. As the result of the poetic duel hearts were linked and betrothals arranged. All the young people of marriageable age participated in the conteſts ; all the marriages of the year were settled there. Each assembly was not only a feſtival of general harmony, but also a general marriage feſtival. It was in a feſtival of

[1] See p. 130 sqq.

youth, a festival of love, that the component groups of a local community revived their traditional amity.

There appears to be no tangible difference between the marriage contract and a covenant of amity or of loyalty and comradeship in arms. Is the singer singing as a soldier to a comrade, or is he thinking of his wife when he sings [1] :

> For death, or life, or toil,
> To thee myself I join.
> I take thy hand in mine,
> With thee I would grow old.

[1] LXVIII. THE DRUM (*Pei fêng*, 6).

1. The beaten drum resounds.
2. We leap into the fight.
3. Make strong both Town and Ts'ao :
4. We alone, to the south we go.

5. 'Tis Sun Tzŭ-chung who leads us
6. In accord with Ch'ên and Sung.
7. For me can be no return . . .
8. My sad heart is tormented . . .

9. We camp . . . we make a halt . . .
10. And now we lose our horses . . .
11. We go to seek for them . . .
12. We go beneath the forest . . .

13. For death, or life, or toil,
14. To thee myself I join.
15. I take thy hand in mine,
16. With thee I would grow old.

17. Alas, what tribulations . . .
18. No hope, for me, of life . . .
19. Alas, how all forsake . . .
20. None keeps, with me, his faith . . .

Events set forth by *SMC.*, iv, 194 sqq. : An expedition sent, after he had killed his brother, the duke Huang of Wei, by Chou Hsiu, in league with the princes of Ch'ên and Sung, to attack the prince of Chêng who had received Ping, a fugitive prince of Wei, and proposed to set him up in opposition to Chou Hsiu.

3. The capital of Wei. Ts'ao is a town in Wei.
5. Sun Tzŭ-chung : the Kung-sun Wên-chung.
8. Cf. LIX, 4.
12. A mountain forest is called Lin. (Mao.)
13 and 14. An agreement of military comradeship. (Chêng.) Five men form a squad. Cf. *Chou li, Ta Ssŭ-Ma.*
15 and 16. An oath of loyalty. (Chêng.) Cf. xii, 4, 10, 16, and see *Li chi, Nei tsê,* Couvreur, p. 667.
13–16. Wang Su : Thought of the married people of the state of Wei who desired to live together until death and not to spend days of suffering parted from one another.

THE ANCIENT FESTIVALS

No doubt, in a war-song, it is the loyalty of his comrades-in-arms that the soldier invokes.[1] If, however, this explanation be doubted,[2] it is because the words of the soldiers' oath correspond to those of the marriage vow.[3] Might it then be that an agreement between comrades was modelled upon the marriage contract? The ancient language makes no distinction between comrade and husband, between the faithful vassal and the faithful husband, between friend and lover. The commonest word used to express any of these meanings—which the written character symbolizes by two hands—indicates either member of a pair. Very often a young girl applies it to the man to whom she wishes to give herself.[4] It is also commonly used of a bird which is being sought as a mate by another bird. Might it be then, that every union is believed to have as its prototype the union between husband and wife? Princes of the same surname spoke of themselves as brothers.[5] Of those whose surnames differed there were some who were bound by treaties, and these referred to one another as sons-in-law and fathers-in-law.[6] Might it then be that the matrimonial alliance is the basis of all alliance?

Feudal princes of the same surname seemed to be previously united by community of spirit. Between them no contract was needed; they were forbidden to give one another their daughters in marriage.[7] To unite themselves by marriage,

---

20. The faith solemnly affirmed in the vow of comradeship. (Chêng.)
Cf. line 16, and LXVI, 51, as well as *Yung fêng*, 3, 1, 1, and *Pei fêng*, 10 (Couvreur, p. 39).
Cf. *Ch'in fêng*, 8 (Couvreur, 142).
A war song. Theme: the oath.

[1] Spoken by one soldier to another. (Chêng.)
[2] Wang Su: A husband's thoughts of his wife.
[3] Especially line 16, which occurs so often in the love-songs. See, for example, LXVI, 51. Compare the expressions given under the notes on line 20 on page 194.
[4] Cf. L, 16.   [5] Cf. *Hsiao ya*, i, 5, line 6: Couvreur, 180.
[6] Or, again, if there be a difference of age, or as a mark of respect, paternal uncle; *Li chi*; Couvreur, 90. Cf. *Hsiao ya*, i, 4; Couvreur, 178.
[7] Cf. *Cho yü Chin yü*, iv, 8: Different names, different Virtues. Different Virtues, different natures. If they are of different natures no matter how close may be their relationship, a man and a woman can mate and found a family. Same family

or to bind themselves by covenants was, on the other hand, permissible for princes of different surnames, but not for all. Certain princely families—not belonging to the same union of ſtates—regarded each other as being of a spirit so antipathetic that any dealings between them muſt be disaſtrous [1] ; a marriage or an alliance would have brought calamity. It would have been a misfortune for one to hazard its Fortune beyond the traditional bounds of its own relations. On the other hand, the special propensities of allied families, although different, had yet an affinity which juſtified friendship. Between such families, and between them only, there exiſted relations sufficiently close to admit of the interchange of diplomatic relations and of girls sent as wives. This interchange always kept within certain limits, whereby each of the families concerned, continuing to entruſt its happiness to the same proved associates, kept itself in close touch with its kindred, was a principle of good fortune. Thanks to it, federal union was foſtered in a ſtate of unchanging cohesion.

name, same Virtue : same Virtue, the same mind. The same mind, the same tendencies. When they have the same tendencies, no matter how diſtant their relationship, a man and a woman may not mate for fear of taint ; and, out of deference, they avoid it. Taint produces discontent ; discontent and dissensions induce calamities. Calamities result in the extermination of the family. That is why when a wife is taken, she should not be of the same surname as the husband. Dissensions and calamities are feared. Thus when Virtues are different, families are united in marriage. When Virtues are identical they are united by righteousness.

[1] *Kuo yü, Chou yü*, ii, 1, Marriage unions are the ſteps by which come good fortune and ill. If through them fortune be sought within (the limits of traditional relationships), good fortune results. If it be sought outside these limits, ill fortune results. (Here follow examples of ſtates which adhered to these matrimonial regulations and prospered). All were able to seek happiness within the limits (of their traditional relationships) and kept themselves in close relation with their kin. (Here follow examples of ſtates which were extinguished because they failed to observe these regulations.) They all sought happiness outside (the limits of approved relationships) and were eſtranged from their relatives.

Cf. the commentary of Wei Chao : When a wife is sought within the circle of traditional relationships, a real mate is obtained and good fortune follows. Observe that the exaɔt meaning of *Fu*, happiness or good fortune, is a long poſterity, that is to say, the perpetuity of the princely house.

Cf. *SMC.*, iv, 398. We have made matrimonial alliances and thus the origin of our intimacy is ancient.

Also, *SMC.*, iv, 466. As reason for the seleɔtion of an heir-apparent is given the faɔt that his mother bore the same surname as that of the wife of Hou Chi, anceſtor of the royal house.

THE ANCIENT FESTIVALS

Envoys and brides brought regular evidence of the strength of the union and, moreover, they were its guarantee. But a state whose existence depends upon war and tillage jealously conserves all its men ; the envoys remain but a short time in the state to which they are sent and only under exceptional circumstances do they stay as hostages. The state to which they went was always anxious to detain them : every hostage was given a woman to attend him ; an attempt was made to bind every guest by marriage.[1] Marriage formed, indeed, what were regarded as the most stable relationships ; a girl is wedded once and for all. That is why she is not jealously retained by her family. She is destined to become a permanent hostage in another family, in which she will be the representative of her own family.

To take a wife outside the confederation or in one's own family would have been to deprive the confederated states of an accredited representative[2] ; and to marry a girl into her own family or outside the group of allied states would have been to deprive them of a guarantee. The two-fold prohibition against marriages between relatives and between those who are not of the same traditional league appears to be a negative aspect of the obligations laid upon the narrow, homogeneous groups which are made exclusive by the permanent system of alliance which binds them. This alliance demands that all the girls of every family shall be reserved for the interchange which shall develop in each individual group the sense of general solidarity.

If complete exclusiveness were permitted in the lesser groups, the higher unity which comprises the groups traditionally

---

[1] Cf. *SMC.*, iv, pp. 7, 26, 43, 281 (two cases). The girl is given in marriage in order that the feelings of guestship may be strengthened. Ibid., 283, 289–94–31, 285, 289.

[2] Cf. *SMC.*, iv, 279. The sister of a prince, defeated by her husband, puts on mourning at the proclamation of the rejoicings which are held to mark the victory and obtains a treaty for her brother.—Other instances : IV, 55 and 44. In certain instances the woman appears to be so strongly attached to her own family that she is almost like an enemy let into the house of her husband : *SMC.*, iv, 458 (a wife betrays her husband for her father).

197

associated would be endangered. This exclusiveness is lessened by the exchange of individuals, by which the composition of the groups is altered. The chief method of exchange is marriage, wherefore the marriage alliance is regarded as a means to unity. It serves to bind the social contract which it is desired to make lasting, and it is also regarded as indestructible. The social compact requires to be renewed at intervals, wherefore a festival was devoted to the celebration of the marriages of the year. While family exclusivism was weakened by marriage outside the family, the rule of marriage within the federation of states proves the greater importance of the community, and this is the reason why the families within the union are obliged to bring together all their sons and daughters without exception in a collective ceremony. When a local community, celebrating one of its seasonal festivals in its holy places, manifested anew the strength of its union, the various exogamous groups, suddenly abandoning their accustomed seclusion, whose immediate purpose was an interchange of daughters, brought together at one stroke all the young people [1] whom they had

---

[1] The festivals gather together in the holy place all the young people of marriageable age. They pair off for the first time and the festival concludes with sexual intercourse. The festivals have thus the distinct characteristics of a festival of initiation. The commentator on the *Hsia Calendar* has preserved a recollection of it. To a passage which reads : *In the second month the boys and girls enjoyed themselves together in great numbers*, he adds a note : *the coming-of-age cap was presented to the youths and they took wives.* (Observe that the commentators on the *I li* were still disputing as to whether the coming-of-age ceremony was celebrated at any particular time of the year.) This is the only information we possess concerning the initiatory character of the sex contests. In view of the fact that the *Shih ching* has been preserved by the learned dictators of orthodox morality, it is not surprising that there is in the *Shih ching* an entire absence of information on the point. A doubly interesting fact will be established by comparison. In his *Fastes*, iii, 523 sqq., Ovid has described at length the festivals of Anna Perenna, which are very similar to the festivals of mountains and rivers. They were held on the banks of the Tiber, the couples lying on the grass (526, *accumbit cum pare quisque sua*). They drank steadily (532), they sang and acted the songs (535), they danced (538), the girls sang licentious verses (675, *cantent . . . obscena puellæ*). The occasion was the celebration of a pseudo-marriage between Mars and Anna (see Harrison, *Themis*, 197 sqq.).—Two lines of Martial complete the description given by Ovid. They show the existence of a wood consecrated to Anna Perenna (Martial, iv, 64, lines 16–17) :—

Et quod virgineo cruore gaudet
Annæ pomiferum nemus Perennæ.

until this moment kept strictly within the limits of family life. These young people, overcome at first by their still unimpaired sense of their inherent difference, and then becoming conscious of the awakening of their hidden affinities, met and paired off in a contest in which their complex feelings burst forth in song and transformed themselves into a love which immediately established harmony between them for life.

Because it really especially tends to promote the interchange of persons who proceed to lessen the force of family particularism, the marriage union is considered a particularly powerful agent for the upkeep and the strengthening of social unity. But is its power due to this fact alone ? and, on the other hand, has the love contest no other aim than that of making closer the union between local groups ?

It is not only the exchange of persons that is capable of bringing into exclusive groups the consciousness of a greater unity : there is also the exchange of goods. It is by the generous use of their crops, by not keeping them all for their individual use, by consuming in company the produce of all their private fields, that the people of neighbouring villages, gathered together by districts, revived the sense of their affinities in the celebration of the Pa Cha festival. The exchange of goods [1] no less than diplomatic exchanges ; the orgy, no less than sexual licence, could thus work for the increase of general harmony. On the

These two lines are perfectly clear. It is very interesting to observe that our commentators on the classics are no less prudish and ingenious than the Chinese commentators. In defiance of all the texts, they have suggested the substitution of *pudore* or *rubore* for *cruore* as being more decent and more pleasing, because they are unwilling to admit what is indicated by the blood of maidens. See Friedlander, i, 371. Cf. the notes of Glotz Ordalie in *La Grèce primitive*, p. 69 sqq., upon the connection between springs, rivers, wells, and virginity. See especially the notes on the καλλίκορον (παρθένιον) (ἀνθέον, cf. χουρηίον ἄνθος) φρέαρ of Eleusis ; on the λουτρόν νυμφικόν in Troas (λαβέμου, Σχάμανδρε, την παρθενίαν; and on the spring Κισσοεσσα at Haliarte (τὰ προτέλεια θύειν).

[1] It has already been remarked that the festivals of youth have about them a suggestion of a fair ; cf. LXIII and LXVI. Cf. App. III, Billet. It will be observed that the site of the ' wall of song ' of Japan is the public square ; that the daughter of Tzŭ Chung danced in the market-place ; and that the gatherings outside the gates of the villages, like the festival of Kao Mei, were held in the suburb devoted to trade.

other hand, the betrothal festival, with its contests, still retains sufficient grounds for being kept up when the rivalry or the unity of local groups becomes weakened. This is the case among the Lolo, with whom one or the other has declined to such a degree that the young men and girls have gained the right (at least among certain tribes) to sing together even though they belong to the same village.[1] The most enduring, the chief function of the singing contest is not that of bringing local groups together. Yet it has been employed for this purpose, as we have just seen, and has even been so employed in preference to other practices which would have served the same purpose satisfactorily.

Although there may have been love-song contests in the autumn, they played an infinitely more important part in spring. The young men came to fetch their brides in autumn but it was in spring that they mated. The study of the Pa Cha, that autumn festival from which sexual rites have almost completely disappeared, has shown that it formed an introduction to that phase of rural life in which solitary groups live the life of the family. This is the period of indoor work, when men and women are reunited. The spring festivals, on the other hand, are the prelude to the period of field-work during which local groups certainly live apart, but during which men and women form distinct bodies, occupied with different types of work. Before family exclusivism became emphasized in domestic life, the unity of local communities was strengthened by an autumn festival, and, in the same way, before sex opposition became weakened by corporate life, was not the spring festival with its contest an attempt to draw the sexes together by means of general betrothals?

The sung contest, while expressing the complexity of the social unity, also revived it in two ways. It brought together the young people of different villages and of opposite sexes, and at the same time it weakened the antagonism of the secondary groups as well as that of the sex groups. The

[1] Cf. App. III, Bonifacy, p. 272.

opposition of local groups, like that of the sexes, is at the basis of Chinese corporate life, but while the former is merely a question of geographical position, the latter depends upon a division made according to work, and this is the more stable of the two, being apparently fundamental. If society is indeed divided from the beginning into two groups according to sex, a festival which brings these two halves of the community together and reconciles them, restores its original unity, wherefore sex union must appear to be the basis of all alliance. In a more complex society in which, in consequence of the over-emphasis of division, certain groups traditionally associated find themselves united in one community, the marriage union could not fail to be regarded as the most effective means to union. That is why the love contest which settled all the marriages of the year had the right of priority in the seasonal festivals of rural Harmony, and especially in the great spring festival.

By reason of the fact that, in origin and substance, sex union was a principle of social unity, it could not fail to be regulated. The corresponding duties of federal endogamy and family exogamy were, it appears, only the first, the most general and the simplest of the rules to which all marriage unions must conform. These rules doubtless became more detailed as the composition of the community became more complex. I see evidence of this severe regulation in the fact that love remained totally unacquainted with the torments of desire and the impulses of passion. Indeed, in the extemporized songs, it always retains a suggestion of impersonality. It expresses itself not according to the unconstrained play of fresh inspiration, but in phrases or sayings better suited to the expression of the ordinary emotions of a crowd than the special feelings of individuals.[1] When, in the course of the contest, and in the heat of the struggle, the participants approached to challenge each other and extemporize face to face, their inspiration did not spring from the special store of their soul, the individual

[1] Cf. p. 85 sqq.

ſtirring of their heart, the ecſtacy of their spirit, but modelled itself, on the contrary, upon traditional themes, following a dance rhythm to which all yielded under the impulse of collective emotions. It was by means of proverbs [1] that they declared their dawning love. But that this declaration of love could find expression in proverbs was due to the faৎ that the feeling itself was not caused by any personal feeling of inclination, preference or choice. Had it been otherwise, if the participants had been impelled towards each other by an inſtinৎive inclination, it is beyond the bounds of possibility that they should never have given a hint of personal feeling. They would not always have addressed themselves to some person indefinite, impersonal and unspecified. New lines would usually be indicated by other devices than mere descriptive auxiliaries ; variants would show some originality, whereas, on the contrary, the imagery of the love-songs is charaৎterized by the moſt monotonous uniformity. The reason is that even in the duels in which they challenged each other as individuals, the youths and girls were primarily representatives of their sex and ambassadors of their respeৎive family groups. Even then they were not following their fancy, but fulfilling a duty. It is not, in faৎ, beauty deſtined for him alone, diſtinৎive grace which attraৎs a man to the beloved, but, usually, it is to her preſtige that he yields and to the influence of her virtue that he submits, while, so far as the girl is concerned, the qualities which force a man upon her as a fore-ordained husband, are inherited and not personal. Since the feelings of love, with their air of impersonality, have yet a sort of appearance of compulsion, it would seem that there was no more real power of seleৎion in the marriage preliminaries than unreſtrained imagination in the poetic conteſt. In classical times betrothals were arranged without any freedom of choice, and by order of an intermediary. Would such a cuſtom have been possible if, in the firſt place, there had been freedom of choice ? Is it not significant that, according to

[1] Cf. App. I.

tradition, the sex festivals of spring were presided over by an official who bore the definite title of Intermediary ? [1]   It would appear that the contests in which love was generated, far from being occasions for individual preference and for licence, simply brought together young people who were intended for one another and were under the necessity of loving one another.   They fell in love immediately, with an impersonal and compulsory love, such a love as must exist between persons to whom unity is no less necessary than kinship between relatives.   Probably the engagements made by the intermediary did not conform to all the prescribed rules of selection which in olden times did not admit of freedom of choice, but they conformed, at least in theory, to the rule that personal inclination should carry no weight in the arrangement of marriages. Consequently, love did not make its appearance as, or turn out to be, an impulsive, immoderate sentiment, stirring up trouble and anarchy.

It is, indeed, a remarkable fact that, in the eyes of the Chinese, it is not love which is a cause of disunion and strife, but particularly marital affection, love between husband and wife, and it is also remarkable that it is this particular type of love which has provided the raw material for poetry of a personal character.   An ancient law required that all the wives of one man should be related among themselves, and even, in the beginning, that they should be sisters (= cousins [2]).   By this means occasion for jealousy between them was eliminated

---

[1] It will be observed that what seemed detestable to the commentators was not so much the gatherings of the sexes or even sexual intercourse, as private agreements and individual trysts. Cf. X, notes ; L, 13, notes and particularly XLIV, pref.

[2] Concerning sororal polygyny, see Granet : *La polygynie sororaie et le sororat dans la Chine ancienne.* See *Tso chuan*, Yin, 1st year, Legge, 3 ; Ch'êng, 8th year, Legge, 336 ; Tu yü. It is essential that they should all belong to one family in order that all three, being closely bound by ties of blood, sex dissensions may be pacified. Ch'êng, 9th year, Legge, 370 ; Yin, 7th year, Legge, 22 ; Chuang, 19th year. Ho Hsiao : The end desired is that, when one of the wives has a son, there may be two others to take pleasure in him ; by this means, which prevents jealousy, the number of descendants is increased.—Hsiang, 23rd year, Legge, 500. Add *SMC.*, iv, 26, 78, 68 ; iii, 178, 193, 239, 258, 366 ; and i, 53.   This custom is often recalled by the songs IX, LXI. *Wei fêng*, 3 ; *Shao nan*, ii ; *Hsiao ya*, iv, 4 (Couvreur, 200) ; *Ta ya*, iii, 7 ; Couvreur, 405.

and the children of each were loved by the others as they were by their own mother.[1] This sororal polygyny [2] (marriage of sisters) probably originates from a still older form of marriage in which each family group must take all the wives, not only for one member but for all his brothers, from a single family. All the households of relatives were thus identical in form. All the wives, all the sisters-in-law, had the same mind and the same interests as their husbands. Marriage, while helping to strengthen social unity, while weakening the exclusivism of the secondary groups to the benefit of this unity, did not introduce into them an element of separation much more powerful than that consequent upon the opposition of the sexes. But it was enough that matrimonial alliances were no longer arranged according to severe rules in order to permit, not indeed a choice of husband according to personal preference, but a choice of alliance according to the individual interests of each group. Thereafter, all the wives of one husband, all the brides of one generation, being no longer taken of necessity from a single family, homogeneity ceased among the female members of each family group, and elements of separation entered into the group through those households in which the couples were not all uniform. Thus rivalries became possible, with consequent injury to family unity. Favouritism towards a wife, a sister-in-law, or a daughter-in-law, and, in particular, the love of a wife who could brook no rival, became evident sources of dissension.[3] Since, moreover, internal strife manifested itself in a matrimonial instability which made itself felt throughout the alliances ratified by the marriage,[4] the love between husband and wife might appear to be a cause of disorder in the family, and, in addition, of disorder in the community. These results of the marriage union are entirely contrary to its original function. They were due to the new fact that the matrimonial alliance which had become freer—

---

[1] Cf. *SMC.*, iv, 68.
[2] Cf. *Polygynie sororale.*
[3] Cf. LXVI and *Pei fêng*, 1.
[4] *SMC.*, iv, 27, and 58–9.

in consequence of some complication or instability in the social structure which made its control too difficult or too unpopular —was turned to account principally for confederacies or struggles for power. Previously, in a society simpler and in a better position to control it strictly, it had been a chief means in the strengthening of public order.

The spring contests held their own as popular customs even after the part which they played was guaranteed by other means through the rise of the power of the princes. The two-fold regulating influence of the prince, the official worship of mountains and rivers, the laws of the government, by bringing order into nature and among men, by controlling seasonal work and sex relations, proceeded to perform the many functions of the old festivals. Along with the knowledge of their original functions, respect for the rules derived therefrom was also lost. It is possible that the rural festivals, particularly during periods of disorder, degenerated into debauchery and sex licence. Hence the contempt in which they were held and the strange fact that to native scholars they appeared as evidences of anarchy, in spite of the fact that their original purpose had been the strengthening of social unity.

The ancient festivals, the record of which has been preserved for us by the *Shih ching*, appear as festivals of union which, in the ordered life of the Chinese peasants, marked the periods of the assemblies of local and sex groups. They made clear the social compact, which, to the local communities, was a source of strength and stability. They ordered the course of social life. But, because their order happened, as a matter of fact, to coincide with the natural order of the seasons, they were also credited with having power to insure the normal course of things and the well-being of nature. Thus their potency expanded and took various forms. Their sanctity and all their virtues extended to the traditional places where they were held. Then, when the alliance which, to begin with, was revived at periodical intervals in the holy places, came under the control of a princely family, the faithful were provided with human

205

mediators in close touch with the powers which they had originally externalized in things, and with which the power of the prince was then identified. At the court of the prince, the leader of the worship, a process of elaboration of the original material went on, and from it issued an official ritual, so distorted that it is not possible at first sight to discover the origins of the practices which somehow survived in the guise of popular customs.

CONCLUSION

I have endeavoured to describe the most ancient facts of the religious history of China. An old anthology of poems has furnished the material required. I have not made a hasty selection of the facts in my text. I have studied the *Kuo fêng* as a whole, taking into account its recent history and the story of its beginnings. *I have taken the document itself as a basis* : the origin, preservation and interpretation of the old songs are so many facts which must be considered in close relation to the material provided by the texts. *I did not attempt the interpretation of the texts until after I had obtained a clear view of the work as a whole.*[1] When I had grasped the unity of the whole it was easier to group the facts which appeared to be related with unwarped judgment and without prejudice, and thus to discover the foundation of the old institutions. Taken in this way, the study of the text and that of the facts, have a close relation one to the other, and the conclusions arrived at in definite stages, reinforce each other. It only remains to arrange systematically the observations made in the course of *this progressive two-fold study of literary and religious history.*[2]

The love poems which form the greater part of the *Kuo fêng* are drawn from an ancient stock of popular songs. *These songs were composed by means of poetical themes which originated in an assembly devoted to traditional improvisation. This was carried on by alternating choirs of young men and young women*

It seems to me that the first essential in methodical examination is to start from a critical consideration of all the data both in the work of observation, by which the facts are ascertained and verified, and in the theoretical elaboration of those finally accepted.

[2] A certain number of these observations, those, for example, concerned with poetic rhythm, or the origin or purpose of the exogamic rule, are given with the greatest generality. *It should be understood that the only intention is to bring out clearly what the Chinese facts may suggest* and to give direction to wider investigations bearing upon the problems concerned.

who engaged with one another in a contest in the course of the seasonal festivals of ancient peasant communities.

When they held their great periodical assemblies, the peasants of ancient China suddenly emerged from the seclusion of a monotonous private life to share in a solemn festival hallowed by tradition which was concerned with their noblest ideals. They left their little patch of ground, their quiet village and their loneliness to consecrate that federal under-standing which meant the security of each little group. They hallowed it by a supreme act of faith, by the most dread and efficient communion : they introduced the younger generation to public and sexual life simultaneously, thereby endowing the young people with the requisite status to become hostages themselves, to take part in the exchanges, thanks to which the matrimonial partnership could, in the course of home life, recall the compact of union and ensure its observance.

The authority of tradition, the solemnity of the festival, the importance of the rites and the number of those who took part in them, all combined to give to the holy orgy an unusual emotional force. How intense must have been the emotions animating the crowd! But also how complex, especially in those who took the principal parts in the rites.[1] Strangers owing to the behaviour proper to each sex and the characteristic dispositions of their families, thrust suddenly into each other's presence and made to take a leading part, a mysterious, unique part under the eyes and the direction of a whole people, the young people approached each other with minds charged with anxiety and hope, imbued with respect, suspicion, dread and caution, and yet compelled to follow the behests of unavoidable attraction.[2]

---

[1] Poetical language is a special form of expression corresponding to a special activity. Poetical expression always commands respect. It is suited to religious activities : poetry is the language of the prophets. The prophecies recorded in the *Tso Chuan* and by *Ssŭ-ma Chien* are nearly all in the form of songs improvised by inspired youths (T'ung Tzŭ). Cf. *SMC.*, iv, 275 ; i, 282 ; *Tso Chuan Hsi,* 5th year ; Legge, 148 ; Chao, 25th year, Legge, 709.

[2] Cf. the courting ceremony of the ball game as practised by the Thos and the Miao-tzŭ, concurrently with the poetical contest. See pp. 138 sq.

CONCLUSION

The force of these mixed and powerful emotions led them to face each other in a duel in the course of which their feelings sprang into life and finally expressed themselves. *They failed to find adequate expression in the meagre language of everyday life : for their true expression these solemn emotions demanded a solemn language, the language of poetry.*

Two choruses of young men and young women, in which each actor is overflowing with the most intense emotion, advance towards each other. Their opposition, their coming together, as their meaning becomes more and more apparent, force from their inmost beings an expression of the sentiments which have taken complete possession of them, which are manifested by their whole bearing, by gesture and by voice, by a gesticulated and spoken mime. Still strangers to each other, they stand face to face, the observed of a whole assembly ; the good repute of a whole family depends upon their demeanour. *Pricked on by emulation the two choirs engage in a tourney wherein both gesture and words have to respond to each other ;* so the arrows of opposed armies cross each other in the air. Each side in turn flashes its reply, just as two sides of players hurl the ball toward each other : no sooner does it return to the first side than it is flung back, to be again returned ; and this goes on till the game ends. In the same way, so long as the tourney lasts, the alternations of mimic improvisations are repeated ; this repeated alternation is the principle of the rhythm characteristic of the language of poetry.

The Chinese song, most simple in form, consists of a series of slightly modified couplets ; each couplet consists in the juxtaposition of two strictly correspondent phrases. The earliest poems are nothing but a sequence of distichs [1] and the

---

[1] Each distich is a couplet of two phrases, each with its own meaning and relating to the same general idea. The distichs appear actually as couplets of four verses alternately rhyming—the reason for this will be seen presently—but the two first verses of the couplet, and also the two last, are only in fact the two hemistichs of the same verse, for the thought is only completely expressed at the end of the associated verse. The pause is frequently indicated by a final particle. Cf. XXII, 2, 4, 6, 8, and LII, 2, 4 ; 14, 16 ; also XLVI, 6, 8.

distich is the elementary form of poetry. In reality, in order to express their sentiments, the actors who face each other gradually outline them with the help of such vocal gestures as accompany a figure in a ballet : thus they work out two symmetrical designs. These two designs, placed in opposition and similar, are composed of a number of practically equal elements : the two phrases forming the halves of a distich contain very nearly the same number of words.[1] On both sides of the design of the whole vocalizations and movements correspond : the yoked phrases are composed of words musically corresponding, the musical correspondence being more strongly emphasized in the rhyming words ending each phrase.[2]

The symmetrical elements of the design correspond in meaning : the words of the alternate sentences pair, and there is either parallelism or antithesis[3] between the pairs. In short, the opposing designs are like symmetrical curves with analogous functions defining the whole : the pairs of balancing words play similar syntactical parts in each phrase.[4] *Two phrases presenting such a system of correspondences form a couplet.*

The alternation of symmetrical gesticulatory actions results in the use of correspondences, which is the principle of versification ; while skilfully modified repetition of the distichs is the principle of poetical composition. But when the rules of the art of versification became fixed, another art came into being, that of using

---

[1] Each half of the distich is a phrase usually of eight words. The sense finishes at the eighth word (just as among the Lolos at the fifth : cf. Vial. *Les Lolos*, pp. 17–18). All are not always needed for the sense ; for the sake of symmetry padding is used, meaningless words introduced at the end (finals cf. No. XXII) or at the beginning (IX, 1–2).

[2] The rhyme is of the assonance type (cf. Vial, *Lolos*, p. 17) : it is often accented by employing a final particle. The ideal is that the sounds of the paired words should correspond musically, as in the school game of the Tui-tzŭ.

[3] For example, XLVI :—

In the south are lofty trees,	No one can rest beneath them.
Nan yu ch'iao mu	*pu k'o hsiu hsi*
By the Han are strolling girls,	But one may not solicit them
Han yu yu nü	*pu k'o ch'iu ssŭ*

[4] Same example : *yu* is an epithet like *ch'iao*, *Hai* is a final without meaning like *ssŭ*.

CONCLUSION

ready-made verses in more flexible compositions. This advance
was made the more easy by one fact. Each of the two
elements of a distich was composed of two parts : one described
the subject circumstanced by its relationship to the action
designed by the whole ; the other ultimately described the action
itself. The first parts of each of two elements correspond term
by term ; so also the second. Each exists as a whole in itself, so
completely indeed that one distich regularly rhymed could, by
marking the cæsuras, be regarded as a couplet of four verses
alternately rhyming.[1] *Henceforward it was no longer deemed
necessary that paired verses should follow each other.* Couplets
could be made by interpolating the verses of two distichs.
The art of composition gained in flexibility by the use of both
processes, although the fundamental principle was still the
repetition, gradually modified, of the same elements. Only this
repetition took place in a less restricted order and the poem
evolved two types. Sometimes [2] the repeated elements were
grouped into a refrain, while the invention of shades of difference,
reserved for the couplets, introduced therein a principle of
development sufficient to manifest the cadenced advance of
the idea. Sometimes [3] these gradually modified elements were
placed in the burden of the song in such fashion that each
couplet, taking up the development of the idea, somewhat
behind the preceding and leading it farther forward, carried
on the idea, if I may say so, in an echelon movement.

[1] Cf., for instance, LII,
> The Chên and the Wei have overflowed
> The youths and maidens come with orchids
where the real rhyme is the seventh word, a meaningless particle. And LXVI,
> So great is the breadth of the Han, it cannot be crossed by a ford.
> So vast is the river Chiang, it cannot be crossed in a boat.
where the real rhyme, being in the eighth word, a particle, the cæsura, marked by
another meaningless word (secondary rhyme) placed fourth, sharply divides the
subject, the great flow of water, from the action which is the basis of the verse,
the crossing.
[2] Cf. *The Han*, XLVI, *Grasshoppers of the Meadows*, LIX.
[3] Cf. *The Dead Hind*, LXIV ; *The Bamboo Stalks*, XLV ; *The Ospreys*, LVI.
The perfected form of this would be the *pantoum*. Skeat (*Malay Magic*, p. 483)
supplies evidence of the fondness of the Malays for these poetical contests.
Pantoums appear to be alternating songs.

FESTIVALS AND SONGS OF ANCIENT CHINA

The sentiments to which the contest, in which they took shape, gave expression in verse, were also, by this mimic tourney, presented in figurative form. Intense and collective, impersonal and complex, direct, earlier than any analysis, concrete in a superlative degree, simple emotions of the soul, *they only found adequate expression in the movements carried out by the alternating choirs.*

These movements are of two kinds. Sometimes elementary, they are simple gestures, utterances and body movements so closely connected that *the vocal gesture* retained for ever, in its short characteristic music, all the concrete flavour, all the summoning force of a whole representation.[1] Doubtless the chief effort of original invention for these poetical contests was directed toward finding [2] descriptive auxiliaries [3] ; the search for them has been of first importance in the formation of the Chinese volcabulary,[4] which is very rich in concrete expressions ; it has also been of first importance in the creation and history of ideographic writing [5] in which the ideogram

---

[1] Cf. p. 89 sqq. The comments affirm both the astonishingly concrete nature of these descriptive auxiliaries, which makes them untranslatable and impossible of analysis, and their great wealth, big with so much symbolism. For example, the expression *Kuan kuan*, cf. LVI, in *The Ospreys*, is enough to depict a certain fashion of flight and call by couples and, at the same time, evokes a whole series of sexual customs common to men and birds.

[2] Witness the number of variants existing ; see notes to the songs.

[3] A noteworthy feature of these auxiliaries is their formation from a redoubled vocal gesture. The same appears among the Lolo (cf. the expression *leu-leu*, in the first couplet of The Complaint of the Wife, see App. III) and the same may be said of the descriptive suffixes of the *Ewé* (cf. Lévy-Bruhl, *Les Fonctions mentales dans les sociétés inférieures*, p. 183 sqq.) always used in duplicated form. It might be interesting to inquire why. It is evident that the repetition of the vocal figure increases its intensity ; but why only doubled ? So far as Chinese is concerned one remark deserves to be recorded. Many are the doubled expressions in which an object is represented under two antithetical and conjoined aspects, under the aspect of the *Yin* and also under that of the *Yang* ; cf. App. II and *Shuo wên. BTKK. (HCCC.)*, 651b, p. 11, v°, and 653, p. 4, v°. Can it be that these vocal ideas were doubled because they were invented by a double chorus of men and women ? I suggest this hypothesis at all events : I am the more inclined to believe it because it is, above all, a matter of rhythm : the verses of the *Shih-ching* are mostly made up of doublets of two characters.

[4] Note, for example, the great number of terms for concrete sentimental states which all seem derived from primitive descriptive suffixes. Cf. p. 89 and the notes.

[5] I cannot help believing that the gestures, which formed an integral part of the expression found by men to represent objects, came to suggest and guide the growing

CONCLUSION

comes in to restore to the word, always associated with the thing
seen, the help of a sketch and of gestures which depict it. Some-
times, the image, more complex, appears from the organization
of rhythmical movements. Each of the figures delineated by
the alternating choruses, which are standing face to face, is like
a reply to the other side, and each can be substituted for that
which it repeats. Usually one of the two juxtaposed sentences
describes a phenomenon relative to persons, and is more directly
intelligible ; the other, describing the circumstances of that
phenomenon, or if one prefers it, the natural phenomena
in symmetry with it, seems to refer rather less directly to the
act illustrated by the whole.[1] As a result of the rhythm or,
if one prefers it, as the result of a figure of speech, one of these
two formulæ placed in apposition appears as the *symbolic double*
of the other : *a natural image seems to express indirectly and as by
allegory the human fact with which traditional experience associates
it.* By what seems very like artifice, the natural correspondences
seem to become something like images as we conceive them.
However, far from their invention depending upon a play of
fantasy aided by a developed system of syntax, the rhythmic effect
from which they proceed, which is the first principle of poetry,
does nothing but show, under various aspects which tradition
has consecrated, the mysterious bond between men and things.

Whence comes that virtue or that attraction with which
the allegory and the symbol are endowed ? Very early in their
history, as we know, the verses of the *Shih ching* were discovered
to be full of a profound meaning, which, as soon as it was
thoroughly understood, itself communicated virtue.[2] They

system of writing. I think also that if Chinese writing remained fundamentally
ideographic throughout the ages it was because the voice was insufficient wholly to
express the concrete ideas inherent in the words when it was not accompanied by
sketch or gesture. It is well known that a Chinese will often sketch with his
fingers the characters correspondng with the words he utters. Cf. Lévy-Bruhl,
Les Fonctions mentales, p. 167 sqq.

[1] As an example :—

> The Chên and the Wei have overflowed.
> The youths and maidens come with orchids.

[2] See p. 50 sqq., and p. 74 sqq.

213

spoke with a strange authority : songs of praise, their power made well-doing inevitable ; satires, their compelling force forbade evil. To say to a Princess : " Do your duty as a wife " is a simple piece of advice ; but to force her into the way of virtue one had only to quote: " In harmony the ospreys cry . . . in the river, on the rocks." [1] For these are symbolic words. Words have a more persuasive force when they are spoken in an indirect form ; and the ancient anthology from which it is taken gives to the sentence quoted a venerable air which is heightened yet more by the historical memories with which it is illustrated.[2] But not even that could enforce complete and immediate submission. How then is it that what seems to us a simple image has the force of a formula of constraint ? It is not a simple image, at least in the sense in which we apply the term : *in the themes of the improvised songs are engraved those correspondences which actually existed between the phenomena of Nature and human observances.* Hibernating animals, for example, seek their retreats when men retire into their dwellings [3] ; such regular recurrences show the ways of Nature under the guise of human customs and both are perceived as a unity. The correspondences inscribed in the poetical themes showed the unity of natural and social rules, and their authority came from this. Human observances were endowed with new majesty because their force seemed to penetrate into the domain of Nature. Natural events in their turn assumed a moral value and served as *emblems* for the rules of social life. By remaining within their dwellings men allowed animals to live through the winter season : and, when animals stopped up the entrances to their dens, they gave warning to men that it was time to adopt the habits suitable for winter. The governing principles in social life were not only manifested in human observances, but were inscribed on the formulæ which enjoined them, and these were equally

[1] *The Ospreys*, LVI, p. 106.
[2] For example, with regard to ospreys, the legendary memory of the virtues of the consort of King Wên.
[3] See p. 174 sqq.

CONCLUSION

powerful and imperative. *It was similarly in formulae as imperative and powerful as the emblematic themes that the natural inevitable facts of human habit were proclaimed.* As men's thoughts were brought to bear upon them, the significance of these allegorical formulæ grew richer and richer. Their fundamental sanctity made them suitable for avatars of every kind ; like the practices to which they corresponded, they were used to multiple ends, interpreted to meet new needs. Interpretation could work its will with them more easily than with actual observances ; and it proceeded to actual misinterpretation, which, indeed, became unavoidable as soon as the current morality differed too widely from that of the period in which the emblematic formulæ originated.[1] But the effectiveness of these diverted formulæ, of these elaborated allegories, remained constant, for, in their very shape, their character of natural correspondences was still evident.

These emblematic formulæ, with their constraining force, originated in the contests of courtesy. This fact may help towards an understanding of the meaning of the *proverb competitions* of which the *Shih ching* provides an example, though one of considerable obscurity.[2] In a competition of this kind, each of the opponents endeavours to establish a correspondence between the proposition which he hopes to make the successful one and a series of hallowed sayings which cannot be gainsaid without a certain suspicion of irreverence with regard to the stock of national wisdom.[3] He proceeds to prove this proposition by means of what I shall call *analogic rhythm* and over-

---

[1] See for example the symbolical interpretation of the poems LVI, LIX, and LXVII, B, in terms of the innovations in the marriage ritual of a noble.

[2] *The Dew on the Roads*, XI, see App. I. Cf. the competitions in poetical set phrases among the Malagasy. Perhaps *SMC.*, iv, 63, is an instance of homeric duel. It is noteworthy that it took place in the course of an aquatic festival.

[3] This method may take two forms. Sometimes the constraining force of parallel hallowed formulæ is used directly. This is reasoning by exact analogy (or by analogy professedly exact). Sometimes the force is used indirectly. This is the kind of reasoning by false analogy which takes the following form : If you maintain . . . you might just as well maintain (this or that absurd analogy). Reasoning by *irony, per absurdum*.

215

whelms his opponent beneath a host [1] of venerable formulæ. He whose formulæ are first exhausted is defeated, that is, he whose fund of traditional learning is less, who is unable to discover in the popular stock, valid proofs, an effective correspondence.[2] The all-important part played in the history of Chinese thought by what has been called the *Chinese sorites* [3] makes it clear that this is the main factor in the art of proof. The sorites consists of a chain of propositions, the correspondence of which is affirmed by the analogic rhythm with which they are elaborated. In the early natural correspondences, the formal bond established by analogic rhythm was nothing more or less than the natural and obvious expression of an internal bond resulting from the traditional juxtaposition, imposed, essential, of the facts expressed by the juxtaposed formulæ. Thereafter, this internal bond had to be taken for granted as soon as the rhythm manifested the logical bond which was definitely associated with it, its unmistakable sign, its clear manifestation. This is why *every correspondence, even when it is artificial, by the very power of the analogic rhythm* [4] *which serves to establish*

---

[1] The proverb competition assures victory to the competitor best provided with the logical armament supplied by the traditional fund of wisdom. It compels each of the opponents to develop his argument at length. This lavish treatment—*copia* is a quality which every orator finds necessary—is in itself a part of the proof, a logical part.

[2] In the competition in sayings, the art, in reasoning by analogy, consists in supplying analogies rich in resonance.

[3] See M. Masson-Oursel's contribution, Esquisse d'une théorie comparée du sorite, *Rev. de metaphysique et de morale*, Nov. 1912. See also *Rev. philos.*, July, 1917, and February, 1918. In my opinion M. Masson-Oursel is mistaken in only considering the sorites from the point of view of strictly formal logic. It was the real solidarity, the real relationship, between the formulæ brought together which constituted the strength of the primitive sorites. This solidarity was made manifest by the analogic rhythm of the elaboration. The formal bond, which at a later stage, became the essential element, was originally no more than the perceptible aspect of a real bond.

[4] When a Chinese author develops his thought in the form of a sorites, the development has always a strongly marked element of rhythm. Usually the rhythm is further accentuated by the employment of a connecting particle. The rhythm suggests the idea that the formulæ brought together have a definite relationship, and the connecting particle helps to make this impression more intense. The sorites is sometimes found in a more elaborate form. The concepts juxtaposed by formulæ similarly brought together are then related two by two and united by a connecting particle in such a way that the second formula takes over one of the concepts of the

it, unites the formulæ it brings together to such an intimate degree that a natural association between them comes to be assumed. Consequently, a proposition which is put forward for acceptance by the deliberate establishment, by analogic expansion, of a correspondence between it and certain hallowed formulæ, immediately takes over from those formulæ their character of traditional, sacred truth. This it does by assuming a solidarity which, although formal, is yet inherent in the nature of things. An opponent is challenged to deny the particular proposition which is inserted in the chain, without denying at the same time the most revered and most potent hallowed formulæ.

When the young people of a district were brought together for the tourney in which the future husband and wife were first to feel the birth of love, it was by invoking—like two advocates [1]—a double series of poetic precedents that they won their suit. They persuaded one another to obey the traditional rules which bade them unite, by weaving, as they stood face to face [2] a double chain of venerable analogies. A kind of mutual enchantment resulted, in course of time, from their twin litanies.[3] All they had to do was to sing to one another in turn the ancient love formulæ : they had only to repeat these formulæ with the slightest of shades of difference at each couplet ; their

preceding formula. The consequence of this is a kind of reasoning by progressive stages in which the primitive solidarity between the formulæ seems to be directly established between the elementary concept themselves. *The development then seems to prove not an equivalence between the formulæ, but relations of inclusion between the concepts.* See the magnificent example of a sorites at the end of the *Ta Chuan.* *Li chi* ; Couv., i, 787.

[1] See the *Dew on the Roads*, XI and App. I. The amorous disputations carried on in the form of alternating songs are called by the same name as juridical disputations. The duke of Shao is supposed to have heard such amorous disputations beneath a holy tree. Cf. *Shao nan,* 5 and 6.

[2] Among the Thos, the lovers are placed back to back during this poetical incantation. They turn round and face each other for the ball game. See p. 141, and App. III.

[3] Observers have remarked the monotony and long-drawn out nature of this sung courtship. Among the Thos, the gallant may be compelled to utter a long complaint and then to begin all over again. But he *always* ends by getting what he set out to get. Cf. App. I. In certain European songs we find a kind of argumentative element and something resembling a litany. The *Magali* type of song is an example. A Chinese example is given in App. I, p. 250.

improvisation was entirely traditional. Their inventive genius was not governed by any originality of feeling or of choice ; it was not ſtimulated by the necessity of gaining a new cause by new arguments. Their cause was an old one, and its result determined ; the various ſtages were definitely fixed in advance. It was sufficient for the young people to play their part in the conteſt. If they allowed themselves any improvisations, *these improvisations came simply from the rhythm of the dance*, and hardly ever went beyond the discovery of a few concrete images, a few vocal geſtures.

When society changed its form and love, become more free,[1] developed into a personal sentiment, then and only then, personal invention modified the art of the song. As manners changed firſt in noble circles, it was a court poetry [2] which took the place of popular poetry.

This court poetry took over from its predecessor the rules of the poetic art. Still incapable of developing vocal geſtures for itself, at leaſt it drew effeſts of correspondence from the rhythm and so created new images.[3] In order to develop an idea it enshrined the traditional themes in a more supple type of composition.[4] It was often content, by means of a slight

[1] The earlieſt poems of the personal type are all on the theme of the deserted wife. Cf. LXVI and *Pei fêng*, 10 ; Couv., 39. This is because the feudal organization of the polygamous household (cf. p. 204) implied the play of rivalry between wives, and so the appearance of personal feelings. This allowed fantasy a place in the field of love.

[2] Court poetry certainly, but that of rural, peasant courts. The Chinese lordships were invariably village lordships ; the manners of the nobles were ſtill ruſtic. It was this faſt which made the transition possible. The majority of the songs grouped under the heading *Village Loves* muſt have originated in such an environment. See, for example, the songs of the *serenade* type. Cf. XLII, notes. (For serenades in Formosa, see App. III.) In Japan, it would seem that this court poetry developed along original lines. There is the example of the feudal cuſtom of the poetic duel in a kind of court of love for the conqueſt of a beauty. (See App. III and *Kojiki* Chamberlain's trans., p. 530.) This was an *adaptation of the primitive tourney to feudal manners*. There we have a body of material which would be of great intereſt in a ſtudy of the origins of *courtly love*.

[3] Cf. *The Little Stars*, LXVII.

[4] See p. 133 sqq. These traditional themes provided the essential landscape of the poetic scenes. The use of ancient themes, cuſtomarily known as *literary allusions*, has always played an important part in the poetic art of China. This is because, juſt as the rhythm charaſteriſtic of the poetic form originated in the organization of the ancient conteſts, so the background capable of awakening the

CONCLUSION

modification, to introduce an allusion which gave an air of circumstance to an old development.[1] Apart from this element of topicality, these learned productions are hardly to be distinguished from popular songs. They were preserved in the same collection by the same body of interpreters.

It would be difficult to account for the collection of these popular songs at a remote period if something of their sacred character had not continued to be associated with them. Many of them remained attached to the marriage rites,[2] more or less well understood according as the rites had more or less changed. In this case, the ritual function of the songs secured respect for them. Others survived because, thanks to the vagueness of their language and the relationship between the notions of love and of friendship,[3] thanks especially to the symbolic plasticity of the poetic formulæ,[4] it was possible, by making use of the constraining power that was in them, to employ the songs, in the guise of satires or panegyrics, as exhortations with the power to reform morals.

---

kind of emotion characteristic of poetry was taken from the scene of the festivals. Consequently, the most hallowed images, far from losing their savour, best retained their power. In its rhythmic forms and in its emotional material, Chinese poetry preserved a traditional air. The hallowed landscape did not impose itself only upon the poetic imagination. It is to be found in painting. Holy places were a favourite subject of the artist, and it is not unreasonable to assume that the characteristic features of the sacred landscape gave a definite style to landscape painting in general. It is certain that, by looking at the painting of a hallowed landscape, the beneficial results of the same influence as that which emanated from the verses of the *Shih ching* were secured. To possess the reproduction of such a landscape is the same thing as possessing, in one's own home, the assistance of a beneficent influence. This nfluence might still be secured, when it was not possible to make a pilgrimage, if the typical features of the holy place were reproduced naturally but on a smaller scale. This may perhaps be an explanation of the success, both in China and Japan, of that art of gardening which, by the employment of tiny rocks, dwarf trees, and rare plants, reproduces, in minute proportions, the characteristic aspect of those High Places where the religious genius and the artistic genius of the race awoke together.

[1] *SMC.*, iv, 231. Note the importance of geographical localizations. To seek a friend upon such and such a river = to seek the friendship of the lord of such and such a country. Cf. LIVB.

[2] Especially the poems interpreted as evidence of the noble practice of post-nuptial abstinence. LVI, LIX, LXVIIB.

[3] See pp. 29 and 194 sqq.

[4] For example, *The Gourd*, L.

FESTIVALS AND SONGS OF ANCIENT CHINA

The old songs, invested with a new purpose and a new meaning, were sung at courts where poems were being produced which differed very little from themselves. When collected they took the form of a loose anthology which became a unity only when all the poems it included were interpreted in accordance with uniform principles. It was asserted that, like those which were being produced at the moment, all had a learned origin and all possessed the character of counsels of political morality. The courtiers who, at the seignorial council, made use of the symbolic power of the poetic formulæ, definitely fixed the interpretation of the songs when they wrote those collections of Harangues and " Gestes " [1] which they intended to become the basis of their Prince's education. In these collections they put a number of quotations taken from the songs which they associated to a definite historical event.[2] From their time onwards, the Anthology itself, now that it was made to serve the purpose of education, took on the appearance of a *Classic*. The hallowed character of the poems which composed it passed on to their interpretation and this became irrevocable, beyond the reach of profane hands.

Such is the history of the document.[3] It is only one aspect of the history of the facts upon which the text is based.

---

[1] Such as the *Kuo yü*, the *Lieh nü ch'uan*, the *Tso chuan*. The differentiation of historical collections in collections of harangues or of " gestes " is Chinese.

[2] All the stories in the *Lieh nü chuan* end with a quotation from the *Shih ching*. Note the analogy of biblical quotations. An allegorical theme is used as a text in such a way that its capacity to drive home a moral or its value as an instrument of proof is carried over to the development of the idea put forward.

[3] A systematic study of the *Shih ching* and Chinese poetry in its earliest form should take into account the fact that several types of poetical composition have developed from the forms invented in the tourneys. So were created : (1) *A poetry of the calendar*, concerned with the relation of different forms of work to definite days. *The Seventh Month* (XXI, and p. 53) is the best example of this type. It has provided material for the sayings later set out in peasant calendars. (2) *A prophetic, gnomic, and satirical poetry*, of which Ssu-ma Ch'ien, and the *Tso chuan* afford numerous examples. (Cf. *SMC.*, v, 29 ; iv, 275). It seems to have been the work of young people only. (3) *A panegyric poetry*, of a Pindaric type, based on heroic legends, and genealogical (*Shang sung*, 3 ; Couv., 462 ; *Ta ya*, 25 ; Couv., p. 347) ; on the nuptial eulogy (*Ta ya*, 3, 7 ; Couv., 403, and *Wei fêng*, 3 ; Couv., 65) ; the commemoration of investiture (*Ta ya*, 3, 5 ; Couv., 396) ; commemoration of the founding of seignorial towns (cf. Couv., 360). (4) *A ritual poetry*, consisting

Conclusion

The festivals of Ancient China are great assemblies which mark the tempo of the seasonal rhythm of social life. They correspond to short periods during which people come together and social life is intense. These periods alternate with long periods in which people are scattered and social life is practically at a standstill. At each of these assemblies, the pact of union which forms the little local groups into one community receives new sanction in an orgy regulated by tradition. *The orgy, in which the exclusiveness of these usually firmly sealed groups is relaxed as the result of a collective incitement, allows to each one of them a possibility of exchange.* These exchanges, concerned with things but mainly with individuals, put each of the groups in possession of pledges, and, especially, of hostages, which form a permanent guarantee of loyalty to the fundamental pact. *Matrimonial alliances are the basis of the system of guarantees between confederated groups.* Consequently, the essential feature of the ancient festivals is the sexual orgy which makes possible matrimonial exchanges. When they take place, all the unmarried young men and women, that is to say, those who have not yet come to take their part in the business of the community,[1] are brought together that they may receive, together with sexual initiation, the power to enter into the matrimonial bonds which, through them, will maintain the solidarity of the federated groups. *The festivals, then, have the appearance of festivals of youth. The most striking rite is a tourney of dance and song, a rhythmic contest, in which love springs up between those predestined by the traditional rules of the community to marry.*

The nature of these festivals is explained by the very forms of ancient society. They do not, because of the principle inherent in them, pass beyond the circle of human interests; they even appear to have no other aim than the regulation of

---

of festival songs (*Pin fêng*, 1 ; Couv., 160 ; ibid., pp. 439, 441), or of temple hymns (cf. Couv., 459, 460). (5) An elementary form of dramatic poetry, developed out of the primitive tourney itself, with its alternating choruses, interrupted, perhaps, by improvisations in dialogue, and the mimicry of its dances.

[1] An important feature of these festivals is that they are festivals of initiation. See p. 198 and the note.

sexual relations, but they mark, in fact, a unique moment in social life : *that in which, suddenly brought to a pitch of extreme tension, it is able, by its almost miraculous intensification, to inspire in those from whom it emanates an irresistible faith in the efficacy of the practices they carry out in common.* The members of the little local groups, when, by a sudden collective effort, they find anew that community which is their supreme strength, are stupified under the impression that they are suddenly attaining that ideal of harmony and lasting peace which, at that moment, appears to them with renewed prestige. Each individual, in his enthusiasm, imagines that the virtue of the actions in which he is taking part is unlimited, that it passes beyond the circle of human life and extends to all the universe. It seems to him that the continuousness, the harmony of the world, are a consequence of the social stability and social cohesion which he feels to be his own work. Thereafter, although the general activity is fully comprehensive and is displayed in very diverse forms during the course of the festivals, its extraordinary intensity, the prestige of its solemn manifestation, and, above all, its success and its far-reaching power, distinguish this strange activity from that of everyday life. *It appears to be of a sublime and peculiar order, as appertaining to the religious order.* The practices of the ancient festivals, simple gestures of a collectivity inspired by hope, are sacred practices ; they are the elements of a cult. Similarly, the feelings of confidence in the virtue of these gestures which are capable, it is thought, of exercising a decisive influence upon the destinies of man and of the natural environment in which he lives, are the foundation of the beliefs from which has developed the dogmatic basis of Chinese religion and Chinese thought.

Thanks to the study of the ancient festivals, it is possible to describe the form of Chinese society at a remote age. *The inhabitants of a district formed a community, a fundamental grouping which, in consequence of the division of labour, was broken up into elementary groups of two kinds,* social life being governed by a rhythmic system of organization. The first principle of distribution is the technical division of labour between the sexes. Men and women form two corporations, each of which, at the due time, is busied in those works which are appropriate to it. *Each sexual corporation has its own kind of life, its own habits and customs, and these set it in opposition to the other corporation.* The other principle is that of the geographical distribution of the soil. The members of the community share the soil between them by families, and, *in each family group, living separated from the others, there develops a spirit of particularism.* In each domestic domain, the men and women of a local group pursue their occupations independently. During the fine season, the period for the hard work in the fields, which is the business of the men, the women have only to gather mulberry leaves in the orchards and look after the silk-worms in the houses. During the season in which the severity of the climate permits no work in the fields, the men have only the simple task of repairing the buildings. This is the dead season, but, during it, the women are fully employed making thread and weaving. *In this way, the sexes succeed one another, working according to a system based on the alternating rhythm of the seasons.*

Diversity of occupations draws a line of demarcation between men and women even in winter when they are together. During the summer, when they hardly see one another, this distinction is at its maximum. On the other hand, it is in winter that the demarcation is strongest between the local groups which are then confined to their family villages. *But, throughout the year, isolation is the rule, the monotonous life of little groups restricted to everyday private concerns. There is no such thing as social life except at the moments when the alternation of the kinds of life is marked. These are the occasions for a general assembly in which the community recovers its former unity.* The spring assembly has a more strongly marked character of *sexual orgy* because it serves to introduce the season in which the antagonism of the sexes is at its keenest. That of autumn is rather an *orgy of eating* because it comes before the period in which the isolated local groups, by laying up stores of supplies, will be able to strengthen their independence.[1] *In both, competitions and tourneys depict the system upon which the community is organized, and imprint its image on every heart.* Here we have the essential function of these festivals, unique occasions of social life in a society wherein the density of population is too weak to maintain permanently that agglomeration which would make possible the daily exercise of a governmental power.

The most important of the ancient festivals of concord were those of spring. They were those in which sexual rites occupied most place. Thanks to these rites, the antagonism of the sexual corporations vanished for a moment, and, by the bringing together of its two parts, the fundamental group recovered its cohesion. The sexual approach, which has as its aim the union of a couple, and by which is secured the fusion in a single whole of parts antithetical yet closely bound together, is essentially a principle of alliance : it is able to bring about cohesion between elements peculiarly heterogeneous. Hence its use. Sexual union, in a homogeneous group, has no value : endogamy would be a contradiction in terms. So, *when a division of labour based on geographical considerations reinforces the working of a division based upon technical considerations ; when the structure of the basic group implies not only a division into sexual corporations, but also a division into local groups, allied indeed, but distinguished by a certain specific character, each elementary group within which, its homogeneity being complete, matrimonial alliance would be an absurdity, refrains from making use of this principle of cohesion except to mark its solidarity with the neighbouring groups.* It is constrained to practise *exogamy*, and, at the same time, only to take part in matrimonial exchanges *within the community*, to the advantage of the common union.[2]

---

[1] See the analysis of the festival of the Pa Cha, p. 168 sqq.

[2] The theoretical importance of this remark lies in the fact that, if it is correct, it shows that every study of exogamic regulations will be vitiated so long as it only takes into account their negative aspect. The prohibition of marriage within a group goes hand in hand with the prohibition of marriage outside another group. This leads to an obligation to marry within a certain definite circle. In other words, there is a circle of relations within which *connubium* exists, and in which marriage is obligatory. *Exogamy is the negative side of positive matrimonial obligations.*

Conclusion

The potent results of the sexual rites explain the extent of their character of dread. They are able to bring together in a brief communion people who ordinarily live apart, who are usually filled with antipathy for one another. It is a dramatic moment for the individual : then love awakens, then poetry is born. It is a terrible moment for the social body whose future and prosperity are at stake. There is no other act which it is so important for the community to supervise. Both sexual initiation and betrothal take place before all, controlled by the collective body in accordance with the traditional rules. Any unlawful association between the sexes would bring about a general disturbance of social relations. Marriage, therefore, is strictly regulated : no place is left in it for fantasy or personal choice. *At the proper moment, an order which is issued by all*[1] *imposes upon the new members of the community compulsory feelings of love in conformity with the system of social organization.* Between individuals of different sexes these feelings are analogous to those of the friendship[2] which compulsorily unites the members of neighbouring groups.

The sexual tourneys are the most important of the practices which the vague faith with which the assembly is surging adorns with that efficacious power peculiar to religious acts. But, taken as a whole, the varied activity of the crowd was a religious activity. All its gestures were the elements of a cult, but *of a comphrehensive cult in which each practice, far from having a definite purpose,*[3] *did no more than express, in different ways, the feeling of the success of the social enterprise.* In ancient times the cult presents the same features as the social activity. Like the latter, it is concentrated in time and space, limited to the times of the assemblies, *to the festival periods,* attached to the place where these reunions took place, *the holy place.*

---

[1] This idea materialized in the conception of the great intermediary presiding over the general celebration of marriages, and in that of a divinity who acts as patron at this festival. See p. 202 sqq.

[2] Hence the fundamental relationship of the ideas of love and friendship between which the language does not distinguish.

[3] See p. 163 sqq.

Like it again, it emanates equally from all the members of the community; there is no distinction between the faithful and the officiant; it is just possible to say—since all activity implies both action and reaction—that all in turn play each of these two parts.[1]

In these festivals, which took the place of all other types of worship, all the earliest beliefs originated. First, the idea that religious practices possess an efficacy, which, peculiar and undefined, goes beyond human interests strictly so called. As soon as the Chinese began to believe that their cultural actions determined the course of natural phenomena, they pictured to themselves the course of nature on the model of the activity of the festivals. As, in their assemblies, they strove to realize the benefits of the social order, they conceived also in them the idea of the natural order. As they came to picture to themselves, after the manner of their practices, the rules from which order was to spring, they imagined that nature, since it followed certain customs, followed customs analogous to the social rules of which they themselves had just become conscious.[2] To sum up, *the origin of the principles which, in Chinese thought throughout the ages, govern the course of the world, is to be discovered in the structure of society in ages long past, or, more exactly, in the representation of this structure afforded by the practices of the ancient festivals.*

1. The world is governed by the *Yin* and the *Yang*. These are the two primary categories of thought. By virtue of a bipartite system of classification, all things belong either to the *Yin* or to the *Yang*, are of one kind or the other. But these are two concrete categories, two cosmogonic principles. The *Yin* and the *Yang*, the female principle and the male principle, bring about the harmony of the world by coming together, a coming together conceived upon the model of sexual union.

---

[1] The choirs placed face to face sing in turn. In the same way, the arrangement of the festival of the Pa Cha has an antithetical character, and an alternating rhythm governs the order of the ritual acts.

[2] See the analysis of the festival of the Pa Cha, p. 168 sqq.

CONCLUSION

As we have seen, all the members of the social body belong to one or the other of two sexual corporations, and the order of society depends upon the collaboration, according to a definite rhythm, of these antithetical groupings. In the festivals during which the system of social organization becomes evident to the eye at the same time as it comes into being, each individual sees the general harmony proceed from a contest in which a chorus of men is set in opposition to a chorus of women, a contest which culminates in the union of the sexes. He then imagines *that all life results from the antithetical activity, the closely knit activity, of two sexual groups which divide the world between them and come together in union at definitely regulated times.* That is why, to the Chinese, the principles of classification are also real principles—that is why the categories of thought are concrete and have the validity of cosmogonic principles—that is why *the two kinds in which all creatures are divided appear as two cosmogonic principles possessed of sex.*

2. Space, in Chinese thought, is not a simple extension, resulting from the juxtaposition of homogeneous elements, an extension whose parts, all qualitatively similar, are capable of being imposed one upon another. On the contrary, it is an organized whole, composed of extensions of different kinds, male and female, *Yin* or *Yang*, which are placed face to face ; it is a grouping of extensions set front to front. Each of the sexual corporations had a place set apart for its particular work, that the proper distance might be observed. The men went to work in the sunlight of the fields ; the women in the shade of the orchards or under cover of the houses. Particularly on the ground where the festivals were held, each corporation, to avoid all contact with the other, had to have a definite place set aside for it. In the valleys, on the slopes of the holy place, the men placed themselves on the sunny side, the women in the shade.[1] The masculine position, the *adret*,

[1] I must confess that no text, for obvious reasons, expressly states that the men and the women were placed in the positions I have attributed to them. But see App. III, pp. 262 and 267, where valuable information is given by Legendre and Colquhoun.

227

was *Yang*; the feminine position, the *hubac*, was *Yin*,[1] or rather it was the *Yin* and the *Yang*. The words whose primitive meaning was ' adret ' and ' hubac ' were definitely chosen to designate the two concrete categories, a certain indication that the distribution of the members of society and of all things into two groups was first perceived under its spatial aspect. It was conceived with the assistance of the spectacle afforded by the distribution of the actors in the festivals. Consequently, the category of space was placed under the dependence of the essential categories of *Yin* and *Yang*. The existence of two kinds of extension is admitted. This is not all. The Chinese idea of space was derived from the appearance of the holy place at which the tourney was held, or rather, from the appearance of the ballet figure formed by the two opposing groups of men and women. *As the evolutions of the two opposing choruses outlined a figure of which all the elements, corresponding unit to unit, and face to face, contributed to give one significance to the whole, space was considered as a definite whole composed of surfaces of contrary kinds brought face to face.*[2] Finally, too many rhythmic sensations and visualized impressions of movement remained incorporated in this representation of space for it not to have a tendency to relate itself with that of time.

3. Time, for the Chinese, is not a monotonous duration made up of a succession of qualitatively similar moments according to a uniform movement. On the contrary, it seems to them to be constituted by the repeated alternation of two periods of opposite kinds, *Yin* or *Yang*, male or female,

---

[1] To convey the original meaning of the words *Yin* and *Yang*, I make use of two terms borrowed from those in use in Alpine districts. Yin = hubac = *ad opacum* = shady slope, north of the mountain, south of the river. Yang = adret = *ad rectum* = sunny slope, south of the mountain, north of the river. Such having been the primary meaning of the words *Yin* and *Yang*, it seems to me impossible (granted that the *Yin* is specifically feminine and the *Yang* masculine) that the place for the women was not on the ' hubac ', and the place for the men on the ' adret '.

[2] Hence a very peculiar notion of the Centre, conceived as a point of convergence of antithetical forces, brought together at a radiant influx. There *would seem to be a connection between the idea of a centre and that of a holy place, of an ancestral centre.* In Chinese, the idea of centre calls up those of concord and harmony.

corresponding time for time. The sexual corporations, in order to preserve their independance, divided the work of the year between them. One season belonged to the men for their work in the fields, another to the women for their work at home, and both sexes succeeded one another alternately. During the festivals it was especially necessary to organize this alternation of the activities of the sexes, in order to avoid a confusion of the activities of the sexes. In the contest, the choirs of men and the choirs of women answer each other in turn. The time of the festival is taken up by the repeated alternation of symmetrical musical periods corresponding time for time. *The idea of a series of periods coupled and defined by the alternating song of male or female voices is at the root of the Chinese conception of time, which considers it no more than the alternating rhythm of the concurrent activity of the Yin and the Yang.*[1]

4. Neither time nor space, since both are subject to the separation of the *Yin* and *Yang* categories, forms a homogeneous whole. There are two kinds of extension and two kinds of duration. Durations and extensions of a contrary kind are in opposition, whereas a duration relates itself to an extension of the same kind. This relationship, by pairs,[2] of the notions concerning space and time is easily appreciated when we know that the concept of both has shaped itself according to the idea presented to the mind by a mimed scene, in which the voice and the gestures of two opposing choirs of contrasted type, expressing the same rhythm, a moving figure corresponded to each musical period. *Hence the close association of the principles of alternative correspondence and of symmetry of position which are the basis of time and space.* These principles are only a dual consequence of the necessity of giving a definite and appropriate part to each group of actors of different kind during the festivals. But the contest is only a dramatic representation of the social

---

[1] The critical points at which the alternating rhythm changes, the moments of transition between the two kinds of life—*the times of festival, are conceived as a reunion, a sexual coming together, a rendezvous of the Yin and the Yang.* See p. 127 and notes.

[2] Winter, night, north. Summer, day, south, etc.

structure of long past ages in which the division of labour between the sexes was the primordial fact. Society is split up into two sexual corporations. All things belong either to the *Yin* group or the *Yang* group. The collaboration and union of the sexes assure social production and the increase of the group : the *Yin* and the *Yang* unite sexually and are the original creators. Men work in the sun in the fields ; women in the houses. The *Yang* is the creating principle of sunny slopes, of the South, of light ; the *Yin* of shady slopes, of the North, of darkness. The work of men, which is the main work, is at its intensest in the fine season, the period when farmers spread over the whole country : the *Yang* is the principle of summer, of work. It is a principle of expansion.[1] Women carry on their occupations at the period when human activity is least intense, when everyone lives in his own dwelling, pushed back upon himself : the *Yin* is the principle of the dead season, of winter ; it is a principle of withdrawal, of inertia, of activity turned inwards and become latent. So, we see, *the ancient rules of the division of labour which regulated social activity, provided thought with principles of order. These were concrete principles, active principles which served as a directing plan to the conception of the world and seemed to preside in a real manner over natural evolution.*[2]

[1] See the old calendar preserved in the *Shu ching* and Ssŭ-ma Ch'ien. Cf. p. 165, and notes, and App. II.

[2] I may here put forward briefly the hypothesis to which this work has led. A close analysis brings us to consider the *Yin* and the *Yang* as a *pair of group-forces, endowed with sex, standing in a frontal relation to one another, alternating.* It may be shown that the organization of the contests is sufficient to account for all the constitutive elements of these complex ideas. Such is the proof of the hypothesis that these fundamental conceptions have their origin in the primitive festivals of China, a logical proof and, in my opinion, basic. The state of the documents does not allow us to bring forward a proof of historical order of equal value ; there is no text which says expressly that when the alternating choirs took up their positions facing one another in the sacred valleys, the girls were on the shady slope and the boys on the sunny slope. But, if it had not been so, the Chinese words which originally meant ' adret ' and ' hubac ' could never have had the fortune they have had. It is perfectly comprehensible if we accept the contrary suggestion.

Besides, there is a decisive reason why we should admit that the position of the sexes in these tourneys was that which our hypothesis requires. We see clearly why this arrangement was adopted. It is inconceivable that the division of labour,

CONCLUSION

An important date in the history of Chinese civilization is that of the foundation of seignorial towns. Society changed its structure when the increased density of the population made possible the existence of permanent agglomerations.

We find no trace of a town not governed by a lord, and the beginning of a feudal dynasty is always marked by the foundation of a town.[1] A permanent agglomeration, indeed, first makes it possible for men to have daily relations with one another. When social activity is a feature of everyday life, festivals which, at considerable intervals, renew the sense of the benefits of social organization, are no longer sufficient to maintain order. Control at every instant becomes a necessity : men brought together by life in towns need a government. The lord who governs becomes the principle of the social order just as the festivals used to be ; his governmental power is invested with that same august character which was a feature of the ancient festivals. It is endowed with a regulative virtue whose action extends to men and to things. The holiness of the chief radiates all around him. It penetrates those of

as it was apportioned between the sexes, was not accompanied by representations relating the women on the one hand to the gloomy season and the shady places in which they performed their tasks and, on the other hand, the men to broad daylight and the sunny days on which they worked. As a direct consequence of the elementary division of labour there would be a predisposition to place the choirs of girls on the shady side and those of the boys on the sunny side.

The concrete principles of classification were originally conceived from a spatial point of view, but the range of the image which formed the directing plan at their conception was determined by the primary fact of an organization of labour based upon a rhythm alternating between two sexual corporations. The Yin and the Yang which, at first, seem to be categories into which the different species fit themselves, are essentially *two groups possessed of sex whose rhythmical activity presides over the creation of all things.* There is a further confirmation of our hypothesis in the fact that it takes into account, not only all the constitutive elements of the notions which we are trying to explain, but also their relation to one another and the rank which they assume. Further authority might be secured for it by reference to the studies of comparative sociology. MM. Durkheim and Mauss, in their authoritative work upon primitive systems of classification, have pointed out the similarity between the Chinese system of classification and the systems employed by certain primitive peoples, for which the documentary material available permits us to assume an origin analogous to that implied by our hypothesis. See *Année sociologique*, vol. vi.

[1] Note that when a dynasty begins to realize that its power is waning and wishes to renew its mandate, it tries to make sure of success by establishing a new capital. See *Shih ching* ; Couv., 360.

his subjects who come into closest contact with him and confers upon them fitness to exercise governmental functions. In this way is created a body of nobility consisting of officials. The holiness of the chief extends to his residence. This becomes a holy place where assemblies are held, where exchanges of every kind take place. The lord builds temples there, he sets up markets there. Around himself, henceforth, human activity localizes itself as it formerly concentrated itself in the holy place of the assemblies. Similarly, this activity extends throughout the whole year, though it still retains something of its periodic nature. The gatherings at the court at which vassals pay their homage, the fairs held at the market, still, by taking place at stated times, give an element of rhythm to social life, but, generally speaking, life has now taken on a new character of permanence, and, for this reason, all its institutions are modified.

The opposition of the sexes continued to be one of the cardinal rules of society : it took a new form. The activity of the males, particularly of those in close attendance upon the lord, lost nothing of its nobility. Quite the contrary. But while the men were frequently summoned to meetings at the court, the women were normally excluded from them. They lived in the seclusion of the gynæceum,[1] constantly occupied in their household duties, kept aloof from the solemnities of public life. *The opposition between the sexes, which remained considerable, seemed to be determined by a difference of value between man and woman.* Sexual contact, which more and more inspired fear, was dreaded because the man, when he approached a woman, seemed to compromise his august character. As soon as woman was cut off from public life, it was felt that she was too impure to have any right to share in it. The seclusion in which she lived, which appeared to be imposed upon her because of this impurity, became stricter

---

[1] The house remained the concern of the women. The man ascribes to himself the domain of everything outside the house. The women are confined in the gynæceum. See *Li chi, Nei tsê* ; Couv., i, 659.

and ſtricter. The practices which accompanied sexual union were considered so many remedies intended to combat the fatal influence which emanated from the woman ; sexual rites disappeared from the religious ceremonies, and traces of them are only to be found in those ceremonies which have more of a magic character.[1] Finally, women no longer took part in public worship, except in rare inſtances, survivals of some importance however, as, for example, when they appeared as prieſtesses of the High Places.[2] The only other part they played was in the worship of anceſtors, and this was a semi-private worship.[3]

By a symmetrical evolution, marriage practically ceased to be a public concern. While the old communities had, to all intents and purposes, only a domeſtic policy and that, so to speak, inalterable, the lords developed a syſtem of diplomacy with varied and changing purposes. They made use of the matrimonial alliance to build up diplomatic connections, to aid them in their ſtruggles for influence. Consequently, at leaſt in noble circles, matrimonial unions, inſtead of being imposed by traditional rules, come to depend upon the momentary policy of the head of the family. *Marriages, inſtead of being contracted in a solemn ceremony, under the control of the whole community, are entered upon at the beheſt of political expediency,* at a time determined by the requirements of diplomacy and only when the necessary precautions have been taken to ward againſt the danger of sexual acts.

Unions contracted outside the traditional circle of allies, especially those which did not observe the exogamic rule, were ſtill considered disaſtrous. In them were discerned the deeper causes of the ruin which overtook lordships. But the marriage of the lord was of greater importance in itself than all the marriages in his country. As all the hallowed powers once set free in the feſtivals now seemed to be concentrated

---

[1] For example, the magic rites to bring rain. Cf. *Li chi*, Couv., ii, 339.
[2] Cf. Ssŭ-ma Ch'ien, Chav., iii, 452.
[3] The miſtress of the house plays a leading part in this. It is well to note the precautions which muſt be taken to avoid contact with her. Cf. *Li chi*, Couv., ii, 339.

in the virtue of the lord, so the marriage of the chief now appeared to have as much influence on the national life as the general celebration of marriages had formerly possessed.[1] The gynæcea of the lords, in which, in the form of quarrels due to personal love and jealousy, the struggles for influence characteristic of feudal diplomacy had their repercussion, appeared to be so many centres of anarchy whence disorder and social instability spread. As the nature of woman was considered fundamentally pernicious, it was considered that the wife of the prince would ruin the state unless the virtue of her husband was strong enough, by the exercise of its sovereign influence, to ensure that she should change her nature and become worthy to be the regulator of the manners of the country.

As soon as a nobility came into existence, and, with it, noble manners, the feelings of contempt which kept women secluded and remote from every form of public life, the fear inspired by contact with a woman, became motives strong enough to degrade the festivals of youth to the level of popular customs.[2] Besides, the functions which these festivals had formerly fulfilled were now attributed to the lord. All the multiple beneficent power of the festivals had originally been incorporated in the places where they were traditionally celebrated. It was from these places that harmony between the citizens, the happiness and fruitfulness of marriages, the prosperity of the year, had seemed to issue. They governed the life both of men and of nature, giving children to the households, rain and sun to the crops. Everything seemed to spring from their tutelary power : the faithful believed that they themselves were descended from these *ancestral centres.* The most direct descendants, those whom a hallowed genealogy permitted to bear the name of the great ancestor, formed a race elect, a mighty race, *whose chiefs shared between them by a kind of collegiality with the holy place, the virtue which*

---

[1] See the commentaries relating to the marriage of the Prince in *Li chi* ; Couv., ii, 367, and the comments to the *Ospreys*, lvi.
[2] This is the tradition of the Chou li and of Chêng Ki'ang Ch'eng. See p. 126.

CONCLUSION

confers fitness to govern men and things.   They maintained this virtue by the cult they paid to the holy place, they fed it with the homage which, through them, the faithful brought. But, when they had become heads of a permanent government, they needed, to reinvigorate their controlling power, a more direct cult, one more a matter of everyday life than the periodical festivals of mountains and streams had been. Specialized in religious practices, surrounded by a body of specialists, they ended by setting up distinctions in the all-inclusive activity of the earlier ages.   In this way they prepared the way for a breaking up of the original cult and found means to set up in their towns the different temples to which they could frequently go to give themselves a new lease of authority. The holy places remained the *external soul of their power*; *they shared their fortunes*, some, accompanying a seignorial race in its fall, became simple places of popular pilgrimage; others, with the rise of a dynasty, became the object of a national worship,[1] which, as religious thought brought about the discrimination, was addressed sometimes to the Mountain, sometimes to the River.[2]

There was no lord who had not a town, no seignorial town which had not its market, its temple of the ancestors, its altar of the god of the soil.[3]   These were the urban successors to the rural holy place.   In the market took place the exchanges which gave the air of a fair to the festivals of youth.   It is worthy of note that the market-place continued to be the place of rendezvous,[4] as though exchanges in goods could not be carried out without commerce in people.   The ceremonies at the temple of the ancestors made manifest the relations established between

[1] See, in Ssŭ-ma Ch'ien (Chav., vol. iii, p. 422) the attempts made by the lords of Ch'in to associate themselves to the holy places, and ascribe to them a national cult.

[2] For example, the cult of T'ai Shan. Cf. Chavannes, *le T'ai Chan*. See *Shih ching*; Couv., p. 457.

[3] See in the *Shih ching*, the odes commemorating the foundation of towns. Couv., pp. 403 and 360.

[4] Cf. poems LXIII and LXVI. Note that it is in the southern outskirts of the town, the place where exchanges always took place, that the festival of Kao Mei was held.

the members of human society. The ancestors are the guardians of the social order : from them is asked the *Mandate* which gives authority to make the most important decisions of life ; marriages and alliances are contracted under their control ; through their intervention children are granted.[1] The god of the soil, though attenuated and removed from his original environment, is the direct heir to the hallowed power of the holy place. The latter manifested itself in the wealth of vegetation ; it seemed to be resident and resident only in a sacred wood, then in a holy tree, and, finally, in a stela carved out of a hallowed substance,[2] a stela which could be moved about and which the lord set up near his residence. The god of the soil was implored to ensure the regular alternation of the seasons, for only so could society exist. In his presence, by means of rhetorical disputations, a relic of the ancient tourney, certain cases were decided, especially those concerning sexual matters.[3] The Duke of Shao heard a matrimonial case, pleaded in alternate verses, beneath a tree, supported by the veneration of all the assistants.

So the all-inclusive activity of a religious kind, which once had been apportioned to certain definite parts of the year and certain parts of the country, became, in the long run, entirely dissociated from considerations of time and space. It was taken from the collective field and made the speciality of a particular body. Once deprived of its fullness, economic and political affairs having been partly laicized, what remained, that is to say, religious activity properly so called, less dependent upon the body of social facts and subjected to the analysis of a body of interpreters, little by little came to be adapted for special purposes, so that a *ritual technique* came into being. The ancient practices, which were of the most diverse nature, also possessed a certain vague efficacy. Thanks to the systematic classification carried

[1] See the story of the birth of Confucius. It shows the transition from the old usages to the new. Cf. Chav., *SMC.*, vol. v, 289.
[2] Cf. *Chou li, Ti kuan, Ta ssŭ t'u and Luan yü, Ai kung wên :* pine for the Hsia, cypress for the Yin, mulberry for the Chou.
[3] Cf. *Dew on the Roads*, XI, and *Shao nan*, 5 ; Couv., 20 ; cf. App. I.

CONCLUSION

out by scholars, each of these practices was credited with a particular purpose. The ancient festivals were reduced to a clutter of rites which the different systems of religious thought distributed up and down the calendar.[1]

The action of those who, in the seignorial courts, had become the guardians of the religious traditions, made itself felt in a similar way in beliefs as well as in practices. Thanks to the speculations of the schools of religious interpreters, *the analysis of the primitive notions of Yin and Yang supplied the intellectual element which served as the governing principle in the setting up of a ceremonial technique.* In another direction, the ancient beliefs underwent the direct influence of the new social order. That bringing into prominence of personalities which is at the basis of a feudal organization, which goes on simultaneously with the development of ancestor worship, appeared, in the field of belief, as a *conception of individualized religious forces.* Thus mountains and rivers were conceived under the appearance of heroes, dukes, and counts.[2] The art of genealogy, an essential factor in feudal policy, was employed to organize, for diplomatic purposes and in the form of heroic legends, the history of local cults. We have, for example, legends worked out on the theme of *miraculous birth.* The facts here are

[1] We find that the primitive rituals gradually disintegrated. The different practices gave place to distinct ceremonies marked out in accordance with variable principles. Sometimes they were associated with solar dates, sometimes to a day in the cycle, sometimes to a kind of mnemotechnic date (e.g. the third day of the third month; cf. the calendar of Ch'ing Ch'u). The ceremonies of the dismembered festivals were spread throughout the months as so many *holidays.* The number of festivals seems to have increased as their duration grew less. A crude attempt at a logical distribution of the rites coincides with their disintegration as definite wholes. For example, the ninth day of the ninth month became the great day for climbing the mountains (cf. de Groot, *Fêtes d'Emouy*, p. 530), the fifth of the fifth month, that of rites performed on water (ibid., p. 346). But the climbing rites, far from being kept for autumn, are found also in spring (seventh and fifteenth days of the first month; cf. Ch'ing Ch'u). And, similarly, the water rites were also practised in one of the autumn months (seventh and fourteenth days of the seventh month, ibid.). I shall be content with these summary notes. They will serve as a counsel of prudence to those who try to seek the *origin* or the significance of the festivals by a consideration of their date or of the rite which seems to play the chief part in them.
[2] See p. 182.

237

frequently doublets, and they are only the more instructive on that account, for they show the importance which the princely families attached to a heroic origin, and furnish proof of the paucity of the schemes which presented themselves to the imagination of the genealogists. The following are practically the only types of miraculous conception [1] : pregnancy is brought about by a meteor which the heroine has seen, by a footprint in which she has placed her own foot, by an egg which she has swallowed, a flower, a seed, or a communication from an ancestor in dream. Of these types of legend, all, or two at the very least, are related to the festivals of mountains and streams. We may be sure that the genealogical legends of the pregnancy of Chien Ti or of the birth of Count Lan, find their origin, in every detail, in the practices of the ancient festivals and ancient beliefs regarding ancestral centres.[2]

The need of personifying sacred forces, felt even outside the framework of feudal religion, produced from the ancient national customs a certain number of popular myths sufficiently vigorous to exist without the assistance of an official cult. From the old festivals in which a chorus of men and a chorus of women carried on, at the rainy season and in the water, a tourney of courtesy which ended in sexual connection, was born the *myth of the battle and final union of the dragons who were masters of the rain*.[3] And the essential rites of the festivals of youth are still current in our own day throughout the Far East in the form of a *stellar myth, the story of the Weaver*.[4] From this constellation Chinese [5]

---

[1] See p. 187 sq. The legend which appears to present the greatest degree of originality, that of conception after placing the foot in a footprint, seems to have some relation to the cult of sacred places (sacred stones).

[2] Cf. pp. 157 and 187 sqq.

[3] See p. 151 sq. The rites of Lu and the beliefs of Chêng clearly show the relation of this myth to the ancient festivals.

[4] An example of the kind of interpretation which seems to me most dangerous is to be found in de Groot's account of this myth (*Emouy*, 436–44).

[5] In China (see *Hsi Ching Tsa Chi* and the *calendar of Ch'ing Ch'u*) children's figures are set floating on the water. (Cf. rites of Chêng, p. 158.) Cf. Groot, *Emouy*, 443. The *Hsi Ching Tsa Chi* mentions ceremonies beside the pool of the Hundred Children. These are ceremonies of purification.

and Japanese [1] women hope to secure skill in their work and to obtain children. All through the year, the Weaver lives a life of solitary labour on the shores of the Milky Way, but, on the seventh night of the seventh month, this virgin of the skies, like a peasant woman in days gone by, crosses the heavenly river [2] and goes to join the Neatherd.

[1] In Japan, on the day of the festival of the dead, BON-ODORI, couples used to sing songs in the thickets. (Cf. App. III, p. 260.) That is, in the middle of the seventh month. The feast of Tanabata, the Weaver, occurs a few days previously. In China, the Buddhist festival of the dead still takes place on the same day. It should be noted that the fourteenth (7 × 2) of the seventh month is the ancient date of the autumn sacrifice of purification which corresponds with that of spring (the third of the third month).

[2] She crosses it followed by a cortège of magpies. The magpie is a symbol of marriage (cf. IX) ; de Groot, *Emouy*, 440 ; *Fêng su chi*.

TABLE OF CONCORDANCE OF ODES

Order in the Anthology					Order of Study	
Section and No.		Couv. Page	Legge Page	No.	No.	Section and No.
Chou nan,	1	5	1	LVI	I	Chou nan, 6
,, ,,	3	8	8	LVIII	II	Kuei fêng, 3
,, ,,	5	10	11	VI	III	Hsiao ya, VIII, 4
,, ,,	6	10	12	I	IV	Ch'ên fêng, 5
,, ,,	8	12	14	XIX	V	Shao nan, 13
,, ,,	9	13	15	XLVI	VI	Chou nan, 5
,, ,,	10	14	17	XLVII	VII	Yung fêng, 5
Shao nan,	1	16	20	IX	VIII	Pin fêng, 3
,, ,,	3	18	23	LIX	IX	Shao nan, 1
,, ,,	6	20	27	XI	X	Chêng fêng, 20
,, ,,	8	23	29	XIV	XI	Shao nan, 6
,, ,,	9	24	30	XXII	XII	Pei fêng, 16
,, ,,	10	25	31	LXVII	XIII	Chêng fêng, 16
,, ,,	12	26	34	LXIV	XIV	Shao nan, 8
,, ,,	13	27	35	V	XV	Chêng fêng, 11
Pei fêng,	6	35	48	LXVIII	XVI	Yung fêng, 7
,, ,,	9	34	53	L	XVII	Ts'ao fêng, 2
,, ,,	10	39	55	XLIX	XVIII	Wang fêng, 8
,, ,,	16	48	67	XII	XIX	Chou nan, 8
,, ,,	17	49	68	XXXIX	XX	Hsiao ya, VIII, 2
Yung fêng,	4	55	78	XLIV	XXI	Pin fêng 1
,, ,,	5	56	80	VII	XXII	Shao nan, 9
., ,,	7	58	83	XVI	XXIII	Chêng fêng, 19
Wei fêng,	4	67	97	LXVI	XXIV	Ch'ên fêng, 3
,, ,,	5	70	101	XLI	XXV	Ts'ao fêng, 1
,, ,,	7	72	104	XLVIII	XXVI	T'ang fêng, 10
,, ,,	10	75	107	XXVIII	XXVII	Wang fêng, 10
Wang fêng,	8	82	120	XVIII	XXVIII	Wei fêng, 10
,, ,,	9	83	121	XLIII	XIXX	Ch'ên fêng, 4
,, ,,	10	84	122	XXVII	XXX	Chêng fêng 12
Chêng fêng,	2	86	125	XL	XXXI	,, ,, 10
,, ,,	7	92	133	XXXII	XXXII	,, ,, 7
,, ,,	8	92	134	XLII	XXXIII	,, ,, 18
,, ,,	9	93	136	XXXVI	XXXIV	Ch'en fêng, 7
,, ,,	10	94	137	XXXI	XXXV	Chêng fêng, 14
,, ,,	11	95	138	XV	XXXVI	,, ,, 9
,, ,,	12	95	139	XXX	XXXVII	T'ang fêng, 11
,, ,,	13	96	140	LI	XXXVIII	Chêng fêng, 17
,, ,,	14	96	141	XXXV	XXXIX	Pei fêng, 17

Order in the Anthology				Order of Study	
Section and No.	Couv. Page	Legge Page	No.	No.	Section and No.
Chêng fêng 16	98	143	XIII	XL	Chêng fêng, 2
„ „ 17	98	144	XXXVIII	XLI	Ch'i fêng, 4
„ „ 18	99	145	XXXIII	XLII	Chêng fêng, 8
„ „ 19	100	146	XXIII	XLIII	Wang fêng, 9
„ „ 20	101	147	X	XLIV	Yung fêng, 4
„ „ 21	101	148	LII	XLV	Wei fêng, 5
Ch'i fêng, 4	106	153	LI	XLVI	Chou nan, 9
T'ang fêng, 5	124	179	LXI	XLVII	Chou nan, 10
„ „ 10	129	185	XXVI	XLVIII	Wei fêng, 7
„ „ 11	130	186	XXXVII	XLIX	Pei fêng, 10
Ch'in fêng, 4	137	195	LIV	L	„ „ 9
„ „ 7	141	200	LVII	LI	Chêng fêng, 13
Ch'ên fêng, 1	145	205	LXII	LII	„ „ 21
„ „ 2	145	206	LXIII	LIII	Hsiao ya, III, 2
„ „ 3	146	207	XXIV	LIV	Ch'in fêng, 4
„ „ 4	147	208	XXIX	LV	Ch'en fêng, 10
„ „ 5	148	209	IV	LVI	Chou nan, 1
„ „ 7	149	211	XXXIV	LVII	Ch'in fêng, 7
„ „ 10	151	213	LV	LVIII	Chou nan, 3
Kuei fêng, 3	154	217	II	LIX	Shao nan, 3
Ts'ao fêng, 1	155	220	XXV	LX	Hsiao ya, VII, 4
„ „ 2	156	222	XVII	LXI	T'ang fêng, 5
Pin fêng, 1	160	226	XXI	LXII	Ch'en fêng, 1
„ „ 3	167	235	VIII	LXIII	„ „ 2
„ „ 5	170	240	LXV	LXIV	Shao nan, 12
Hsiao ya, III, 2	199	279	LIII	LXV	Pin fêng, 5
„ „ VII, 4	293	391	LX	LXVI	Wei fêng, 4
„ „ VIII, 2	307	411	XX	LXVII	Shao nan, 10
„ „ VIII, 4	310	414	III	LXVIII	Pei fêng, 6

APPENDIX I

NOTES ON ODE XI

CONTESTS IN PROVERBS

XI. *The Dew on the Roads*

1. (Boy.)	The roads are dew-covered :
2.	Why then neither morning nor evening ?
3. (Girl.)	The roads are too wet with dew !

4. (Boy.)	Who says that a sparrow has no beak ?
5.	How could he bore into my roof ?
6.	Who says thou art single ?
7.	How couldſt thou blame me ?
8. (Girl.)	Although thou mayſt blame me ?
9.	The marriage is not arranged !

10. (Boy.)	Who says a rat has no teeth ?
11.	How could he tunnel into my wall ?
12.	Who says thou art single ?
13.	How couldſt thou blame me ?
14. (Girl.)	Although thou mayſt blame me,
15.	Even then I follow thee not !

XI. *Pref.* 1.—The dew on the roads (shows) the Count of Shao deciding lawsuits. An indication of the manners in times of sadness and lawlessness. Beginning of the reformative influence of chaſtity and fidelity. No uncouth lad can insult a chaſte maiden.

The Count of Shao was a virtuous contemporary of King Wên and the laſt sovereign of the Yin. To this latter unhappy prince was due the lawlessness and immorality of which the effeĉts were exhibited by this youth. King Wên, by his virtue, will re-eſtablish morality ; already his influence is making itself felt, as is proved by the chaſte conduĉt of the girl. (Cf. Chêng.)

1, 2, 3. The firſt five ceremonies of marriage took place in the twilight of early dawn ; the sixth (the marriage procession) in the twilight of evening (*I li*, Marriage).

Dew shows the date, second month of spring. (Chêng.) (Cf. X, 2 ; LIV, 2.) In autumn, in the ninth month, dew becomes hoar-frost (end of the cycle of vegetation) : hence the autumn dew belongs to the eighth month (second month of autumn). It follows that the spring dew marks the second month (the corresponding month in spring) : hoar-frost then becomes dew (beginning of the cycle of vegetation).

Chêng recalls the fact that the second month is the marriage month.

According to Mao, verses 1, 2, 3, are metaphorical, to be explained like this : what traveller does not wish to be starting early and to continue till evening ? But fearful of getting wet (through travelling in the dew) he starts neither morning nor evening. Similarly how should a maiden, asked in marriage by an uncouth suitor, not be willing to marry him ? But inasmuch as the rites will not be performed she will not marry him. The fear of walking in the dew is symbolic of the fear of a breach of the rites. (Cf. K'ung Ying-ta.)

According to Chêng (who holds that marriages must take place in the second month of spring) the young man only presents himself when there is too much dew, that is in the third or fourth month. And, in addition, offers an insult to the girl by failing to perform all the ceremonies.

7. According to Mao's view one must render the meaning as : summon me to court and drag me to prison.

9. The marriage rites have not been performed : that is to say the ritual pledges have not been tendered. (Mao.) The pledges have been tendered coercively, but not accepted, for no intermediary has arranged the contract. (Chêng.)

The difficulty of the poem lies in the obscurity of the analogies quoted in verses 4–7 and 10–13.

The commentators are of opinion that the girl originated this line of reasoning to justify her refusal. Her line of argument would be thus : You summon me to court; people will say : It is manifest then that there is a contract between you and me, a promise to marry, but that induction is erroneous ; it is as if one, seeing a hole in his roof, should say : the sparrow that made it has a horn. The suit which you enter against me is similar to but not identical with a suit entered by a suitor against his affianced wife. As a matter of fact we are not engaged.

To me this interpretation appears impossible for two reasons :—

(1) The argument uses a word which can only mean husband. Thus the argument is made from the man's side and in his favour ;

(2) It is impossible to maintain that the analogy is faulty in the continuation of the argument : if a rat tunnels into walls it must be because it has teeth. [Latter-day commentators ingeniously explain that canine teeth are implied, which are lacking in rodents ; then

the analogy would be erroneous. Besides the fact that this subtlety is inadmissible, there still remains the fact that the word referred to above proves the speaker a man.]

I think then that the reasoning by analogy being led by the man the analogies are admissible : hence I have used the word beak and not *horn*. Avowedly it is a hypothesis, but this translation is undoubtedly less ridiculous than that proposed for " teeth ". I attribute verses 4–7 and 10–13 to the man. On the other hand, the word " to follow " (15) is only employable by a woman. (It is a woman's destiny to follow ; cf. theory of the three followings or obediences.) I attribute to the woman verses 14–15, and, by symmetry, 8–9. Finally, since the dew symbolizes the time of the spring festivals, the first two verses seem to me to be a summons on the part of the man, and the third an evasion on the part of the girl.

The poem thus appears to me to be a dialogue.

Themes : Spring meetings ; meteorological.

In the Chou Li (*Ti kuan, mei shih*) it is stated that the intermediary used to decide questions of morals (cf. XLIII, pref.), beside the god of the soil of dethroned dynasties. The relationship of the god of the soil with these sacred groves is recognized. The Count of Shao, arbiter in the suit now under consideration, is represented judging disputes about morals under a tree revered by everyone (cf. *Shao nan*, 5). If we also recollect that the intermediary is held to preside over spring festivals (*Chou li*, ibid.), and that these take place in the sacred groves, we shall readily admit the relationship between the legal formulæ employed in suits concerning morals and the verses improvised in the contests.

The calendar of Ch'ing Ch'u indicates (for the seventh day of the first month) a ritual ascent. People climbed up to the heights in order to recite verses. Reciting verses on high places is a custom which, in the mind of the Chinese, has remained connected with the idea of magical incantations.

Finally, I understand verses 7–8 as meaning : challenge me to a poetical duel, and verses 13–14 as meaning : call me by magic incantations. Such reciprocal incantations constitute a poetical duel.

Perhaps we might compare with XI No. 10 of *Hsiao ya*, iii. Cf. also No. 8 of *Yung fêng*. Couv., 59.

This poem is very difficult to understand. Only with certain definite reservations do I offer the translation given above and the attempt at interpretation that follows it. The commentators admit rightly enough that it is a dispute between a man and a woman concerning a marriage already planned, which he wishes to conclude and she declines. But they believe that the discussion is a real lawsuit, and that the poem—although the first two verses express the ideas of the man—is a speech by the girl. I hold, on the other hand, that the debate is purely formal, that the poem briefly presents a contest in love songs and that the dialogue, which continues through fifteen verses, shows how boys and girls courted each other at the spring betrothals.

Now for my reasons. It is allowed that the expression *shih chia* (9) is taken in a secondary sense (housekeeping, marriage, cf. I, 4–8). In my opinion, it follows that *chia* (6–12) is also taken in a secondary sense. But if it means husband the verses which contain it and the developments into which these verses enter are necessarily spoken by the man (4–7) (10–13). On the other hand, the word *ts'ung*, to follow, can only be used by a woman : therefore, she speaks verse 15 and the preceeding verse 14, which belongs to it : I grant also that, for the sake of symmetry, she also speaks verses (8–9). Hence the allocation of the speeches.

The line of thought runs thus : (1–2) The lad invites the girl to go with him to the spring festival ; this is the season for it (1, dew, cf. X) : why should she not join him there at the fitting hour ? (2, the two twilights, cf. IV, XLI, and *I li*, Marriage). The girl refuses : it is too late ; the time is past (3, too dewy, cf. X, 1, 2) ; (4–7) the boy argues with her. (8–9) Second refusal of the girl. (10–13) Argument repeated on a new theme. (14–15) Renewed refusal.

This allocation of the verses presumes that each of the young people says it is the other's fault (the lad : 7, 13 ; the girl : 8, 14). This would be inadmissible if there was a real suit with plaintiff and defendant. On the other hand, the explanation is simple if the matter is a love debate.

What is the subject of debate ? The boy is content to repeat what amounts to this : " You refuse, but the simple fact that you object to my request proves that we have begun negotiations," a mode of reasoning supported by proverbs similar to our : " There is no smoke without fire." This argument is so strong that the girl can only reply by simple declarations of her determination. That such an argument is admissible permits of only one explanation : The young people are really destined to marry and neither doubts that they will marry in the end. Nor do the commentators doubt it : as they say, the girl only refuses because the rites have not been duly performed. To advance too quickly to the inevitable final stage would compromise her honour (cf. LXIV, 9–11) : Her resistance shows her value, for, though the result is not in doubt, it is important for the self-respect of both antagonists that the battle should be protracted. For the girl to delay her consent, for the boy to obtain a speedy avowal, these are the sole ends of the debate : its interest lies, not in the result, but in the duration, of the contest.

So the lovers' debate is not basically a trial : the result being certain, the contestants struggle only for honour and by courtesy : their conflict is merely formal ; it is a game, a joust. Just as the youthful Miao-tzŭ throw the ball from one to the other for some time before avowing their love, so the young girl, who first of all does not wish to walk in the dew, answers the verse of her suitor by other verses in which she declines his offer (cf. the reverse of this, LII, 5–7). And if the song still ends with a refusal it means that, as among the Thos, a lengthy courtship is needed and several attempts must be made to gain the girl's consent.

Since the issue of the suit is not doubtful, since the young people will not fail to reach the appointed end, the arguments need no change. It is enough to repeat them, in varying guise, just as the ball is thrown to and fro as many times as may be necessary. That is why the youth only repeats his arguments, and why his skill is only used in putting them into new shape.

If my analysis is correct, the poem under discussion is an example of those poetic duels whence love is born. It shows us the nature of the courtship which aroused this sentiment in the minds of the individuals upon whom it was imposed as an obligation.

The lovers' dispute opens with a very general declaration by the youth. Here we are at the spring festival of betrothals ; is it not time for us to marry ? To which the girl replies by a simple evasion : it is too late. (Compare with this the opening of a very similar contest in verses 7–10 in LXVI.) The poetical battle is joined with the first thrust ; it proceeds in a series of engagements all similar to each other (the song exhibits two almost identical). The lad quotes a proverb ; next he establishes a parallel between his axiom and his thesis, and ironically invites the maiden to refute his double proposition. The maiden refutes nothing, being solely intent on not confessing defeat.

The first argument derives all its force from the fact that it is a saying from the calendar : as an emblematic formula borrowed from a seasonal ritual it is endowed with compelling force : whoever summons its aid fetters his adversary and is sure of victory ; but not immediately. The saying from the calendar lacks personal application, does not directly influence the particular individual : in order to affect the opponent some connecting links, such as secondary arguments, are needed. These consist of parallelisms drawn between the thesis maintained and a proverbial axiom. By reason of these parallelisms the conclusions share in the authority of the proverb. The character of necessity attached to the natural phenomenon referred to by the proverb is carried over in its entirety to the conclusions which have been essentially associated to it. The youth forbids the girl to deny that she has an intended husband (himself), under penalty of denying at the same time that a sparrow has a beak or a rat teeth, just as he had already withdrawn from her all right to maintain that the time for their union had not arrived by pointing out on the road the dew symbolic of the spring festivals. But whilst a saying from the calendar is the emblematic formula of a definite social rule, thus carrying an immutable meaning, the proverb is only a traditional saying, and the moral significance associated with the natural phenomenon to which the saying relates is neither precise nor invariable. The proverbial saying does not connote recurrences unfailing and solemnly established; homely and indetermined in its application, it is liable to various corollaries: more adaptable, more manageable than the saying of the calendar, it lends itself more easily to particular examples and personal ends. Hence its use. The proverb is the means of drawing the desired conclusion from the premisses contained in the emblematic formula. It reinforces this conclusion by conferring upon it a natural correspondence which commands respect. The emblematic formulæ of the calendar are real commandments: they are insufficient because one legal phrase does not make a speech. An image impressed upon the mind by personal observation, a metaphor imagined by one's own ingenuity, add nothing to the force of an idea for their novelty deprives them of all weight. On the other hand, a wealth of proverbial sayings furnishes those venerable images which assure victory in a poetical contest: they command respect because they are felt to be related to the emblematic formulæ, and, because they are adaptable, they may serve as emblems and support the particular propositions that one wishes to prove. And he who talks in proverbs will be victor in this lovers' debate.

To ally a personal proposition to unescapable truths by means of venerable metaphors is not done without artifice: art is needed to bridge the interval between the law and its application. The interrogative form is the means of concealing the bridge and disguising the artifice. He who presents his case and a natural correspondence simultaneously in the shape of a question and so opens the attack, forces the adversary to defend at his most vulnerable point, to answer so that every response, save the one desired, is ridiculous. And thus, while the opponent cannot escape from the constraining force of proverbial analogy, the coercive force of irony is added: whence comes this? It does not result only from the use of artifice in language. If the ironical query paralyses the opponent at a weak point, if he

APPENDIX I

cannot answer freely, it is because he is not really questioned, the fact being that the question goes over his head and is addressed to the general conscience. This conscience is summoned to support the validity of the argument, while an air of absurdity, of paradox, or heresy is imposed upon any contrary proposition. Just as, in order to persuade, one does not employ personal arguments that lack authority, but borrows subjects from the public stock, of which the authority is indisputable, so one does not endeavour to obtain the consent that one demands by a voluntary avowal, but by the pressure of public opinion. The constraining force which irony, like the proverb, possesses, a force which has caused it to be adopted as a supplementary weapon, comes from this, that a formula presented interrogatively both in form and content is a forcible appeal to the respect due to the common wisdom.

It is by repeated interrogations, by a multitude of proverbs, by a series of ironical analogies, that consent is secured. It is to be noted that, in the case now being considered, no counter-attack is made on the assailant who seeks an avowal. One of the antagonists remains passive, and only the other uses the weapons of proverbs and irony. The contest thus takes on the shape of a speech punctuated at equal intervals by the simple declaration of a resistance still maintained. Is this not because, by the rules of the game, only one of the contestants has the right to use irony and proverb ? Since the marriage is settled already, it is only a matter of overcoming the resistance of one of the parties to its speedy consummation : so the essential thing in the poetic duel is to overcome resistance as quickly as possible and force an avowal. By the skill he shows in making use of the classical lines of persuasion the lad will compel the maiden not to prolong unduly the refusals which she is bound to give by the rules of the traditional play between bashfulness and love. Thus will he establish his ascendancy and create the influence which will cause her at last to yield consent. That lover will most quickly attain his ends who is best skilled in the use of the constraining power of irony and proverbs : that is to say, he is most worthy of being loved who has the keenest appreciation of the common wisdom. The forces that constrain to an avowal of love are impersonal, and the qualities which inspire love are also impersonal. If courtship is carried on by singing in ironical fashion a string of proverbial analogies, it is because love is not born of any sudden admiration for the good qualities of the individual, but comes from the victory of a sentiment of obligation over private feeling. By its urgent appeals to common wisdom, the incantation succeeds in silencing the sentiments of esprit de corps—domestic and sexual—the sentiments of modesty

249

and of honour, and thus allows the awakening of love : a sentiment opposed to all particularism, the source of union and concord, the mainstay of public order.

It may be useful to compare with Ode XI the Malagasy poems found in the collection of M. Paulhan (*Les Hain-teny Mérinas*) on pages 39, 115 (especially p. 123), 183 ; cf. preface, particularly pp. 52 sqq. and 58 sqq. The following is an example (cf. p. 39) :—

" (A man speaks) :—

> Perchance you thought yourself the mighty rock
> That chisel will not scratch ?
> Perchance you thought yourself the mighty rock
> That water will not erode ?
> Or did you think yourself the brushwood dry
> That fire will not burn ?
> Or did you think yourself the sikidy-coloured cock
> That iron threatens not ?
> Or did you think yourself the bull of clay
> Whose horns will not be aimed at ?
> Where will you find
> The smith who will not burn himself ?
> Where will you find
> The water-carrier who is not wet ?
> Where will you find
> The fire-maker who will not sweat ?
> Where will you find
> The walker who will not tire ?

" And shortly afterwards the woman replies again :—

> Oh ! I am tired of refusing,
> Let it be yes.

" Then they clasp hands and go away like a canoe without anyone to paddle it."

Compare the European songs which have at the same time an appearance of légal argument, and of a litany, such as that of Magali.

NOTE.—When I wrote the above I knew nothing of any Chinese version of the Magali theme. Since then, in March, 1919, in Peking, good fortune enabled me to be present at a very curious Chinese play, to which my attention was directed by M. d'Hormon. It was a piece seldom put on the stage, but included in the *Hsi K'ao*: its title is *Hsiao Fang-niu*, i.e. The Shepherd Boy; it has been translated into French, not very accurately, but very cleverly (the translation appeared anonymously in the *Journal de Pékin*, on 8th February, 1918, under the title " Une Soirée au Théâtre Chinois "). The play is a pastoral ballet with a flute accompaniment of extreme simplicity. The Chinese regard it as imaginative, but really it is a very close imitation of a love song contest.

The actors are a shepherd boy and a young woman he meets out for a stroll. Under pretext of reward for some information the shepherd asks her to sing, and she consents on the condition that he responds. Courtship begins. It is in three parts :—

(1) The girl sings a song of which the words are only an excuse for the musical accompaniment. " *Erh-lang yeh-yeh* is in yellow clad." The boy, under cover of the music, slips in a declaration of love : " I love your tiny feet." The girl asks him to marry her : he will ask his mother. "Done," she says, but let him first strike the gong: he declines, then he yields. The scene is repeated twice.

(2) After this the boy proposes to the girl four sets of four conundrums. She solves them.

(3) Thereupon, without further parley, begins a duet which is a Chinese version of the Song of Magali. The understanding is perfect.

Below is a translation of this song, made according to the principles which I have followed in the translation of the *Shih ching*, and in such a way as to suit the rhythm of the flute accompaniment. The Provençal song is notable for its tone of affectionate courtesy and its basic Christian ideas : in the Chinese is a mixture of Buddhist beliefs and crude indelicacies. One verse: " Be thou the wench and I the bachelor," is an allusion to the amorous diversions of the principal characters of a very famous work of a light nature, the *Hsi Hsiang-chi*, the maid Hung Niang and a young student of good family, Chang Chi.

Shepherd.	Before your house,	a bridge there stands.
	And welcome or not,	I'll stroll upon it.
Girl.	Don't you go,	don't go there.
	I'll have my sweetheart,	a big sword has he !
		(repeat)

251

Boy. A big sword has he?
Well, and what of that?
A spurt of red blood,   my head falls off.
There I am dead,   and mingle with the shades.
I turn into a ghoſt,   snatching at your flesh!
                                              (*repeat*)

Girl. Snatching at my flesh?
Well, and what of that?
I'd have my sweetheart   he is a wizard.
Two raps, three raps,   he sends you rolling.
He takes you and throws you,   to the edge of the path.
                                              (*repeat*)

Boy. To the edge of the path?
Well, and what of that?
I turn into the branch,   hidden in the mulberry.
Wait until you come,   to pick the mulberry leaves.
The branch gets caught on you, your skirt is torn.
                                              (*repeat*)

Girl. My skirt is torn?
Well, and what of that?
I'd have my sweetheart   he is a carpenter.
Two cuts, three cuts,   you are lopped off.
He takes you and throws you,   to the depths of the fish-
                                   pond.   (*repeat*)

Boy. To the depths of the fish-pond?
Well, and what of that?
I turn into the eel,   hidden in the fish-pond.
Wait until you come,   to draw up the water.
You are the maid,   I am the gay gallant.
                                              (*repeat*)

Girl. You the gay gallant?
Well, and what of that?
I'd have my sweetheart   to fish with a net.
Two meshes, three meshes,   there you are caught.
I have your flesh to eat,   your sauce to lick.
                                              (*repeat*)

252

Appendix I

Boy. My sauce to lick?
Well, and what of that?
I turn into a bone,   hidden in your bowl.
Wait until you come,   to lick your sauce.
The bone becomes lodged   deep in your throat.
                                        (*repeat*)

Girl. Deep in my throat?
Well, and what of that?
I'd have my sweetheart   and he sells senna.
Two doses, three doses,   and you are cleared away.
He takes you and throws you,   away on the midden.
                                        (*repeat*)

Boy. Away on the midden?
Well, and what of that?
I turn into the bee,   hidden in the midden.
Wait until you come,   and go to make water,
The bee begins to buzz,   On the flowers you've put
                               there!   (*repeat*)

Girl. On the flower I've put there?
Well, and what of that?
I'd have my sweetheart   he's a fine archer.
Two shafts, three shafts,   and you would be dead.
Go and pay your visit,   to the grand justiciary![1]
                                        (*repeat*)

Boy. To the grand justiciary?
Well, and what of that?
Before the great judge,   I shall summon you.
You will then be dead,   mingling with the shades.
And we shall be reborn,   so that we may wed.
                                        (*repeat*)

---

[1] Yen-wang or Yen-luo-Wang, the most celebrated of the judges in the Buddhist Hell.

APPENDIX II

NOTES ON ODE XVI

Beliefs with regard to the Rainbow

The classical explanation of Ode XVI rests upon the hypothesis that the rainbow is a celestial monition directed against sexual irregularities (Mao, 1, 2). This implies that it is itself considered an abnormal phenomenon, a disorder of nature, and so, as one avoids looking at an immoral woman, one never points a finger at a rainbow (Chêng, 1, 2).

Moreover, the rainbow furnishes two themes to the calendar. One is set down for the third month of spring (*Yüeh ling, Li Chi*; Couv., i, p. 346), when the rainbow first appears. The other is set down for the first month of winter (tenth month) (id., p. 392): the rainbow hides and is seen no more. Hence the appearance of rainbows is normal from the third to the tenth month, or at any rate during the third and the tenth months. Must there be also sexual irregularities during the same period? And is it possible that such never occur before the second or after the tenth month.

The rainbow is usually represented by two characters (see *Shuo wên* (*HCCC.*), 651*b*, p. 11, v°, and 653, p. 4, v°). The learned say that one of the characters is a term representing the lighter portion of the colour bands, and the other the darker. The bands, whether light or dark, are vapours or emanations, the light being male, *Yang*, and the dark female, *Yin*. So the bow is made of the *Yin* and *Yang* vapours, which are terrestrial and celestial emanations. The rainbow is also conceived to be an emanation resulting from the union of *Yin* and *Yang*.

Again, it is never seen after the tenth month: for then begins a period of rest for heaven and earth (*Yüeh ling, Li Chi*; Couv., i, p. 393). Terrestrial emanations no longer ascend, celestial no longer descend. The *Yin* and the *Yang* no longer mingle. A rainbow is an impossibility. But it reappears in spring, because the terrestrial emanations as they rise mingle with the celestial which are descending. (*Yüeh ling, Li Chi*; Couv., 336.)

The oppositions and conjunctions of the *Yin* and the *Yang* produce the alternation of the seasons. If the rainbow is a product of the *Yin* and the *Yang* in conjunction, how comes it to be an emblem of irregular unions? Chinese writers appreciate the difficulty, and this is how they meet it.

254

Appendix II

The firſt explanation ſtarts with the likeness between the words for " rainbow " and " attack ", " assault ". The rainbow is the result of a battle between the pure *Yang* and the emanations of the *Yin* (see *Shih ming*, chap. 1). From the idea of fighting we can, at a pinch, extraĉt the idea of disorder. There is ſtill the difficulty that the disorder resulting from the more or less violent conjunĉtions of the *Yin* and the *Yang* is a necessity in the universal order.

A second explanation is more specious. Every rainbow is not a sign of disorder, only certain rainbows. The bow *muſt* appear in the eaſt or the weſt, according to whether the sun is setting or rising, and so illuminating the eaſt or weſt respeĉtively (Chu Hsi). During the morning the rainbow muſt appear in the weſt, then illuminated, and, in the afternoon, in the eaſt, upon which the sun is shining. A rainbow seen in the eaſt in the morning (such as that in the Ode) is inauspicious. It is, moreover, easy to see how it is the true emblem of an immoral woman. " The bow," says Ch'êng Tzŭ, " appears in illuminated quarters, in the weſt in the morning, and in the eaſt in the afternoon. If it appears in the eaſt (in the *morning*) it certainly results from an emanation from a dark place (i.e. *Yin*) on its way to unite with *Yang*. Let the *Yang* call and the *Yin* respond, let the man go (to seek a bride) and let the woman follow (her husband to be) : this is as it should be. But let the *Yin* go of its own initiative to unite with the *Yang* (as is here the case) and that is hateful. That is why no one points at (the abnormal rainbow seen in the eaſt in the *morning*). A girl marrying (on her own initiative) without the proper rites resembles (such a) rainbow.

Thus there are rainbows and rainbows. That which proceeds, as is proper, from the initiative of the *Yang* and from an illuminated quarter is correĉt and seemly : it is symbolical of a regular union and (in the same way as one can associate with an honourable man) one might point at it.

Thus is juſtified the interpretation by Chêng and Mao of Ode XVI, and at the same time the physical and metaphysical problems which it raises are solved. The only difficulty is this : The theory thus conſtruĉted absolutely contradiĉts the opinions of the authors of the interpretation which it is trying to juſtify. They are sure that every rainbow is an emblem of forbidden union, a sign of prohibition, and they do not say, nor does the ode, that the bow at which one muſt not point appears in the eaſt in the morning.

It is intereſting to find both physics and metaphysics advanced by the necessity of clarifying the commentary on an ode ; it makes one wonder whether the whole theory of the rainbow is not conneĉted with the ſtory of the ode.

The subject-matter of the images in the love songs was gathered up in the course of the festivals of the seasons. The rustic themes were borrowed from the scenes amid which the festivals necessarily took place. They were celebrated at the beginning and at the end of the winter season. During the winter, the dry season, rainbows do not appear. But when the winter had passed and the lads and lasses gathered in the fields, they saw the rainbow in the heavens. The phenomenon that impressed them at the solemn moment of their union became the emblem of it: the rainbow was associated with the idea of the sexual union.

The festivals, regularly recurrent, led to an understanding of a conception of the regularity of the natural order: one could conceive the ways of Nature on the model of human observances. To the betrothals celebrated by the local communities a counterpart in Nature was sought: the rainbow supplied the need. Being an emblem of sexual union, it came to be regarded as itself a marriage. But what was the nature of the nuptials?

During the cold season men lived retired, hidden away in their fast-closed dwellings. During the summer they spread out over the sunny fields where they expended all their energies. It seemed to them that the two controlling factors of their lives also controlled the changes of season. One of these, the *Yang*, was the principle of growth, of activity, of light—the lord of summer. The other, the *Yin*, was the principle of inertia, of darkness, of seclusion—the lord of winter. Such were the most ancient Chinese conceptions of the course of things. Such also they appeared as set out in that old calendar of mystic mould which the *Shu ching* has preserved (see *SMC.*, i, 48 sqq.). They provided the framework in which all human knowledge was fitted.

All things which could be brought into opposing pairs were classed in either the *Yin* or the *Yang* category. Cold and heat, light and shade, sky and earth, sun and moon, etc., all sprang from one or the other. And as they served to classify things so also they served for the analysis and explanation of phenomena. They appeared as the cosmogonic principles by which all things in the universe were brought into being. The nuptials celebrated by Nature during the sexual festivals of spring and autumn were the nuptials of the *Yin* and *Yang*. At these periods intermediate between the seasons under their control they opposed each other and united with each other as the sexual corporations faced each other in the contests and united in betrothals. This union took place in the rainbow.[1] Earth and sky

---

[1] And also in rain. Theme of unions and combats of dragons.

were conjoined by it ; it was made up of the resplendent emanations of the one and the murky exhalations of the other. These festivals of Nature, these solemn nuptials, compelled veneration. Just as in these days no one stretches out his hand toward the north-east, the home of the gods, so, in ancient times, no one dared point at the rainbow.

When the prestige of noble customs had condemned as gross and immoral the old customs kept up by the humbler folk ; when the influence of civilizing princes like King Wên of Chou and Duke Wên of Wei began to produce its effect, the rustic betrothals were looked at askance as the customs of serfs. For the convenience of scientific explanation, the nuptials of the *Yin* and the *Yang* continued to be celebrated, and, astronomical entities as they were, the playthings of learned speculation, their abstract union shocked no one's modesty ; and, further, the most elaborate rules—the calculations of astronomers—governed their meetings. But the rainbow in which their nuptials were once displayed, the phenomenon closely bound up with popular rejoicings, shared the evil repute of those rejoicings. And, like the rustic festivals, from being holy they became vile. The rainbow ceased to be sacred and became impure. When the sexual festivals, of which it was the emblem, were banned, it became the emblem of forbidden unions. It then became necessary to exercise ingenuity in discovering how the *Yin* and the *Yang* conjoined shamefully therein. It appeared clear that the disgrace of their union originated in those happenings, which, according to the new laws, made a marriage irregular. Nothing is so contrary to the rules of correct behaviour than the immodesty of girls who go before their husbands. The rainbow could only be a union in which the *Yin* unduly took the initiative. In a venerable text it was discovered that a rainbow appeared in the east. It was enough to admit that it was a matutinal rainbow, and consequently that it came out from that portion of the horizon unexposed to the sun, to be able to warrant the conclusion that it originated in a brazen provocation on the part of the *Yin*, the dark principle, and that it was an abnormal and shameful rainbow. Finally, from all these arguments about the texts calculated to bolster up an absurdity, from all the deductions based on the slenderest scientific theories, there emerged, for the physicists, an accurate observation of the appearing points of rainbows at various hours of the day : with the help of fantastic principles and false deductions they had discovered an experimental fact.

As to beliefs, it is not uninteresting to observe that, if there was a change in the feelings with which the rainbow was regarded, it was due to the connection between what was sacred and what was impure. How the change came can be explained. Usually the rainbow appears after the rain ; it marks the end of it ; this was doubtless the reason why, when the calendars became more elaborate, the themes relating to the rainbow were put at the ends of the periods of spring and autumn rains, in the third and the tenth months, that is to say considerably after the equinoxes. Now in a strict system of astronomy, only the equinoxes are the actual moments, the regular moments, of the union of the *Yin* and the *Yang*. Similarly, when exact dates were fixed for the festivals and, recognizing the impossibility of destroying the ancient customs, an attempt was made to regulate them, that festival at which the official intermediary presided over the rustic unions was fixed for the spring equinox. On the other hand, it would seem as if the merry-makings in which the sexes united were succeeded by a period during which all approach was forbidden. After the beginning of house-keeping in the autumn, the married pair lived separate for some time. In the same way, after the betrothals in the spring came the reason of rustic labour when the sexual corporations lived apart, the period of engagement, when the affianced couples met only at night and by stealth, unknown to their parents, during which they doubtless refrained from union. In the new calendar, where the sayings were methodically classified and allocated to different dates, it was found that the prohibited periods coincided with the dates marked by the rainbow themes. This may perhaps explain why the rainbow as a symbol of sexual union became the sign of union at prohibited times, the symbol of forbidden, inauspicious, and impure union. We may adduce the following as proof. The *Yüeh ling* fixes the spring equinox for the royal ceremony of celebrating the return of the swallows (just as the *Chou li* fixes that date for the great festival of marriages). But the *Yüeh ling* also says that, after the equinox, a herald, ringing a small handbell with a wooden tongue, gave warning to the people in these terms : " Soon thunder will be heard. If women do not carefully watch their behaviour and conduct they will bear undeveloped children (i.e. will miscarry)." The violation of the prohibition following the spring festival is penalized by miscarriage. Now, if in the *Yüeh ling* prohibition is indicated by the thunder theme, in the *Chi chung Chou shu* miscarriages are connected with rainbow themes, that is with seasonal rules relating to the date thereby indicated. Hence, in this calendar the rainbow indicates the spring prohibition. In my opinion this explains how it became the symbol of prohibited unions.

APPENDIX III

ETHNOGRAPHICAL NOTES

R. KARL FLORENZ. *La Poésie archaïque du Japon*. Premier Congrès
International des Études d'Extrême-Orient, Hanoï, 1902,
p. 41 sqq. Compte rendu analytique.

"The most ancient poems of Japan are those preserved in the
Kojiki (712) and the Nihongi (720): they number about two
hundred. They are inserted in the historic text at the places where
they best seem to fit, but the order of their insertion is far from being
that of their composition. They can be dated, generally speaking,
from the fifth to the seventh century . . . their most frequent theme
is sensual love; their usual form of expression, simile. There is none
of the poetic imagery which later constituted the basis of the Japanese
language. The most common form of poetic expression is the simile,
but allegory occurs. On the other hand, examples of the personification
of abstract ideas and sentiments are rare in the archaic poetry . . .
The characteristic feature of the *naga-uta* is the parallelism of the con-
stituents of a phrase as in ancient Hebrew poetry. But in addition
to those forms common to all languages, Japanese poetry has three
ornaments peculiar to itself. These are: the *makura kotoba* "pillow
words", the *jo* "introductions", and the *kenyogen* "words of double
meaning". *Makura kotoba* are stereotyped epithets, like the epithets
of Homer, attached invariably to particular words, although their
relation to such words, at least in modern poetry, is often difficult to
discover. The *jo* are developed *makura kotaba*, sometimes running
to several verses. The *kenyogen* are words of double meaning belonging
to different phrases which they link together. This last artifice, which
with us would be placed in the category of puns, in Japanese poetry
sometimes produces graceful effects. Alliteration is also found.

A particular custom deserving of mention is the *uta-gaki* "line of
song", or *kagai* "alternate songs". Two groups gathered in the
public square and drawn up facing each other, sang alternately; the
choruses were punctuated with improvisations. One singer stepped
forward and improvised a song to which a member of the opposite
group extemporized a response in the same manner. The youths
used this means of declaring their love or paying court to her whom
they had chosen. She replied in song. Sometimes it amounted to a

battle of song between the rival sides : the most famous is that which
the Nihongi chronicles in the year 498, which took place between
the eldest son of the Emperor Niken (later Buretsu Tenno) and a
noble named Shibi for the hand of Kaga-hime. The nobility
abandoned the custom of *uta-gaki* under the influence of Chinese
ideas, but it has survived in the country in the *bon-odori*, the dances at
the Buddhist festival of the dead."

KOJIKI (trans. B. H. Chamberlain) (*Trans. of the R. Asiatic
Society*. Reprint, 1920).

pp. 20–21. *Dialogue before Intercourse*

—O venuste et amabilis adolescens !

—O venusta et amabilis virgo !

p. 22.

—Ah ! what a fair and lovely maiden.

—Ah ! what a fair and lovely youth.

pp. 91 sqq.—Love dialogue which concludes : " quamobrem ea
nocte non coïerunt sed sequentis diei nocte auguste coïerunt." Observe
in the song of the woman : " Being a maiden like a drooping plant,
my heart is just a *bird on a sand-bank by the shore* ; it will now indeed
be a dotterel. Afterwards it will be a gentle bird . . ." Cf. *Shih ching,
Pei fêng*, 10, 1. 6. *Chou nan*, 1, 1. 1.

p. 95.—Marital dispute.

p. 155.—" As for red jewels, though even the string (they are
strung on) shines, the aspect of (my) lord (who is) like unto white
jewels is (more) illustrious." " As for my younger sister, whom I
took to sleep (with me) on the island where light the wild duck, the
birds of the offing, I shall not forget her till the end of my life."

pp. 179–80.—" Seven maidens on the moor of Takasazhi in
Yamato : which shall be interlaced ? " Three alternate couplets
follow, then :—

" In a damp hut on the reed-moor having spread layer upon layer
of sedge mats, we two slept."

p. 267.—" Hereupon, when presenting to him the great august
food, princess Miyazu lifted up a great liquor cup and presented it to
him. Tunc Herae Myazu veli orae adhaeserunt menstrua. Quare
[Augustus Yamatotake] illa menstrua vidit et auguste cecinit dicens :

Ego volui reclinare (caput) in fragili, molli brachiolo (tuo quod est
simile) vallo impingenti acutae falci in Mone Kagu in caelo formato
quasi cucurbita—ego desideravi dormire (tecum). Sed in ora veli
quod induis luna surrexit.

APPENDIX III

Tunc Herae Myazu augusto cantui respondit, dicens :

Alte resplendentis solis auguste puer ! Placide administrationem faciens mi magne domine ! Renovatis annis venientibus et effluentibus, renovatae lunae eunt veniendo et effluendo. Sane, sane, dum te impatienter expecto, luna suapte surgit in ora veli quod ego induo.

Quare tunc (ille) coivit (cum illa)."

pp. 308–309.—Dialogue :—

" O the maiden of Kohada in the back of the road ! Though I heard of her like the thunder, we mutually intertwine (our arms) as pillows . . . I think lovingly ah ! of how the maiden of Kohada in the back of the road sleeps (with me) without disputing."

pp. 412 sqq.—Contest between the emperor Sei-nei and the prince Shibi for the hand of a beautiful woman.—See the note on the order of the couplets.

GRENARD *in* DUTREUIL DE RHINS. *Mission scientifique dans la Haute Asie.* 2nd p. — *Le Turkestan et le Tibet.*

p. 357.—(In Tibet) " they are fond of double choruses, of men and women, standing opposite each other and answering each other verse by verse, advancing or retiring in time to the music. They devote themselves to these exercises mostly in spring and a certain air of solemnity envelopes them : the time is settled in advance ; the males and females who take part must have performed their ablutions and be dressed in clean clothing as for a religious ceremony. To dance casually for amusement and not in accordance with prescribed regulations would be considered immodest. The Tibetans are accustomed to sing while engaged in their labours, ploughing, sowing, and reaping."

p. 352.—(The wedding) " ends in a grand feast and in joint songs executed alternately by maidens and youths ; he who is found wanting when his turn comes to improvise his distich or quatrain is made to pay a forfeit." (The same customs prevail among the Kagak.)

p. 402.—" Many lakes and mountains possess a sacred character and are worshipped . . . each valley, even if uninhabited, has its guardian spirit ; malicious gnomes live on the rocks and in the grottoes . . . the sources of rivers are guarded by so many serpent-men (lou-klou), which remind us of the naiads and have been likened by the Buddhists to the naga of Vedic mythology. Over all these particular divinities stands the celestial dragon, personification of the cloud and perhaps, more generally, of the cloudy sky, who produces storms, pours the kindly rain, causes floods, sends plague and contagious diseases. He is precisely the dragon of the Mongols and the Chinese : the red tiger is his enemy."

p. 403.—" The water festival is celebrated in September; at this time water is held to possess supernatural properties; everybody bathes in the rivers, thinking thus to prolong life."

p. 401.—" In order to appease the anger of the *manes* who have not received proper burial, the lamas throw balls of *tsamba* into rivers and springs from time to time, and invite all wandering spirits to share them."

E. Rocher. *La Province chinoise de Yun-Nan*, Paris, 1879, 2 v. in-8.

Vol. ii, p. 13.—(Among the Lolos at the time of planting out the rice) " Every evening, after the labour of the day is done, instead of seeking renewed strength for the work of the next day in well-earned rest, the women assemble in groups and go to dance in the meadows or on the grass with the local youth, to the music of the guitar and castanets. Their dances, peculiar and varied, have much in common with those of the Indians. After a round is ended, it is customary for one of the dancers to offer a small glass of rice brandy to the guest of her choice, and, after he has drunk, she drinks also. Each couple does the same until all have drunk. Gradually gaiety gains the ascendancy, songs mingle with the dance, to the same accompaniment, and only night puts an end to these rustic games which are the delight of spring evenings. Each returns home to begin again the next day with even more keenness."

A. E. Legendre. *Le Far-west chinois, Deux ans au Setchouen*. (Paris, 1905.)

p. 292.—(Among the Lolos at Foulin) " being tired of measuring people and finding out their cephalic indices, I went away out of the village and buried myself in a deep narrow valley shut in on both sides by lofty mountains on whose steep sides pastured goats and sheep. *Shepherds and shepherdesses watched them, and from one side to the other answered each other in songs,* flinging to the echoes their simple bucolic ditties, brisk and shrill, but sweetly musical. Wrapt in the calm of a valley, surrounded by nature on a grand scale, it is delicious to listen to the songs of simple souls expressing their most intimate sentiments."

p. 295.—" At night, after dinner, there was a grand gathering of the people of Gué-leou-ka and the neighbouring villages, and, in order to confirm the cordial friendship which existed between Europeans and Lolos, everybody drank from the same jar, using the same pipette. Like the calumet of the Red Indian Sachems the pipette passed from mouth to mouth and an exchange of friendly sentiments began. This little entertainment ended in song. The men sang, but their low notes, suddenly changing to high and very high, sounded inharmonious in the small room in which we were ... The women sang in their turn in a larger room where we were alone ... the sounds, low-pitched and shrill, melted away in a kind of rumble, of modulation full of harmony."

p. 480.—" They went off, youths and maidens, singing merrily, a sickle through the girdle of each, to cut wood or grass in the thickets."

CRABOUILLET. *Les Lolos* (Missions catholiques, v, 1873, p. 108).

" The year begins towards the end of November on a date not the same for all the tribes. On the eve of the new year the young people of both sexes form a single band and climb the mountain to cut wood or dry grasses for a bonfire. This task is performed methodically. They form lines facing one another and cut fern to the accompaniment of improvised songs. The sonorous beauty of these uncultivated voices was not without its charm ... on return to the village each arranges his pile of faggots and at night they light many bonfires ; the houses are lit up by the flames and fireworks maintain a joyful fusillade : the festival ends in general intoxication."

DEBLENNE. In *Mission lyonnaise* (*Récits de voyage*), pp. 249 sqq.

" At certain times in the year, the Miao who are neighbours and members of the same tribe, assemble for certain merry-makings. Each village has a new year festival. The new year does not begin on the same day as the Chinese, but later. About the time of the new year the young men and the young women assemble in order to celebrate a festival similar to that among the Miao of Kuangsi, as recorded by M. Colquhoun, and described under the name of ' Festival of youth among the Thos ' by Dr. A. Billet, in his interesting study of the region about Cao-bang. Dressed in their finest clothes and wearing jewels, the young folk of both sexes assemble at some agreed spot. The young men and women, holding hands and standing face to face in two rows, dance to the sound of the small drum and the *lou-sen* (pan-pipes). Each side having challenged the other, the couples who have paired off proceed to respond to each other in improvised songs. This is often a festival of betrothal. The young men take advantage of the occasion to ask the consent of the girls of their choice, and, if these agree, the couple consider themselves betrothed, subject to the approval of both families. However, as pointed out by Dr. Billet, in certain places these festivals are an excuse for all sorts of excesses for which redress by marriage is never heard of. The defeated in these poetical battles are condemned to drink a certain quantity of spirits, which the conquerors insist upon till complete intoxication supervenes.

SILVESTRE.   Les Thai blancs de Phong-Ho. *BEFEO.*, 1918, No. iv.

p. 25.—After the day's work in the fields the long moonlight, evenings are spent in play. While the confiding parents are in bed, the young men court the girls who respond to their songs.

p. 29.—Before the two families are approached, the young couple find out all about each other during the moonlit evenings after the day's work in the rice fields, that is to say, during the period from the Annamese third to the ninth month. On these evenings, boys and girls meet near the huts while their confiding parents remain inside. The girls spin, their gallants sit at their feet and sing ballads to which the girls reply. These irregular songs, without meaning to us, fill them with pleasure. They laugh and are happy in each other's company. Sometimes these songs are real love songs, and the couple exchange pledges : they are really trial betrothals. Very seldom is their freedom abused.

p. 30.—When a girl, during the moonlight evenings, lets a young man see that she is not untouched by his devotion, the latter tells his parents and, if they approve, they engage two intermediaries to ask the girl from her parents in marriage.

p. 24.—The Thai woman does not sing after marriage.

p. 26.—The men eat together, young boys and children eat separately with the women.

p. 25.—During the new year festival youths and maidens play at shuttlecock. The shuttlecock is a fruit of some kind wrapped in stuff and finished with a tail of a yard or so long, with pieces of thin paper knotted in it, like the tail of a kite. The game is played by two, a boy and a girl opposite each other. The shuttlecock is struck with the palm of the hand. Any boy who misses has his ears warmed by his partner.

p. 47.—Festival of the fifteenth day of the first month. On the fifteenth, all the Thai who own a *seng* perform a certain ceremony. The *seng* is a calcareous concretion occasionally found in the stem of a banana or the trunk of a tree ; it brings good luck. An old man, specially chosen for the purpose, brings a large jar of water from some rapid and puts it down near the window of the hut. He puts all sorts of flowers into the water and then uses it to wash the *seng*, to which he makes the following little speech :—

" This is the fifteenth of the first month, your owner has had you

APPENDIX III

bathed in perfumed waters and now asks you to watch over his family, to protect his property against robbers and to turn aside all illness." The *seng* are then dried with a red cloth and placed on a plate with the chicken which has crowed first and the flowers. The games then begin among the *li-troung*. Men and women face each other and endeavour to throw balls through a plank pierced with a hole and hung between them. Men who win receive a prize of money and women of rings. The two sexes then play at tug-o'-war with a long cane. The women pull towards the village, the men away from it. It is a good omen when the fair sex wins. If, however, the stronger sex wins, there is much to be feared. The losers are sentenced to drink big bumpers of *chum-chum* and have to put up with a full dose of the crudest invective from the winners. Then everybody joins in a game between bowls and catch-ball. The loser has always to get intoxicated.

p. 48.—Flower festival for women only.

A. BILLET. " Deux ans dans le Haut-Tonkin (région de Cao-Bang) " (in *Bul. scient.*, vol. xxviii, Lille, 1895).

pp. 87 sqq.—(The Festival of the Dead) " takes place in the month of March and is celebrated on the same date as among the Annamese. On this day the graves, which are always very simple, consisting of little mounds of earth sometimes surmounted by a tombstone, are repaired by the relatives and friends of the dead and decorated with flowers and little streamers of white paper.

Other festivals, that of the new year, that of Earth, and the curious Children's Festival when, as with us at Christmas, toys and sweet-meats are given to the children, are also found among the Thos.

There is, however, another festival which neither the Annamese nor the Chinese observe. Like the game of Animated Chess, which will be described later, this must be a relic of the ancient customs of the Thos, the original lords of the soil. The festival I mean is that of youth, celebrated some days after the new year. During these days the youths and maidens, clad in their best and bedecked with jewels, meet in the middle of a wide plain, nearly always near a pagoda, under the protection of which they carry on their games. All around are stalls set up by sellers of food, fruit, cakes, and confectionery. At this time also are sold little drums of coloured paper, to the frames of which seeds are attached by strings, the whole being mounted on a handle of bamboo. The handle is rolled round between the fingers, and this shakes the seeds and causes them to strike the stretched paper of the drum with a sound rather inharmonious. Soon the young men have chosen their companions, and then follows a most curious scene which seems to us foreigners extremely comic. The various couples disperse into the shade of the bamboos, pomelo trees, and banyans. Each swain, turned back to back to his companion, as in the scene of *Gros-René and Marinette*, intones a series of lamentations in that nasal and mournful tone characteristic of the popular songs of the Thos. About midday the couples assemble again, and then take up positions in two lines, about fifty paces apart, facing each other as if for a monster quadrille. Each youth holds in his hand a ball attached to a long cord, which he throws towards the maiden of his choice. If she catches it or picks it up it means that the thrower pleases her, and she becomes his " conquest " for the remainder of the festival. If the girl throws back the ball it means that she is not quite pleased with him. The suitor recommences his serenade and the game of ball continues till the girl declares herself satisfied, which usually is not long delayed.

In most of the villages this is really a festival of betrothal. But in some districts it is an excuse for a sort of saturnalia after which rehabilitation by marriage is absolutely unknown. For the district about Cao-Bang this festival takes place in the peninsula of Pho-Yen, near an ancient pagoda containing the statues of many divinities exceedingly well preserved. Every year it attracts a huge assembly of young people and sightseers from the villages in the vicinity, from Cao-Bang to Nuoc-Hai and Mo-Xat, and even from the mountains of Luc-Khu and Tap-Na.

In the merry-makings and games which mark other festivals is found a trace of Annamese or Chinese influence. This is especially remarkable during the festivals of *Tet* or New Year, which come in the early days of February. A more astonishing fact is that some of these games recall those practised by ourselves, such as ball games, knucklebones, spinning tops, kites, or shuttlecocks, which are struck with the foot, as in China, with most remarkable adroitness. The games of dice, cards, dominoes, are all known, but, above all, the sport of *ba-kouan* (a sort of odds and evens), which they play to the extent of wagering all they possess, even to parts of their clothing.

Besides these games introduced from China or Annam, there are two which seem to be peculiar to the natives, the swing, very like the ordinary swing of our public fairs, except that the swing of the Thos is built entirely of bamboo and the cords are replaced by stiff rattans.

Another game, little known in the delta, but very common in Siam, is yet more peculiar to the Thos. Speaking broadly, it is our game of chess, but with this peculiarity : the pieces, kings, queens, bishops, knights, etc., are represented by living persons moved about by the

266

APPENDIX III

players according to the rules of the game . . . (they) are recruited from among the young people of the most highly respected families of the district. To be chosen as one of the players is a greatly coveted honour. This game of animated chess is only played once a year, during the two or three official days of *Tet*. As an exception it may be allowed on the 14th of July.

BONIFACY. "La fête Thai de Ho-bo" (*BEFEO.*, 1915, No. 3, pp. 17–23).

In April and May, 1915, M. Bonifacy was able to observe three famous local festivals : (1) At Binh-lieu ; (2) at Dong-trung-po ; (3) at Na-thuoc. Further, he has heard of gatherings at Bao-lac. These festivals are known as *Ho-bo*, which, according to M. Bonifacy, signifies mixture, promiscuity. Very young girls and matrons take part : no respect at all is paid to exogamy. The women walk about in parties, as also do the men ; after exchanges of alluring glances, sexual relations take place in the jungle ; marriage does not necessarily follow.

M. Bonifacy stresses the agrarian character of the festival ; the sexual rites produce a magical effect on the fruitfulness of the year.

M. Bonifacy, who accepts without criticism the hypothesis of primitive promiscuity, has overlooked the fact that at the time he observed these festivals they had been greatly modified by foreign influence. One fact he notes is significant. Outsiders, for example, Annamese soldiers, may share in the general licence, but, he says, " the Annamese sharp-shooters who take advantage of the opportunity, are only favoured by old women ! " M. Bonifacy has only seen the Thai festivals in a state of decadence similar to that of the festivals of the waters and mountains when the commentators of the *Shih ching* saw them.

COLQUHOUN. *Across Chrysê*, ii, 238.

The Lolos have a festival at the beginning of the first month. They hollow out the trunk of a large tree and make what they call a " trough ". Men and women together strike thereon with a bamboo. The sound resembles that of a drum. Men and women put their arms round each other's waists and the festival ends in an orgy.

Ibid., i, 213.—Account of the festival called *Hoi-ngam* among the Miao-tzŭ (the term *Hoi-ngam* is obscene). On the first day of the year men and women assemble in a narrow valley, the men on one side and the women opposite. They sing. When a lad has made an impression on a girl by his songs, she throws to him a coloured ball.

267

Nearby a fair is held, where the gallants buy many gifts for their sweethearts.

IMBAULT HUART. *L'Ile de Formose*

p. 248.—"When a young man wishes to marry and has found a girl who pleases him, he goes frequently to her door with a musical instrument; if the girl is pleased she goes out to meet him who seeks her. They come to an agreement and then tell their parents. The marriage feast is held in the house of the bride, where the young man continues to reside after the wedding, never going home again. Thenceforward the young man looks upon his father-in-law's house as his own."

O. SAINSON. "Histoire particulière de Nan-tchao" (in *Publ. de l'Éc. de Lang. or. viv.*), 1894.

p. 93.—Su Hsing (who reigned A.D. 1041–4) was fond of walking and liked being in the open. He had a palace built in the eastern capital and there planted many flowering trees. Yellow flowers were planted on the dike of Ch'un têng, and white on the bridge of Yün ch'in . . . In the spring time, in company with his ladies, he set bowls floating on the river downstream from the three Yü An springs to the Chin Chu Liu moat. Men and women sat down, threw flowers at each other, placed them in their hair, and devoted themselves to pleasure day and night. Among the flowers was one with a lasting and penetrating scent and, as Su Hsing liked it, it was called after him. There was another sort of flower that opened when anyone happened to sing, and a plant which shook its branches if fencing went on near it. Hsing used to place singers near the one and fencers by the other to show these wonders.

p. 69.—Miraculous conception while bathing, work of a dragon.

p. 86.—Miraculous conception in a river, due to being touched by a floating stick.

p. 188.—(Miao tzŭ.) Every year in the first month of spring they dance in the moonlight; the men play on pan-pipes; the women shake small bells and sing in chorus. They can keep up movements of arms and legs the whole day without fatigue. They also make coloured balls which a man throws towards her who pleases him. In the evening each one comes back with the woman to whom he has thrown the ball, and the couple remain together till morning. Considerations of the conditions and date of marriage follow. The contract of marriage is prepared to the accompaniment of bronze drums, blaring trumpets, and general thanksgiving.

p. 183.—(Man ch'ieh.) "The (Chinese) twelfth month is their

firﬅ. Since the love of drink is part of their nature, men and women assemble at this time; the men play on pan-pipes, the women the guitar; they pass the whole month in amusement and drinking. They bear privation patiently, filling their bellies with wild plants."

p. 178.—(Ch'ia To). "They are dull by nature and take pleasure in songs and mimes. Men and women for the moﬅ part couple like wild beaﬅs, but those who marry employ an intermediary."

p. 178.—(Pu la.) "As to marriage, they begin by coupling like wild beaﬅs."

p. 171.—(Hei kan i.) "At marriages, the men play on pan-pipes, and the women the guitar and they sing to these. So they amuse themselves. They begin by coupling like wild beaﬅs, and call in the intermediary afterwards."

p. 164.—(P'u jên.) "At marriages, young and old dance to the pan-pipes; they call this the peacock pantomime. The son-in-law puts up a rod from which hang embroidered silk purses containing the five kinds of cereal, and silverware. The members of the two families, men and women, old and young, try to get hold of them. The one who succeeds is the victor."

p. 173.—(Chêng.) "When a young man of these people wishes to marry, he drives oxen and sheep to the dwelling of his intended, then he sprinkles water over her, and that suffices for an engagement."

pp. 264 sqq.—(Translation of an essay in verse by Mr. Yang Chuang-chai.)

"At Tien nan, in the firﬅ month, the signs of spring appear early . . . handsome plum trees, superb peach trees, are laden with blossom . . . They are fond of the swinging basket . . . In the second month the spring is gay and beautiful: the men become excited and ﬅay no longer at home; the water in the ﬅreams is warm in spring and fountains gush out on all sides . . . wine is sold on every side and hairpins and bracelets are seen everywhere. The scented flower is sought and flower-battles are waged in the newly decorated summer-house. Songs are sung at the foot of the jujube trees and some good verse is composed . . . (third month) songs are sung and responded to . . . (ninth month) the women ﬅick jasmin flowers into their hair . . . (tenth month) Everyone reposes in the warm rooms."

"Les barbares soumis du Yun-nan" (Chap. du Tien hi), in *BEFEO.*, viii, 333 sqq.

p. 371.—(Mo hsieh.) "In their leisure hours they sing love songs called *a-ho-tzŭ* and *hsi-pi-ti*. (When they sing) on the tone *shang* they weep. When a couple have sung in harmony, they go off into the valleys or into the woods, and there unite."

p. 353.—(Wo ni.) " When they have drunk wine, a man, to the sound of a reed flute, takes the lead and men and women, hand in hand, circle about, leaping and dancing to amuse themselves."

p. 343.—(Miao Lolo.) " Men and women all go barefoot, but when they dance and sing for amusement they don skin shoes. The men blow into reed pipes; the women dress in bordered garments and sing while they dance, each as she wills."

p. 344.—" For weddings and all occasions of rejoicing they build a shed of pine as banquet and music hall."

p. 378 (Li-su.) " Love charms are made from mountain grasses. A lover has only to conceal one of these charms in his dress to bring the desired one to his side; they are not to be parted again."

p. 336.—(Lolo barbarians.) " The twelfth month brings the Festival of Spring. A wooden base is set up and a plank put across it: a man seats himself at each end, and they amuse themselves by see-sawing up and down."

p. 349.—(P'o i.) " They are extravagant. The festival of the Master of Earth falls in the first month. They borrow all round in order to be well-dressed; but when they have to repay double they do not regret it. There is also the Festival of the Swing, wherein men and women take part equally."

p. 375.—(Na-ma.) " When a man has an intrigue with a girl, the father and mother do not interfere, but the girl must not be seen by her eldest brother. He would slay her lover."

p. 360.—(P'u jên.) " Among them the women choose their husbands."

p. 350.—(P'o i.) Men and women have sexual relations previous to marriage.

p. 348.—" They do not esteem virgins, and, as in the country about the confluence of the (Yang-tse) Chiang and the Han, they are allowed perfect liberty to stroll about and are only kept within at the age of puberty. At the present time, this custom (of confining them) is gradually disappearing."

p. 361.—" At weddings, oxen and sheep are slaughtered: the fiancée is indicated by pouring water on her feet."

p. 355.—(Lu-lu barbarians.) " The couples do not see each other during the day."

BEAUVAIS. " Notes sur les coutumes des indigènes de la région de Long-tcheou," BEFEO., viii, 265 sqq.

(Translating the *Lung-chou Chi liu*) : " Each year during the third or fourth month, the young men and young women of different villages meet together to sing songs in alternating couplets. People from the neighbouring villages, bringing their provisions, come to these gatherings. Each assembly consists of not less than a thousand all about the age of twenty. The natives insist that if these gatherings were prevented or forbidden for any reason, the harvests of the year would not mature and many epidemics would afflict the people."

Another passage from the same work : " The young men and the young girls of this region like to wander about in couples singing songs. As a custom it is not to be recommended, but it is practised all through the province of Yüeh-hsi (Kuang-hsi).

M. Beauvais adds : " These meetings are often merely pretexts for betrothals. The young man and the girl, facing each other, make love by means of these songs in alternate couplets. It must be confessed that these gatherings lead to scenes of licence ; often the couples who have found a secret liking for each other wander off into the jungle or among the thickets to anticipate their honeymoon. The Chinese officials have never been able to prohibit these customs. A rising would have followed shortly after their prohibition."

BONIFACY. " Études sur les chants et la poésie populaire des Mans du Tonkin," p. 85 sqq., *Premier Congrès internat. des Ét. d'Ext.-Orient, Hanoï,* 1902 ; *Compte rendu analyt., Hanoï,* 1903.

(These songs are in Chinese) " The grace of these verses lies in the final rhyme and the periodical recurrence of certain phrases. The written literature comprises : 1st, quatrains, usually in dialogue ; 2nd, sacred songs ; 3rd, romances. To sing the quatrains they form choruses of girls and boys who sing alternately. The sacred songs are used in the raising of spirits, when they are accompanied by dances representing warlike or other deeds ; in exorcisms, when they are punctuated by sacrifices ; at funerals, but this use is not common to all the races. The romances are in verse like our old *chansons de geste.*"

A Wedding Song (" Man quan coc ")

(1) I hear the voice of my love as he comes singing a sweet song.
(2) Coins are attached to my mat ; someone has interlaced four characters.
(3) Coins are attached to my mat ; the four characters are interlaced there.
(4) Soon upon these four characters the *mei* [1] will come together.

[1] *mei* (plum tree) is the symbol of virginity.

271

FESTIVALS AND SONGS OF ANCIENT CHINA

A Love Song ("Man cao lan")

Poor am I.
Going out on the road I meet someone whom I dare not greet.
To the accomplished maiden the wealthy youth! I am poor
and lowly.
I dare not mate with you, Miss, the bond is too honourable
(for me).

BONIFACY. "Études sur les coutumes et la langue des Lolo et des
La-qua du haut Tonkin," in *BEFEO.*, viii, 531 sqq.

p. 537.—(La-qua.) "The young unmarried folk are very un-
restrained and *sing on the mountain*, but the lads may not belong to
the same village as the lasses. This is doubtless a survival of primitive
exogamy."
(Lolo.) "The young unmarried folk are unrestrained. They sing
together even though they belong to the same village. The whole
of the first month is especially devoted to love-making. The young
people are left quite free; it is the Festival of *Con-ci* (cf. *BEFEO.*,
viii, 336), which varies with the tribe."
p. 538.—"The La-qua are very fond of songs which take the form
of dialogue between lasses and lads. These songs end in a cry, *pi houit*.
It is a curious fact that the words are in the Thai language. The
La-qua are unable to give the literal meaning of the songs. They now
know no more than their general meaning."
The Lolo do not sing so often as the *La-qua*, at least before strangers.

A La-qua Song (in Thai)

In this country we have never seen a stranger;
Whence is he, this stranger?
This pleasing stranger has come,
We must sing in his honour.
Whence comes he, this stranger?
Comes he by the river or not?
How many rivers and countries has he seen?
How has he crossed the deep waters?
How fine it is to have travelled a thousand leagues!

APPENDIX III

A Lolo Love Song

The lad. Of what country are you, Miss ?
Where do you dwell, Miss ?
I think of you here.
I have never seen you before.

The lass. You talk cleverly;
You speak sensibly.
If you will be my spouse,
Come near that I may look at you.

p. 545.—(Among the Lolo and the La-qua) the young people come to an understanding and then the young man informs his parents, who send an intermediary. Cf. p. 536.

p. 545.—(At a Lolo wedding) they make pretence of a capture of the bride, singing suitable songs the while.

LE P. VIAL. " Les Lolo," in *Études Sino-orientales*, fasc. A, p. 16 sqq., Chap. IV, " La Littérature et la poésie chez les Lolos."

" *Lolo* literature certainly has, like Chinese, its fixed phrases, its tiresome repetitions, but its charm lies less in the rhythm or cadence of the wording, which is always the same, than in the freshness of idea and sentiment . . . (the) metaphors come in unexpectedly . . . repetitions are frequent and the author uses the same phrases when he refers to the same idea ; the expression of the idea closes with the fifth word . . . this rule—in verse is obligatory, and this is, with a shade of rhyme or assonance, the distinguishing mark of poetry, which only tolerates verses of three or five syllables . . . not every word has a meaning : many are introduced merely for the sake of euphony or to enable a verse to terminate with the fifth word . . ."

" The song, or rather the ballad, belongs to every day. They sing about everything, improvise about everything . . . the girl is particularly adroit at expressing her feelings . . . the only rival to the simplicity of the words is the simplicity of the air, a mere modulation, a sob, a tear, a sigh, always the same tear, always the same sob."

p. 31.—Description of the wrestling matches, among the Gni and the Ashi, as compared with those of the Breton " pardons ".

" When, in any district, the harvest has failed, or the number of deaths rises, the headmen assemble and vow to do battle for one, two, or three days on end . . . When the date arrives, an area is levelled, a piece of land consecrated to this purpose, which may not be changed. . . . The wrestlers strip themselves of all but the lower garment. They begin by putting their arms round each other, then they rub their hands in the sand and are ready. . . . The match ends with a prayer."

p. 35.—(Quotation from a note by Fr. Roux.)

The Chung-Chia-tzŭ of Kuei-chou "are fond of singing; the songs they sing are plaintive, languishing love-songs. Dancing is unknown, but music is held in high honour. Gatherings of the two sexes on the mountains at which there are contests in eloquence and poetry, are still held, but are becoming rare."

p. 26.—Father Vial says that among the *Lolos* " girls and women never dance. The young man passes his evenings gossipping with those of his own age, playing the mandolin or flute, wrestling or dancing". "Conduct is loose, even very loose, but in this respect they do not go beyond what I may call pagan propriety, and, to tell the truth, there is about as much play as passion."

p. 20.   *Complaint of the Wife*

1

Mother, thy daughter is sad,   *Ema, neu cha la,*
Three days ago you went away;   *Se gni ta tche ra;*
Mother, come back, come back,   *Ema, tcho kou ja,*
Mother, I long for thee.   *Ema, ga leu leu.*

2

Mother, thy daughter is sad,   *Ema, neu cha la,*
The tree withers, the root lives: *Se che, ke ma che;*
The root lives, the leaf dries up: *Ke che, chla qui me:*
Mother, thy daughter is sad.   *Ema, neu cha la.*

3

The breezes stir the leaf,
Mother, thy daughter is sad;
The leaf lives once again,
Thy daughter has no more life.

APPENDIX III

4

My father, beſtowing his daughter,
Obtained a jar of wine
Of which I shall not taſte;
For ever thy daughter is sad.

5

My mother, beſtowing her daughter,
Obtained a basket of rice
Of which I shall not eat;
For ever thy daughter is sad.

6

My brother, beſtowing his siſter,
Obtained (for himself) an ox
Of which I shall have no use.
For ever thy daughter is sad.

7

They go to reſt; but I am awake
As if I were a thief.
They arise, but I rise not,
As if I had the plague.

8

Each day I gather pot-herbs,
Three bundles every day,
In three days thrice three bundles;
And ſtill their words are harsh.

9

Mother, thy daughter is sad,
Sad, I go to the wood.
What is there in the wood?
The cicada sings in the wood.

10

Mother, thy daughter is sad,
Sad, I go to the fields,
In the fields there is the grass,
The grass has the grass for its mate.

11

Mother, thy daughter is sad,
Thy daughter has no friend ;
For ever thinking,
Her heart is sad.

Cf. *Wang fêng*, 7. Couvreur, 81.

EITEL. In *Notes and Queries on China and Japan*, vol. i, 1867.
Ethnographical Sketches of the Hakka Chinese.

EXAMPLE OF MOUNTAIN SONGS

I

Now the Sun is risen in the East,
As the mountain tree fears twining creepers,
As the foreign vessel dreads the pirates,
So the young girl fears a handsome lover.

II

Now the Sun has reached its zenith,
Days incessant I continued wooing.
By the heavens we swore to love each other.
Should she false be, may the lightning strike her !

III

Now the Sun shines forth with scorching heat.
At her gate a girl is planting onions.
Every day she sighs, " there are no onions."
Every night she sighs, " I have no husband."

Appendix III

IV

Blazing is the Sun, one hopes for clouds.
Parched are the fields, they hope for water.
Cloudless is the sky, one hopes for showers.
Single is that girl, she hopes for—whom ?

V

Bright the Sun may be and bad the weather,
Trees and flowers gay, the garden dreary ;
Good the plant may be and bad the crop ;
Fine the girl may be and die a spinster !

VI

Don't blame Heaven for sending rain in torrents.
Mind that fearful drought some years ago ;
When for rice were paid cents six and thirty,
And to death were starved the fairest maidens.

VII

Incense burned leaves embers in the censer.
Is the lamp-wick burned there are but ashes.
If you want to woo, then woo two sisters,
Is the one at work, you have the other.

VIII

Once my girl and I walked up yon hill,
When I hurt my foot the blood gushed out.
But she tore her dress to bind my wound.
Pain then racked my foot and racked her heart.

IX

If your sweetheart jilts you, never mind !
Every mountain sends some creeklet forth ;
Every valley has some little water.
If you fail on one side, try the other.

FESTIVALS AND SONGS OF ANCIENT CHINA

X

Ah! the world is worse than ever it was!
Finger-rings are worn as large as door-rings.
Once a lover wanted but one ring.
Now a lover wants a lot of dollars!

XI

Twice I met my sweetheart in the dusk,
And this night we met behind her house.
When somebody passed and looked askant,
But she seized a twig and called her pigs!

XII

Three times barked the watch-dog at the gate.
Surely now my lover muſt be coming.
Hush, my dog, and let me open the door.
With my hand behind I'll lead him in.

EXAMPLE OF THE SONGS OF THE TEA-PICKERS

XIII

In the firſt month when the peach tree blossoms,
When the old year's gone and the new year comes,
When the cool breezes bleach the plumage of the goose,
Then behind their curtains women yearn for love.

XIV

In the next month when the willow blossoms,
Little buds shoot forth and leaflets spread,
When the buds and leaves are glittering with dew,
Then beneath the willows women yearn for love.

XV

In the third month, when the tea trees blossom,
Every maid goes forth to view the gardens,
Every maid then loves to ſtroll about.
But whilſt plucking tea, they yearn for love.

APPENDIX III

XVI

In the fourth month, when the beech tree blossoms,
Standing splendid white with flowers all over,
When no one likes his rice or wine when cold,
In the backroom, at their toilet women yearn for love.

XVII

When then next month, courtyard flowers blossom,
When the swallows seek their wonted haunts,
When the swallows in the garden gambol,
Then whilst gathering flowers, women yearn for love.

XVIII

In the sixth month, when the rice-plant blossoms,
When each blade unfolds, some tender ear,
And each ear seems pregnant with rich corn,
Straining every nerve, then women yearn for love.

XIX

In the next month, when the caltrops blossom,
Crowds of girls go forth to view the gardens,
Crowds of girls go strolling through the fields.
At their wash-tubs, even, women yearn for love.

XX

In the eighth month, when the wild-flowers blossom,
When the old year goes to meet the new year coming,
Then young men like butterflies go roving
Over land and sea—they yearn for love.

XXI

In the ninth month, when the asters blossom,
And the people make fermented wine,
With cold tea or rice I still could manage
But with bed and matting cold—I yearn for love.

XXII

In the tenth month parer trees do blossom,
And the people handle paper-scissors,
Cutting flowers from paper for the fair.
On the ſtreets then selling them, I yearn for love.

XXIII

In the next month, when the snow trees blossom,
And the people handling brooms and besoms
Clear away the snow to open paths,
I too, sweeping off the snow, then yearn for love.

XXIV

In the twelfth month pillow-flowers blossom,
Then I put two pillows on my bed,
It's the famous pair, " the loving wild-fowl,"
Reſting on those pillows—then I yearn for love.

Example of *Responsoria*, playful couplets between two persons
of different sex; one ſtanza is sung by a man and the response muſt
be sung by a woman.

XXV

The Maiden.　Here I've got a thousand cash and one,
　　　　　　Now, my friend, divide them for some persons,
　　　　　　Let not one have more than any other,
　　　　　　Let not one have less than any other,
　　　　　　Who divides these cash that none be left ?
　　　　　　Him I'll marry without go-between.

XXVI

The Youth.　I will try to make out seven portions,
　　　　　　Each a hundred cash makes seven hundred ;
　　　　　　Forty cash then makes two hundred and eighty,
　　　　　　Three to each now, that is twenty-one,

Appendix III

And this altogether makes one thousand and one.
Look, I have divided all your money.
Come now and marry me without a go-between.

XXVII

The Youth. Handsome is my sweetheart grown,
Like the sky's five-coloured clouds ;
Of her body she gives me a part,
All my worldly goods I give to her.

XXVIII

The Maiden. If you love me, rig me smartly out,
I want Swatow-shoes with cloud like horn,
Want a Kuang-si straw hat, quite a beauty,
And some money, too, for playing cards.

XXIX

The Youth. Should I spend my money all for you ?
Sell my best fields all to gain your love ?
Sell my fields, incur my father's wrath ?
Let my wife and children wail and groan ?

XXX

The Maiden. Day and night burn incense, pray to Heaven,
To assist you, love, in making money,
That you might gain many thousand dollars
To redeem the fields you sell for me.

CPSIA information can be obtained at www.ICGtesting.com
Printed in the USA
LVOW11s0420300616

494713LV00002B/85/P